MCSE™ Clustering Using Advanced Server 2000

Jarret W. Buse
Diana Bartley

MCSE Clustering Using Advanced Server 2000 Exam Cram

Limits of Liability and Disclaimer of Warranty

The author and publisher of this book have used their best efforts in preparing the book and the programs contained in it. These efforts include the development, research, and testing of the theories and programs to determine their effectiveness. The author and publisher make no warranty of any kind, expressed or implied, with regard to these programs or the documentation contained in this book.

The author and publisher shall not be liable in the event of incidental or consequential damages in connection with, or arising out of, the furnishing, performance, or use of the programs, associated instructions, and/or claims of productivity gains.

Trademarks

Trademarked names appear throughout this book. Rather than list the names and entities that own the trademarks or insert a trademark symbol with each mention of the trademarked name, the publisher states that it is using the names for editorial purposes only and to the benefit of the trademark owner, with no intention of infringing upon that trademark.

The Coriolis Group, LLC
14455 N. Hayden Road
Suite 220
Scottsdale, Arizona 85260

(480)483-0192
FAX (480)483-0193
www.coriolis.com

Library of Congress Cataloging-in-Publication Data
Buse, Jarret W.
    MCSE clustering using advanced server 2000 / by Jarret Buse and
    Diana Bartley.
        p. cm.
    Includes index.
    ISBN 1-57610-982-8
    1. Electronic data processing personnel--Certification.   2. Microsoft
software--Examinations--Study guides.   3. Operating systems
(Computers)--Examinations--Study guides.   4. Microsoft Windows NT
server.   I. Bartley, Diana.   II. Title.   III. Series.
QA76.3. .B873 2001
005.7'13769--dc21   2001028455

Publisher
Steve Sayre

Acquisitions Editor
Lee Anderson

Product Marketing Manager
Brett Woolley

Project Editor
Karen Swartz

Technical Reviewer
Christian Wolf

Production Coordinator
Thomas Riker

Cover Designer
Laura Wellander

Layout Designer
April Nielsen

Printed in the United States of America
10 9 8 7 6 5 4 3 2 1

The Coriolis Group, LLC • 14455 North Hayden Road, Suite 220 • Scottsdale, Arizona 85260

A Note from Coriolis

Our goal has always been to provide you with the best study tools on the planet to help you achieve your certification in record time. Time is so valuable these days that none of us can afford to waste a second of it, especially when it comes to exam preparation.

Over the past few years, we've created an extensive line of *Exam Cram* and *Exam Prep* study guides, practice exams, and interactive training. To help you study even better, we have now created an e-learning and certification destination called **ExamCram.com**. (You can access the site at **www.examcram.com**.) Now, with every study product you purchase from us, you'll be connected to a large community of people like yourself who are actively studying for their certifications, developing their careers, seeking advice, and sharing their insights and stories.

We believe that the future is all about collaborative learning. Our **ExamCram.com** destination is our approach to creating a highly interactive, easily accessible collaborative environment, where you can take practice exams and discuss your experiences with others, sign up for features like "Questions of the Day," plan your certifications using our interactive planners, create your own personal study pages, and keep up with all of the latest study tips and techniques.

We hope that whatever study products you purchase from us—*Exam Cram* or *Exam Prep* study guides, *Personal Trainers, Personal Test Centers*, or one of our interactive Web courses—will make your studying fun and productive. Our commitment is to build the kind of learning tools that will allow you to study the way you want to, whenever you want to.

Visit ExamCram.com now to enhance your study program.

Help us continue to provide the very best certification study materials possible. Write us or email us at **learn@examcram.com** and let us know how our study products have helped you study. Tell us about new features that you'd like us to add. Send us a story about how we've helped you. We're listening!

Good luck with your certification exam and your career. Thank you for allowing us to help you achieve your goals.

ExamCram.com Connects You to the Ultimate Study Center!

Look for these other products from The Coriolis Group:

MCSE Migrating from NT 4 to Windows 2000 Exam Cram
by Kurt Hudson, Deborah Haralson, Doug Bassett, and Derek Melber

MCSE Exchange 2000 Administration Exam Cram
by David Watts and Will Willis

MCSE Exchange 2000 Design Exam Cram
by William Baldwin

MCSE SQL 2000 Administration Exam Cram
by Kirk Hausman

MCSE SQL 2000 Database Design Exam Cram
by Richard McMahon and Sean Chase

MCSE ISA Server 2000 Exam Cram
by Diana Bartley and Gregory Smith

I dedicate this book, as I did my last book, to my beautiful wife Cassandra and my four wonderful children Devyn, Logan, Caleb, and Little Princess Eilly. And to the future of more to come.

—Jarret W. Buse

෧෧

This book is dedicated to my dear friend, Ryan Johanneson.

—Diana Bartley

෧෧

About the Authors

Jarret W. Buse (MCT, MCSE+I, CCNA, CNA, A+ and Network+) is a technical trainer and consultant specializing in Microsoft products. He has worked in the computer field for nine years and instructs students in the use of various Microsoft products as well as different computer certifications at Micro Computer Solutions of Indiana in Evansville, Indiana. Having a degree in programming, he is still working towards his MCSD, but has yet to find time to pursue the certification. He can be reached at **JARRETBUSE@HOTMAIL.COM**.

Diana Bartley holds a Bachelor of Education degree from the University of Manitoba and over the past several years has earned many industry certifications, some of which include her MCSE, MCT, and MCP+I. She has been actively involved in IT training for several years and currently works for the Entrepreneur and Technology Education Center (ETEC) as a member of the technical team and oversees the engineering program. Diana specializes in technical training for Windows 2000.

Acknowledgments

Thanks to Coriolis for giving me this chance to work with them again and hopefully more in the future. Great thanks to Lee Anderson for his support in giving me this project. Many thanks to Karen Akins Swartz for her assistance in guiding me through the process of completing another book. Thanks also to Diana Bartley for co-authoring this book with me—her talent as an author is greatly appreciated. Among those on the Coriolis team, thanks to Bart Reed for copyediting, Chris Wolf for technical editing, Thomas Riker for production, Laura Wellander for cover design, April Nielsen for interior design, and Brett Woolley for marketing. Thanks to everyone else for their help in making this book possible.

I especially want to thank my beautiful wife, Cassandra, for her love and support not only during this project, but also throughout our lives together with our four children. She knows I will always love her with all my heart, even the fake parts.

I thank my kids for their patience and understanding. My two oldest sons, Devyn and Logan, had to wait to play on the computer until I was finished for the day. My youngest son, Caleb, wanted to get his fingers into everything in my den while I was working. And my Princess Eilly who is starting to crawl and repeat sounds that she hears—you are so adorable.

Thanks to my mom and dad, Geraldine and Jerry Buse, for their support throughout my life in all I do. Also, to my grandmother, Laverne Meyer, for all she has done for me (just remember, Grandma, it will still all be Greek to you) and I wish Grandpa could have seen this.

Thanks to my mother-in-law, JoAnne Plock, for giving me my wife whom I could not live without.

And a hello to my sister-in-law, Selina Plock, and her to her children, my nephew and niece, Tre and Jasmine.

And for all the time you were buried next to the rose bush, thanks for being there, Elvis.

For Sammy who rolls around everywhere every time I leave home.

And again, thanks to God for being with me and inspiring me to go further.

—*Jarret W. Buse*

Acknowledgments

First and foremost, I would like to thank my parents and my son for their patience while I was writing this book. I would never be able to accomplish the things I do without your support. Many thanks to my co-author, Jarret Buse, whose persistence, dedication, and knowledge really made this book come together. Thanks to all my friends and coworkers for their support and encouragement during the past few months. Last, my acknowledgement would not be complete without mention of my good friend and very talented coworker, Ryan Johanneson. You truly are a genius in every sense of the word, and I appreciate all the support you have given me over the past months.

—*Diana Bartley*

Contents at a Glance

Table of Contents

Chapter 10
Installing Microsoft Applications on a Cluster 209

Chapter 11
Optimization   233

Introduction

Welcome to *MCSE Clustering Using Advanced Server 2000 Exam Cram!* Whether this is your first or your fifteenth *Exam Cram* book, you'll find information here and in Chapter 1 that will help ensure your success as you pursue knowledge, experience, and certification. This book aims to help you get ready to take—and pass—the Microsoft certification Exam 70-223, titled "Installing, Configuring, and Administering Microsoft Clustering Services by Using Microsoft Windows 2000 Advanced Server." This Introduction explains Microsoft's certification programs in general and talks about how the *Exam Cram* series can help you prepare for Microsoft's Windows 2000 certification exams.

Exam Cram books help you understand and appreciate the subjects and materials you need to pass Microsoft certification exams. *Exam Cram* books are aimed strictly at test preparation and review. They do not teach you everything you need to know about a topic. Instead, we (the authors) present and dissect the questions and problems we've found that you're likely to encounter on a test. We've worked to bring together as much information as possible about Microsoft certification exams.

Nevertheless, to completely prepare yourself for any Microsoft test, we recommend that you begin by taking the Self-Assessment included in this book immediately following this Introduction. This tool will help you evaluate your knowledge base against the requirements for an MCSE under both ideal and real circumstances.

Based on what you learn from that exercise, you might decide to begin your studies with some classroom training or some background reading. On the other hand, you might decide to pick up and read one of the many study guides available from Microsoft or third-party vendors on certain topics, including The Coriolis Group's *Exam Prep* series. We also recommend that you supplement your study program with visits to **ExamCram.com** to receive additional practice questions, get advice, and track the Windows 2000 MCSE program.

We also strongly recommend that you install, configure, and fool around with the software that you'll be tested on, because nothing beats hands-on experience and familiarity when it comes to understanding the questions you're likely to encounter on a certification test. Book learning is essential, but hands-on experience is the best teacher of all!

The Microsoft Certified Professional (MCP) Program

The MCP Program currently includes the following separate tracks, each of which boasts its own special acronym (as a certification candidate, you need to have a high tolerance for alphabet soup of all kinds):

➤ *MCP (Microsoft Certified Professional)*—This is the least prestigious of all the certification tracks from Microsoft. Passing one of the major Microsoft exams qualifies an individual for the MCP credential. Individuals can demonstrate proficiency with additional Microsoft products by passing additional certification exams.

➤ *MCP+SB (Microsoft Certified Professional + Site Building)*—This certification program is designed for individuals who are planning, building, managing, and maintaining Web sites. Individuals with the MCP+SB credential will have demonstrated the ability to develop Web sites that include multimedia and searchable content and Web sites that connect to and communicate with a back-end database. It requires one MCP exam, plus two of these three exams: "70-055: Designing and Implementing Web Sites with Microsoft FrontPage 98," "70-057: Designing and Implementing Commerce Solutions with Microsoft Site Server 3.0, Commerce Edition," and "70-152: Designing and Implementing Web Solutions with Microsoft Visual InterDev 6.0." Microsoft will retire Exam 70-055 on June 30, 2001 and the MCP+SB certification on June 30, 2002.

➤ *MCSE (Microsoft Certified Systems Engineer)*—Anyone who has a current MCSE is warranted to possess a high level of networking expertise with Microsoft operating systems and products. This credential is designed to prepare individuals to plan, implement, maintain, and support information systems, networks, and internetworks built around Microsoft Windows 2000 and its BackOffice Server 2000 family of products.

To obtain an MCSE, an individual must pass four core operating system exams, one optional core exam, and two elective exams. The operating system exams require individuals to prove their competence with desktop and server operating systems and networking/internetworking components.

For Windows NT 4 MCSEs, the Accelerated exam, "70-240: Microsoft Windows 2000 Accelerated Exam for MCPs Certified on Microsoft Windows NT 4.0," is an option. This free exam covers all of the material tested in the Core Four exams. The hitch in this plan is that you can take the test only once. If you fail, you must take all four core exams to recertify. The Core Four exams are: "70-210: Installing, Configuring and Administering Microsoft

Windows 2000 Professional," "70-215: Installing, Configuring and Administering Microsoft Windows 2000 Server," "70-216: Implementing and Administering a Microsoft Windows 2000 Network Infrastructure," and "70-217: Implementing and Administering a Microsoft Windows 2000 Directory Services Infrastructure."

To fulfill the fifth core exam requirement, you can choose from four design exams: "70-219: Designing a Microsoft Windows 2000 Directory Services Infrastructure," "70-220: Designing Security for a Microsoft Windows 2000 Network," "70-221: Designing a Microsoft Windows 2000 Network Infrastructure, " or "70-226: Designing Highly Available Web Solutions with Microsoft Windows 2000 Server Technologies." You are also required to take two elective exams. An elective exam can fall in any number of subject or product areas, primarily BackOffice Server 2000 components. The three design exams that you don't select as your fifth core exam also qualify as electives. If you are on your way to becoming an MCSE and have already taken some exams, visit **www.microsoft.com/trainingandservices/** for information about how to complete your MCSE certification.

Individuals who wish to remain certified MCSEs after 12/31/2001 must "upgrade" their certifications on or before 12/31/2001. For more detailed information than is included here, visit **www.microsoft.com/trainingandservices/**.

New MCSE candidates must pass seven tests to meet the MCSE requirements. It's not uncommon for the entire process to take a year or so, and many individuals find that they must take a test more than once to pass. The primary goal of the *Exam Prep* and *Exam Cram* test preparation books is to make it possible, given proper study and preparation, to pass all Microsoft certification tests on the first try. Table 1 shows the required and elective exams for the Windows 2000 MCSE certification.

➤ *MCSD (Microsoft Certified Solution Developer)*—The MCSD credential reflects the skills required to create multitier, distributed, and COM-based solutions, in addition to desktop and Internet applications, using new technologies. To obtain an MCSD, an individual must demonstrate the ability to analyze and interpret user requirements; select and integrate products, platforms, tools, and technologies; design and implement code, and customize applications; and perform necessary software tests and quality assurance operations.

To become an MCSD, you must pass a total of four exams: three core exams and one elective exam. Each candidate must choose one of these three desktop application exams—"70-016: Designing and Implementing Desktop Applications with Microsoft Visual C++ 6.0," "70-156: Designing and Implementing Desktop Applications with Microsoft Visual FoxPro 6.0," or "70-176: Designing and Implementing Desktop Applications with Microsoft

Table1   MCSE Windows 2000 Requirements

Core

If you have not passed these 3 Windows NT 4 exams	
Exam 70-067	Implementing and Supporting Microsoft Windows NT Server 4.0
Exam 70-068	Implementing and Supporting Microsoft Windows NT Server 4.0 in the Enterprise
Exam 70-073	Microsoft Windows NT Workstation 4.0
then you must take these 4 exams	
Exam 70-210	Installing, Configuring, and Administering Microsoft Windows 2000 Professional
Exam 70-215	Installing, Configuring, and Administering Microsoft Windows 2000 Server
Exam 70-216	Implementing and Administering a Microsoft Windows 2000 Network Infrastructure
Exam 70-217	Implementing and Administering a Microsoft Windows 2000 Directory Services Infrastructure
If you have already passed exams 70-067, 70-068, and 70-073, you may take this exam	
Exam 70-240	Microsoft Windows 2000 Accelerated Exam for MCPs Certified on Microsoft Windows NT 4.0

5th Core Option

Choose 1 from this group	
Exam 70-219	Designing a Microsoft Windows 2000 Directory Services Infrastructure
Exam 70-220	Designing Security for a Microsoft Windows 2000 Network
Exam 70-221	Designing a Microsoft Windows 2000 Network Infrastructure
Exam 70-226	Designing Highly Available Web Solutions with Microsoft Windows 2000 Server Technologies

Elective*

Choose 2 from this group	
Exam 70-019	Designing and Implementing Data Warehouse with Microsoft SQL Server 7.0
Exam 70-056	Implementing and Supporting Web Sites Using Microsoft Site Server 3.0
Exam 70-080	Implementing and Supporting Microsoft Internet Explorer 5.0 by Using the Internet Explorer Administration Kit
Exam 70-085	Implementing and Supporting Microsoft SNA Server 4.0
Exam 70-086	Implementing and Supporting Microsoft Systems Management Server 2.0
Exam 70-222	Migrating from Microsoft Windows NT 4.0 to Microsoft Windows 2000
Exam 70-223	Installing, Configuring, and Administering Microsoft Clustering Services by Using Microsoft Windows 2000 Advanced Server
Exam 70-224	Installing, Configuring, and Administering Microsoft Exchange 2000 Server
Exam 70-225	Designing and Deploying a Messaging Infrastructure with Microsoft Exchange 2000 Server
Exam 70-227	Installing, Configuring, and Administering Microsoft Internet Security and Acceleration (ISA) Server 2000 Enterprise Edition
Exam 70-228	Installing, Configuring, and Administering Microsoft SQL Server 2000 Enterprise Edition
Exam 70-229	Designing and Implementing Databases with Microsoft SQL Server 2000 Enterprise Edition
Exam 70-244	Supporting and Maintaining a Microsoft Windows NT Server 4.0 Network

This is not a complete listing—you can still be tested on some earlier versions of these products. However, we have included mainly the most recent versions so that you may test on these versions and thus be certified longer. We have not included any tests that are scheduled to be retired.

* 5th Core Option exams may also be used as electives, but can only be counted once toward a certification. You cannot receive credit for an exam as both a core and an elective in the same track.

Visual Basic 6.0"—*plus* one of these three distributed application exams—"70-015: Designing and Implementing Distributed Applications with Microsoft Visual C++ 6.0," "70-155: Designing and Implementing Distributed Applications with Microsoft Visual FoxPro 6.0," or "70-175: Designing and Implementing Distributed Applications with Microsoft Visual Basic 6.0." The third core exam is "70-100: Analyzing Requirements and Defining Solution Architectures." Elective exams cover specific Microsoft applications and languages, including Visual Basic, C++, the Microsoft Foundation Classes, Access, SQL Server, Excel, and more.

➤ *MCDBA (Microsoft Certified Database Administrator)*—The MCDBA credential reflects the skills required to implement and administer Microsoft SQL Server databases. To obtain an MCDBA, an individual must demonstrate the ability to derive physical database designs, develop logical data models, create physical databases, create data services by using Transact-SQL, manage and maintain databases, configure and manage security, monitor and optimize databases, and install and configure Microsoft SQL Server.

To become an MCDBA, you must pass a total of three core exams and one elective exam. The required core exams are "70-028: Administering Microsoft SQL Server 7.0" or "70-228: Installing, Configuring, and Administering Microsoft SQL Server 2000 Enterprise Edition," "70-029: Designing and Implementing Databases with Microsoft SQL Server 7.0" or "70-229: Designing and Implementing Databases with Microsoft SQL Server 2000 Enterprise Edition", and "70-215: Installing, Configuring and Administering Microsoft Windows 2000 Server" or "70-240: Microsoft Windows 2000 Accelerated Exam for MCPs Certified on Microsoft Windows NT."

The elective exams that you can choose from cover specific uses of SQL Server and include "70-015: Designing and Implementing Distributed Applications with Microsoft Visual C++ 6.0," "70-019: Designing and Implementing Data Warehouses with Microsoft SQL Server 7.0," "70-155: Designing and Implementing Distributed Applications with Microsoft Visual FoxPro 6.0," "70-175: Designing and Implementing Distributed Applications with Microsoft Visual Basic 6.0," and two exams that relate to Windows 2000: "70-216: Implementing and Administering a Microsoft Windows 2000 Network Infrastructure," and "70-087: Implementing and Supporting Microsoft Internet Information Server 4.0."

If you have taken the three core Windows NT 4 exams on your path to becoming an MCSE, you qualify for the Accelerated exam (it replaces the Network Infrastructure exam requirement). The Accelerated exam covers the objectives of all four of the Windows 2000 core exams. In addition to taking the Accelerated exam, you must take only the two SQL exams—Administering and Database Design.

➤ *MCT (Microsoft Certified Trainer)*—Microsoft Certified Trainers are deemed able to deliver elements of the official Microsoft curriculum, based on technical knowledge and instructional ability. Thus, it is necessary for an individual seeking MCT credentials (which are granted on a course-by-course basis) to pass the related certification exam for a course and complete the official Microsoft training in the subject area, and to demonstrate an ability to teach.

This teaching skill criterion may be satisfied by proving that one has already attained training certification from Novell, Banyan, Lotus, the Santa Cruz Operation, or Cisco, or by taking a Microsoft-sanctioned workshop on instruction. Microsoft makes it clear that MCTs are important cogs in the Microsoft training channels. Instructors must be MCTs before Microsoft will allow them to teach in any of its official training channels, including Microsoft's affiliated Certified Technical Education Centers (CTECs) and its online training partner network. As of January 1, 2001, MCT candidates must possess a premier certification such as MCSE, MCDBA, or MCSD.

Microsoft has announced that the MCP+I and MCSE+I credentials will not be continued when the MCSE exams for Windows 2000 are in full swing because the skill set for the Internet portion of the program has been included in the new MCSE program. Therefore, details on these tracks are not provided here; go to **www.microsoft.com/trainingandservices/** if you need more information.

Once a Microsoft product becomes obsolete, MCPs typically have to recertify on current versions. (If individuals do not recertify, their certifications become invalid.) Because technology keeps changing and new products continually supplant old ones, this should come as no surprise. This explains why Microsoft has announced that MCSEs have 12 months past the scheduled retirement date for the Windows NT 4 exams to recertify on Windows 2000 topics. (Note that this means taking at least two exams, if not more.)

The best place to keep tabs on the MCP program and its related certifications is on the Web. The URL for the MCP program is **www.microsoft.com/ trainingandservices/**. But Microsoft's Web site changes often, so if this URL doesn't work, try using the Search tool on Microsoft's site with either "MCP" or the quoted phrase "Microsoft Certified Professional" as a search string. This will help you find the latest and most accurate information about Microsoft's certification programs.

Taking a Certification Exam

Once you've prepared for your exam, you need to register with a testing center. Each computer-based MCP exam costs $100, and if you don't pass, you may retest for an additional $100 for each additional try. In the United States and Canada, tests are administered by Prometric and by Virtual University Enterprises (VUE). Here's how you can contact them:

➤ *Prometric*—You can sign up for a test through the company's Web site at **www.prometric.com**. Within the United States and Canada, you can register by phone at 800-755-3926. If you live outside this region, check the company's Web site for the appropriate phone number.

➤ *Virtual University Enterprises*—You can sign up for a test or get the phone numbers for local testing centers through the Web page at **www.vue.com/ms/**.

To sign up for a test, you must possess a valid credit card, or contact either company for mailing instructions to send them a check (in the U.S.). Only when payment is verified, or a check has cleared, can you actually register for a test.

To schedule an exam, call the number or visit either of the Web pages at least one day in advance. To cancel or reschedule an exam, you must call before 7 P.M. pacific standard time the day before the scheduled test time (or you may be charged, even if you don't appear to take the test). When you want to schedule a test, have the following information ready:

➤ Your name, organization, and mailing address.

➤ Your Microsoft Test ID. (Inside the United States, this means your Social Security number; citizens of other nations should call ahead to find out what type of identification number is required to register for a test.)

➤ The name and number of the exam you wish to take.

➤ A method of payment. (As we've already mentioned, a credit card is the most convenient method, but alternate means can be arranged in advance, if necessary.)

Once you sign up for a test, you'll be informed as to when and where the test is scheduled. Try to arrive at least 15 minutes early. You must supply two forms of identification—one of which must be a photo ID—to be admitted into the testing room.

All exams are completely closed-book. In fact, you will not be permitted to take anything with you into the testing area, but you will be furnished with a blank sheet of paper and a pen or, in some cases, an erasable plastic sheet and an erasable pen. We suggest that you immediately write down on that sheet of paper all the information you've memorized for the test. In *Exam Cram* books, this information appears on a tear-out sheet inside the front cover of each book. You will have some time to compose yourself, record this information, and take a sample orientation exam before you begin the real thing. We suggest you take the orientation test before taking your first exam, but because they're all more or less identical in layout, behavior, and controls, you probably won't need to do this more than once.

When you complete a Microsoft certification exam, the software will tell you whether you've passed or failed. If you need to retake an exam, you'll have to schedule a new test with Prometric or VUE and pay another $100.

 The first time you fail a test, you can retake the test the next day. However, if you fail a second time, you must wait 14 days before retaking that test. The 14-day waiting period remains in effect for all retakes after the second failure.

Tracking MCP Status

As soon as you pass any Microsoft exam (except Networking Essentials), you'll attain Microsoft Certified Professional (MCP) status. Microsoft also generates transcripts that indicate which exams you have passed. You can view a copy of your transcript at any time by going to the MCP secured site and selecting Transcript Tool. This tool will allow you to print a copy of your current transcript and confirm your certification status.

Once you pass the necessary set of exams, you'll be certified. Official certification normally takes anywhere from six to eight weeks, so don't expect to get your credentials overnight. When the package for a qualified certification arrives, it includes a Welcome Kit that contains a number of elements (see Microsoft's Web site for other benefits of specific certifications):

➤ A certificate suitable for framing, along with a wallet card and lapel pin.

➤ A license to use the MCP logo, thereby allowing you to use the logo in advertisements, promotions, and documents, and on letterhead, business cards, and so on. Along with the license comes an MCP logo sheet, which includes camera-ready artwork. (Note: Before using any of the artwork, individuals must sign and return a licensing agreement that indicates they'll abide by its terms and conditions.)

➤ A subscription to *Microsoft Certified Professional Magazine*, which provides ongoing data about testing and certification activities, requirements, and changes to the program.

Many people believe that the benefits of MCP certification go well beyond the perks that Microsoft provides to newly anointed members of this elite group. We're starting to see more job listings that request or require applicants to have an MCP, MCSE, and so on, and many individuals who complete the program can qualify for increases in pay and/or responsibility. As an official recognition of hard work and broad knowledge, one of the MCP credentials is a badge of honor in many IT organizations.

How to Prepare for an Exam

Preparing for any Windows 2000 Server-related test (including " Installing, Configuring and Administering Microsoft Clustering Services by Using Microsoft Windows 2000 Advanced Server") requires that you obtain and study materials designed to provide comprehensive information about the product and its capabilities that will appear on the specific exam for which you are preparing. The following list of materials will help you study and prepare:

➤ The Windows 2000 Server product CD includes comprehensive online documentation and related materials; it should be a primary resource when you are preparing for the test.

➤ The exam preparation materials, practice tests, and self-assessment exams on the Microsoft Training & Services page at **www.microsoft.com/ trainingandservices/default.asp?PageID=mcp**. The Testing Innovations link offers samples of the new question types found on the Windows 2000 MCSE exams. Find the materials, download them, and use them!

➤ The exam preparation advice, practice tests, questions of the day, and discussion groups on the **ExamCram.com** e-learning and certification destination Web site (**www.examcram.com**).

In addition, you'll probably find any or all of the following materials useful in your quest for Clustering Services expertise:

➤ *Microsoft training kits*—Microsoft Press offers a training kit that specifically targets Exam 70-223. For more information, visit: **http:// mspress.microsoft.com/findabook/list/series_ak.htm**. This training kit contains information that you will find useful in preparing for the test.

➤ *Microsoft TechNet CD*—This monthly CD-based publication delivers numerous electronic titles that include coverage of Clustering Services and related topics on the Technical Information (TechNet) CD. Its offerings include product facts, technical notes, tools and utilities, and information on how to access the Seminars Online training materials for Clustering Services. A subscription to TechNet costs $299 per year, but it is well worth the price. Visit **www.microsoft.com/technet/** and check out the information under the "TechNet Subscription" menu entry for more details.

➤ *Study guides*—Several publishers—including The Coriolis Group—offer Windows 2000 titles. The Coriolis Group series includes the following:

➤ *The Exam Cram series*—These books give you information about the material you need to know to pass the tests.

➤ *The Exam Prep series*—These books provide a greater level of detail than the *Exam Cram* books and are designed to teach you everything you need to know from an exam perspective. Each book comes with a CD that contains interactive practice exams in a variety of testing formats.

Together, the two series make a perfect pair.

➤ *Multimedia*—These Coriolis Group materials are designed to support learners of all types—whether you learn best by reading or doing:

  ➤ *The Exam Cram Personal Trainer*—Offers a unique, personalized self-paced training course based on the exam.

  ➤ *The Exam Cram Personal Test Center*—Features multiple test options that simulate the actual exam, including Fixed-Length, Random, Review, and Test All. Explanations of correct and incorrect answers reinforce concepts learned.

➤ *Classroom training*—CTECs, online partners, and third-party training companies (like Wave Technologies, Learning Tree, Data-Tech, and others) all offer classroom training on Windows 2000. These companies aim to help you prepare to pass Exam 70-223. Although such training runs upwards of $350 per day in class, most of the individuals lucky enough to partake find it to be quite worthwhile.

➤ *Other publications*—There's no shortage of materials available about Clustering Services. The resource sections at the end of each chapter should give you an idea of where we think you should look for further discussion.

By far, this set of required and recommended materials represents a nonpareil collection of sources and resources for Clustering Services and related topics. We anticipate that you'll find that this book belongs in this company.

About this Book

Each topical *Exam Cram* chapter follows a regular structure, along with graphical cues about important or useful information. Here's the structure of a typical chapter:

➤ *Opening hotlists*—Each chapter begins with a list of the terms, tools, and techniques that you must learn and understand before you can be fully conversant with that chapter's subject matter. We follow the hotlists with one or two introductory paragraphs to set the stage for the rest of the chapter.

➤ *Topical coverage*—After the opening hotlists, each chapter covers a series of topics related to the chapter's subject title. Throughout this section, we highlight topics or concepts likely to appear on a test using a special Exam Alert layout, like this:

This is what an Exam Alert looks like. Normally, an Exam Alert stresses concepts, terms, software, or activities that are likely to relate to one or more certification test questions. For that reason, we think any information found offset in Exam Alert format is worthy of unusual attentiveness on your part. Indeed, most of the information that appears on The Cram Sheet appears as Exam Alerts within the text.

Pay close attention to material flagged as an Exam Alert; although all the information in this book pertains to what you need to know to pass the exam, we flag certain items that are really important. You'll find what appears in the meat of each chapter to be worth knowing, too, when preparing for the test. Because this book's material is very condensed, we recommend that you use this book along with other resources to achieve the maximum benefit.

In addition to the Exam Alerts, we have provided tips that will help you build a better foundation for Clustering Services knowledge. Although the information may not be on the exam, it is certainly related and will help you become a better test-taker.

 This is how tips are formatted. Keep your eyes open for these, and you'll become a Clustering Services guru in no time!

➤ *Practice questions*—Although we talk about test questions and topics throughout the book, a section at the end of each chapter presents a series of mock test questions and explanations of both correct and incorrect answers.

➤ *Details and resources*—Every chapter ends with a section titled "Need to Know More?". This section provides direct pointers to Microsoft and third-party resources offering more details on the chapter's subject. In addition, this section tries to rank or at least rate the quality and thoroughness of the topic's coverage by each resource. If you find a resource you like in this collection, use it, but don't feel compelled to use all the resources. On the other hand, we recommend only resources we use on a regular basis, so none of our recommendations will be a waste of your time or money (but purchasing them all at once probably represents an expense that many network administrators and would-be MCPs and MCSEs might find hard to justify).

The bulk of the book follows this chapter structure slavishly, but there are a few other elements that we'd like to point out. Chapter 14 includes a sample test that provides a good review of the material presented throughout the book to ensure you're ready for the exam. Chapter 15 is an answer key to the sample test that appears in Chapter 14 In addition, you'll find a handy glossary and an index.

Finally, the tear-out Cram Sheet attached next to the inside front cover of this *Exam Cram* book represents a condensed and compiled collection of facts and tips that we think you should memorize before taking the test. Because you can dump this information out of your head onto a piece of paper before taking the exam, you can master this information by brute force—you need to remember it only long enough to write it down when you walk into the test room. You might even want to look at it in the car or in the lobby of the testing center just before you walk in to take the test.

How to Use this Book

We've structured the topics in this book to build on one another. Therefore, some topics in later chapters make more sense after you've read earlier chapters. That's why we suggest you read this book from front to back for your initial test preparation. If you need to brush up on a topic or you have to bone up for a second try, use the index or table of contents to go straight to the topics and questions that you need to study. Beyond helping you prepare for the test, we think you'll find this book useful as a tightly focused reference to some of the most important aspects of Clustering Services.

Given all the book's elements and its specialized focus, we've tried to create a tool that will help you prepare for—and pass—Microsoft Exam 70-223. Please share your feedback on the book with us, especially if you have ideas about how we can improve it for future test-takers. We'll consider everything you say carefully, and we'll respond to all suggestions.

Send your questions or comments to us at **learn@examcram.com**. Please remember to include the title of the book in your message; otherwise, we'll be forced to guess which book you're writing about. And we don't like to guess—we want to *know*! Also, be sure to check out the Web pages at **www.examcram.com**, where you'll find information updates, commentary, and certification information.

Thanks, and enjoy the book!

Self-Assessment

The reason we included a Self-Assessment in this *Exam Cram* book is to help you evaluate your readiness to tackle MCSE certification. It should also help you understand what you need to know to master the topic of this book—namely, Exam 70-223, "Installing, Configuring, and Administering Microsoft Clustering Services Using Microsoft Windows 2000 Advanced Server." But before you tackle this Self-Assessment, let's talk about concerns you may face when pursuing an MCSE for Windows 2000, and what an ideal MCSE candidate might look like.

MCSEs in the Real World

In the next section, we describe an ideal MCSE candidate, knowing full well that only a few real candidates will meet this ideal. In fact, our description of that ideal candidate might seem downright scary, especially with the changes that have been made to the program to support Windows 2000. But take heart: Although the requirements to obtain an MCSE may seem formidable, they are by no means impossible to meet. However, be keenly aware that it does take time, involves some expense, and requires real effort to get through the process.

Increasing numbers of people are attaining Microsoft certifications, so the goal is within reach. You can get all the real-world motivation you need from knowing that many others have gone before, so you will be able to follow in their footsteps. If you're willing to tackle the process seriously and do what it takes to obtain the necessary experience and knowledge, you can take—and pass—all the certification tests involved in obtaining an MCSE. In fact, we've designed *Exam Preps*, the companion *Exam Crams*, *Exam Cram Personal Trainers*, and *Exam Cram Personal Test Centers* to make it as easy on you as possible to prepare for these exams. We've also greatly expanded our Web site, **www.examcram.com**, to provide a host of resources to help you prepare for the complexities of Windows 2000.

Besides MCSE, other Microsoft certifications include:

➤ MCSD, which is aimed at software developers and requires one specific exam, two more exams on client and distributed topics, plus a fourth elective exam drawn from a different, but limited, pool of options.

➤ Other Microsoft certifications, whose requirements range from one test (MCP) to several tests (MCP+SB, MCDBA).

The Ideal Windows 2000 MCSE Candidate

Just to give you some idea of what an ideal MCSE candidate is like, here are some relevant statistics about the background and experience such an individual might have. Don't worry if you don't meet these qualifications, or don't come that close—this is a far from ideal world, and where you fall short is simply where you'll have more work to do.

➤ Academic or professional training in network theory, concepts, and operations. This includes everything from networking media and transmission techniques through network operating systems, services, and applications.

➤ Three-plus years of professional networking experience, including experience with Ethernet, token ring, modems, and other networking media. This must include installation, configuration, upgrade, and troubleshooting experience.

Note: The Windows 2000 MCSE program is much more rigorous than the previous NT MCSE program; therefore, you'll really need some hands-on experience. Some of the exams require you to solve real-world case studies and network design issues, so the more hands-on experience you have, the better.

➤ Two-plus years in a networked environment that includes hands-on experience with Windows 2000 Server, Windows 2000 Professional, Windows NT Server, Windows NT Workstation, and Windows 95 or Windows 98. A solid understanding of each system's architecture, installation, configuration, maintenance, and troubleshooting is also essential.

➤ Knowledge of the various methods for installing Windows 2000, including manual and unattended installations.

➤ A thorough understanding of key networking protocols, addressing, and name resolution, including TCP/IP, IPX/SPX, and NetBEUI.

➤ A thorough understanding of NetBIOS naming, browsing, and file and print services.

➤ Familiarity with key Windows 2000-based TCP/IP-based services, including HTTP (Web servers), DHCP, WINS, DNS, plus familiarity with one or more of the following: Internet Information Server (IIS), Index Server, and Proxy Server.

➤ An understanding of how to implement security for key network data in a Windows 2000 environment.

➤ Working knowledge of NetWare 3.x and 4.x, including IPX/SPX frame formats, NetWare file, print, and directory services, and both Novell and Microsoft client software. Working knowledge of Microsoft's Client Service For NetWare (CSNW), Gateway Service For NetWare (GSNW), the NetWare Migration Tool (NWCONV), and the NetWare Client For Windows (NT, 95, and 98) is essential.

➤ A good working understanding of Active Directory. The more you work with Windows 2000, the more you'll realize that this new operating system is quite different than Windows NT. New technologies like Active Directory have really changed the way that Windows is configured and used. We recommend that you find out as much as you can about Active Directory and acquire as much experience using this technology as possible. The time you take learning about Active Directory will be time very well spent!

Fundamentally, this boils down to a bachelor's degree in computer science, plus three years' experience working in a position involving network design, installation, configuration, and maintenance. We believe that well under half of all certification candidates meet these requirements, and that, in fact, most meet less than half of these requirements—at least, when they begin the certification process. But because all the people who already have been certified have survived this ordeal, you can survive it too—especially if you heed what our Self-Assessment can tell you about what you already know and what you need to learn.

Put Yourself to the Test

The following series of questions and observations is designed to help you figure out how much work you must do to pursue Microsoft certification and what kinds of resources you may consult on your quest. Be absolutely honest in your answers, or you'll end up wasting money on exams you're not yet ready to take. There are no right or wrong answers, only steps along the path to certification. Only you can decide where you really belong in the broad spectrum of aspiring candidates.

Two things should be clear from the outset, however:

➤ Even a modest background in computer science will be helpful.

➤ Hands-on experience with Microsoft products and technologies is an essential ingredient to certification success.

Educational Background

1. Have you ever taken any computer-related classes? [Yes or No]

    If Yes, proceed to question 2; if No, proceed to question 4.

2. Have you taken any classes on computer operating systems? [Yes or No]

If Yes, you will probably be able to handle Microsoft's architecture and system component discussions. If you're rusty, brush up on basic operating system concepts, especially virtual memory, multitasking regimes, user mode versus kernel mode operation, and general computer security topics.

If No, consider some basic reading in this area. We strongly recommend a good general operating systems book, such as *Operating System Concepts, 5th Edition*, by Abraham Silberschatz and Peter Baer Galvin (John Wiley & Sons, 1998, ISBN 0-471-36414-2). If this title doesn't appeal to you, check out reviews for other, similar titles at your favorite online bookstore.

3. Have you taken any networking concepts or technologies classes? [Yes or No]

If Yes, you will probably be able to handle Microsoft's networking terminology, concepts, and technologies (brace yourself for frequent departures from normal usage). If you're rusty, brush up on basic networking concepts and terminology, especially networking media, transmission types, the OSI Reference Model, and networking technologies such as Ethernet, token ring, FDDI, and WAN links.

If No, you might want to read one or two books in this topic area. The two best books that we know of are *Computer Networks, 3rd Edition*, by Andrew S. Tanenbaum (Prentice-Hall, 1996, ISBN 0-13-349945-6) and *Computer Networks and Internets, 2nd Edition*, by Douglas E. Comer and Ralph E. Droms (Prentice-Hall, 1998, ISBN 0-130-83617-6).

Skip to the next section, "Hands-on Experience."

4. Have you done any reading on operating systems or networks? [Yes or No]

If Yes, review the requirements stated in the first paragraphs after questions 2 and 3. If you meet those requirements, move on to the next section. If No, consult the recommended reading for both topics. A strong background will help you prepare for the Microsoft exams better than just about anything else.

Hands-on Experience

The most important key to success on all of the Microsoft tests is hands-on experience, especially with Windows 2000 Server and Professional, plus the many add-on services and BackOffice components around which so many of the Microsoft certification exams revolve. If we leave you with only one realization after taking this Self-Assessment, it should be that there's no substitute for time spent installing, configuring, and using the various Microsoft products upon which you'll be tested repeatedly and in depth.

5. Have you installed, configured, and worked with:

➤ Windows 2000 Server? [Yes or No]

If Yes, make sure you understand basic concepts as covered in Exam 70-215. You should also study the TCP/IP interfaces, utilities, and services for Exam 70-216, plus implementing security features for Exam 70-220.

 You can download objectives, practice exams, and other data about Microsoft exams from the Training and Certification page at **www.microsoft.com/trainingandservices/default.asp?PageID=mcp**. Use the "Exams" link to obtain specific exam information.

If you haven't worked with Windows 2000 Server, you must obtain one or two machines and a copy of Windows 2000 Server. Then, learn the operating system and whatever other software components on which you'll also be tested.

In fact, we recommend that you obtain two computers, each with a network interface, and set up a two-node network on which to practice. With decent Windows 2000-capable computers selling for about $500 to $600 apiece these days, this shouldn't be too much of a financial hardship. You may have to scrounge to come up with the necessary software, but if you scour the Microsoft Web site you can usually find low-cost options to obtain evaluation copies of most of the software that you'll need.

➤ Windows 2000 Professional? [Yes or No]

If Yes, make sure you understand the concepts covered in Exam 70-210.

If No, you will want to obtain a copy of Windows 2000 Professional and learn how to install, configure, and maintain it. You can use *MCSE Windows 2000 Professional Exam Cram* to guide your activities and studies, or work straight from Microsoft's test objectives if you prefer.

 For any and all of these Microsoft exams, the Resource Kits for the topics involved are a good study resource. You can purchase softcover Resource Kits from Microsoft Press (search for them at **http://mspress.microsoft.com/**), but they also appear on the TechNet CDs (**www.microsoft.com/technet**). Along with *Exam Crams* and *Exam Preps*, we believe that Resource Kits are among the best tools you can use to prepare for Microsoft exams.

6. For any specific Microsoft product that is not itself an operating system (for example, SQL Server), have you installed, configured, used, and upgraded this software? [Yes or No]

If the answer is Yes, skip to the next section. If it's No, you must get some experience. Read on for suggestions on how to do this.

Experience is a must with any Microsoft product exam, be it something as simple as FrontPage 2000 or as challenging as SQL Server 7.0. For trial copies of other software, search Microsoft's Web site using the name of the product as your search term. Also, search for bundles like "BackOffice" or "Small Business Server."

 If you have the funds, or your employer will pay your way, consider taking a class at a Certified Training and Education Center (CTEC) or at an Authorized Academic Training Partner (AATP). In addition to classroom exposure to the topic of your choice, you get a copy of the software that is the focus of your course, along with a trial version of whatever operating system it needs, with the training materials for that class.

Before you even think about taking any Microsoft exam, make sure you've spent enough time with the related software to understand how it may be installed and configured, how to maintain such an installation, and how to troubleshoot that software when things go wrong. This will help you in the exam, and in real life!

Testing Your Exam-Readiness

Whether you attend a formal class on a specific topic to get ready for an exam or use written materials to study on your own, some preparation for the Microsoft certification exams is essential. At $100 a try, pass or fail, you want to do everything you can to pass on your first try. That's where studying comes in.

We have included a practice exam in this book, so if you don't score that well on the test, you can study more and then tackle the test again. We also have exams that you can take online through the **ExamCram.com** Web site at **www.examcram.com**. If you still don't hit a score of at least 85 percent after these tests, you'll want to investigate the other practice test resources we mention in this section.

For any given subject, consider taking a class if you've tackled self-study materials, taken the test, and failed anyway. The opportunity to interact with an instructor and fellow students can make all the difference in the world, if you can afford that privilege. For information about Microsoft classes, visit the Training and Certification page at **www.microsoft.com/education/partners/ctec.asp** for Microsoft Certified Education Centers or **www.microsoft.com/aatp/default.htm** for Microsoft Authorized Training Providers.

If you can't afford to take a class, visit the Training and Certification page anyway, because it also includes pointers to free practice exams and to Microsoft Certified Professional Approved Study Guides and other self-study tools. And even if you can't afford to spend much at all, you should still invest in some low-cost practice exams from commercial vendors.

7. Have you taken a practice exam on your chosen test subject? [Yes or No]

   If Yes, and you scored 70 percent or better, you're probably ready to tackle the real thing. If your score isn't above that threshold, keep at it until you break that barrier.

   If No, obtain all the free and low-budget practice tests you can find and get to work. Keep at it until you can break the passing threshold comfortably.

 When it comes to assessing your test readiness, there is no better way than to take a good-quality practice exam and pass with a score of 85 percent or better. When we're preparing ourselves, we shoot for 85-plus percent, just to leave room for the "weirdness factor" that sometimes shows up on Microsoft exams.

Assessing Readiness for Exam 70-223

In addition to the general exam-readiness information in the previous section, there are several things you can do to prepare for the Installing, Configuring, and Administering Clustering Services by Using Microsoft Windows 2000 Advanced Server exam. As you're getting ready for Exam 70-223, visit the Exam Cram Windows 2000 Resource Center at **www.examcram.com/studyresource/w2kresource/**. Another valuable resource is the Exam Cram Insider newsletter. Sign up at **www.examcram.com** or send a blank email message to **subscribe-ec@mars.coriolis.com**. We also suggest that you join an active MCSE mailing list. One of the better ones is managed by Sunbelt Software. Sign up at **www.sunbelt-software.com** (look for the Subscribe button).

You can also cruise the Web looking for "braindumps" (recollections of test topics and experiences recorded by others) to help you anticipate topics you're likely to encounter on the test. The MCSE mailing list is a good place to ask where the useful braindumps are.

 You can't be sure that a braindump's author can provide correct answers. Thus, use the questions to guide your studies, but don't rely on the answers in a braindump to lead you to the truth. Double-check everything you find in any braindump.

Microsoft exam mavens also recommend checking the Microsoft Knowledge Base (available on its own CD as part of the TechNet collection, or on the Microsoft Web site at **http://support.microsoft.com/support/**) for "meaningful technical support issues" that relate to your exam's topics. Although we're not sure exactly what the quoted phrase means, we have also noticed some overlap between technical support questions on particular products and troubleshooting questions on the exams for those products.

Onward, through the Fog!

Once you've assessed your readiness, undertaken the right background studies, obtained the hands-on experience that will help you understand the products and technologies at work, and reviewed the many sources of information to help you prepare for a test, you'll be ready to take a round of practice tests. When your scores come back positive enough to get you through the exam, you're ready to go after the real thing. If you follow our assessment regime, you'll not only know what you need to study, but when you're ready to make a test date at Prometric or VUE. Good luck!

Microsoft
Certification Exams

. . . .

Terms you'll need to understand:

✓ Case study

✓ Multiple-choice question formats

✓ Build-list-and-reorder question format

✓ Create-a-tree question format

✓ Drag-and-connect question format

✓ Select-and-place question format

✓ Fixed-length tests

✓ Simulations

✓ Adaptive tests

✓ Short-form tests

Techniques you'll need to master:

✓ Assessing your exam-readiness

✓ Answering Microsoft's varying question types

✓ Altering your test strategy depending on the exam format

✓ Practicing (to make perfect)

✓ Making the best use of the testing software

✓ Budgeting your time

✓ Guessing (as a last resort)

Exam taking is not something that most people anticipate eagerly, no matter how well prepared they may be. In most cases, familiarity helps offset test anxiety. In plain English, this means you probably won't be as nervous when you take your fourth or fifth Microsoft certification exam as you'll be when you take your first one.

Whether it's your first exam or your tenth, understanding the details of taking the new exams (how much time to spend on questions, the environment you'll be in, and so on) and the new exam software will help you concentrate on the material rather than on the setting. Likewise, mastering a few basic exam-taking skills should help you recognize—and perhaps even outfox—some of the tricks and snares you're bound to find in some exam questions.

This chapter, besides explaining the exam environment and software, describes some proven exam-taking strategies that you should be able to use to your advantage.

Assessing Exam-Readiness

We strongly recommend that you read through and take the Self-Assessment included with this book (it appears just before this chapter, in fact). This will help you compare your knowledge base to the requirements for obtaining an MCSE, and it will also help you identify parts of your background or experience that may be in need of improvement, enhancement, or further learning. If you get the right set of basics under your belt, obtaining Microsoft certification will be that much easier.

Once you've gone through the Self-Assessment, you can remedy those topical areas where your background or experience may not measure up to an ideal certification candidate. But you can also tackle subject matter for individual tests at the same time, so you can continue making progress while you're catching up in some areas.

Once you've worked through an *Exam Cram*, have read the supplementary materials, and have taken the practice test, you'll have a pretty clear idea of when you should be ready to take the real exam. Although we strongly recommend that you keep practicing until your scores top the 85 percent mark, 90 percent would be a good goal to give yourself some margin for error in a real exam situation (where stress will play more of a role than when you practice). Once you hit that point, you should be ready to go. But if you get through the practice exam in this book without attaining that score, you should keep taking practice tests and studying the materials until you get there. You'll find more pointers on how to study and prepare in the Self-Assessment. But now, on to the exam itself!

The Exam Situation

When you arrive at the testing center where you scheduled your exam, you'll need to sign in with an exam coordinator. He or she will ask you to show two forms of identification, one of which must be a photo ID. After you've signed in and your time slot arrives, you'll be asked to deposit any books, bags, or other items you brought with you. Then, you'll be escorted into a closed room.

All exams are completely closed book. In fact, you will not be permitted to take anything with you into the testing area, but you will be furnished with a blank sheet of paper and a pen or, in some cases, an erasable plastic sheet and an erasable pen. Before the exam, you should memorize as much of the important material as you can, so you can write that information on the blank sheet as soon as you are seated in front of the computer. You can refer to this piece of paper anytime you like during the test, but you'll have to surrender the sheet when you leave the room.

You will have some time to compose yourself, to record this information, and to take a sample orientation exam before you begin the real thing. We suggest you take the orientation test before taking your first exam, but because they're all more or less identical in layout, behavior, and controls, you probably won't need to do this more than once.

Typically, the room will be furnished with anywhere from one to half a dozen computers, and each workstation will be separated from the others by dividers designed to keep you from seeing what's happening on someone else's computer. Most test rooms feature a wall with a large picture window. This permits the exam coordinator to monitor the room, to prevent exam-takers from talking to one another, and to observe anything out of the ordinary that might go on. The exam coordinator will have preloaded the appropriate Microsoft certification exam—for this book, that's Exam 70-223—and you'll be permitted to start as soon as you're seated in front of the computer.

All Microsoft certification exams allow a certain maximum amount of time in which to complete your work (this time is indicated on the exam by an on-screen counter/clock, so you can check the time remaining whenever you like). All Microsoft certification exams are computer generated. In addition to multiple choice, you'll encounter select and place (drag and drop), create a tree (categorization and prioritization), drag and connect, and build list and reorder (list prioritization) on most exams. Although this may sound quite simple, the questions are constructed not only to check your mastery of basic facts and figures about Cluster Services, but they also require you to evaluate one or more sets of circumstances or requirements. Often, you'll be asked to give more than one answer to a question. Likewise, you might be asked to select the best or most effective solution to a problem from a range of choices, all of which technically are correct. Taking the exam is quite an adventure, and it involves real thinking. This book shows you what to expect and how to deal with the potential problems, puzzles, and predicaments.

In the next section, you'll learn more about how Microsoft test questions look and how they must be answered.

Exam Layout and Design

The format of Microsoft's Windows 2000 exams is different from that of its previous exams. For the design exams (70-219, 70-220, 70-221), each exam consists entirely of a series of case studies, and the questions can be of six types. For the Core Four exams (70-210, 70-215, 70-216, 70-217), the same six types of questions can appear, but you are not likely to encounter complex multiquestion case studies. It is unlikely that you will encounter a case study format in Exam 70-223, but you will encounter some of the 6 questions types discussed in the following paragraphs.

For design exams, each case study or "testlet" presents a detailed problem that you must read and analyze. Figure 1.1 shows an example of what a case study looks like. You must select the different tabs in the case study to view the entire case.

Following each case study is a set of questions related to the case study; these questions can be one of six types (which are discussed next). Careful attention to details provided in the case study is the key to success. Be prepared to toggle frequently between the case study and the questions as you work. Some of the case studies also include diagrams, which are called *exhibits*, that you'll need to examine closely to understand how to answer the questions.

Once you complete a case study, you can review all the questions and your answers. However, once you move on to the next case study, you may not be able to return to the previous case study and make any changes.

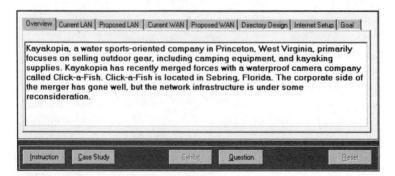

Figure 1.1 This is how case studies appear.

The six types of question formats are:

➤ Multiple choice, single answer

➤ Multiple choice, multiple answers

➤ Build list and reorder (list prioritization)

➤ Create a tree

➤ Drag and connect

➤ Select and place (drag and drop)

Note: Exam formats may vary by test center location. You may want to call the test center or visit ExamCram.com to see if you can find out which type of test you'll encounter.

Multiple-Choice Question Format

Some exam questions require you to select a single answer, whereas others ask you to select multiple correct answers. The following multiple-choice question requires you to select a single correct answer. Following the question is a brief summary of each potential answer and why it is either right or wrong.

Question 1

You have three domains connected to an empty root domain under one contiguous domain name: **tutu.com**. This organization is formed into a forest arrangement with a secondary domain called **frog.com**. How many Schema Masters exist for this arrangement?

○ a. 1

○ b. 2

○ c. 3

○ d. 4

The correct answer is a because only one Schema Master is necessary for a forest arrangement. The other answers (b, c, d) are misleading because they try to make you believe that Schema Masters might be in each domain, or perhaps that you should have one for each contiguous namespaced domain.

This sample question format corresponds closely to the Microsoft certification exam format—the only difference on the exam is that questions are not followed by answer keys. To select an answer, you would position the cursor over the radio button next to the answer. Then, click the mouse button to select the answer.

Let's examine a question where one or more answers are possible. This type of question provides checkboxes rather than radio buttons for marking all appropriate selections.

Question 2

> How can you seize FSMO roles? [Check all correct answers]
>
> ❑ a.   The ntdsutil.exe utility
>
> ❑ b.   The Replication Monitor
>
> ❑ c.   The secedit.exe utility
>
> ❑ d.   Active Directory Domains and FSMOs

Answers a and b are correct. You can seize roles from a server that is still running through the Replication Monitor or, in the case of a server failure, you can seize roles with the ntdsutil.exe utility. The secedit utility is used to force group policies into play; therefore, answer c is incorrect. Active Directory Domains and Trusts are a combination of truth and fiction; therefore, answer d is incorrect.

For this particular question, two answers are required. Microsoft sometimes gives partial credit for partially correct answers. For Question 2, you have to check the boxes next to items a and b to obtain credit for a correct answer. Notice that picking the right answers also means knowing why the other answers are wrong!

Build-List-and-Reorder Question Format

Questions in the build-list-and-reorder format present two lists of items—one on the left and one on the right. To answer the question, you must move items from the list on the right to the list on the left. The final list must then be reordered into a specific order.

These questions can best be characterized as "From the following list of choices, pick the choices that answer the question. Arrange the list in a certain order." To give you practice with this type of question, some questions of this type are included in this study guide. Here's an example of how they appear in this book; for a sample of how they appear on the test, see Figure 1.2.

Question 3

From the following list of famous people, pick those that have been elected President of the United States. Arrange the list in the order that they served.

Thomas Jefferson

Ben Franklin

Abe Lincoln

George Washington

Andrew Jackson

Paul Revere

The correct answer is:

George Washington

Thomas Jefferson

Andrew Jackson

Abe Lincoln

On an actual exam, the entire list of famous people would initially appear in the list on the right. You would move the four correct answers to the list on the left, and then reorder the list on the left. Notice that the answer to the question did not include all items from the initial list. However, this may not always be the case.

To move an item from the right list to the left list, first select the item by clicking on it, and then click on the Add button (left arrow). Once you move an item from one list to the other, you can move the item back by first selecting the item and then clicking on the appropriate button (either the Add button or the Remove button). Once items have been moved to the left list, you can reorder an item by selecting the item and clicking on the up or down button.

Create-a-Tree Question Format

Questions in the create-a-tree format also present two lists—one on the left side of the screen and one on the right side of the screen. The list on the right consists of individual items, and the list on the left consists of nodes in a tree. To answer the question, you must move items from the list on the right to the appropriate node in the tree.

These questions can best be characterized as simply a matching exercise. Items from the list on the right are placed under the appropriate category in the list on the left. Here's an example of how they appear in this book; for a sample of how they appear on the test, see Figure 1.3.

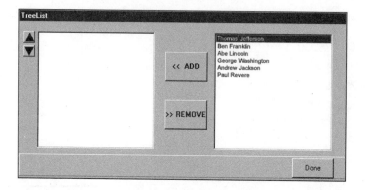

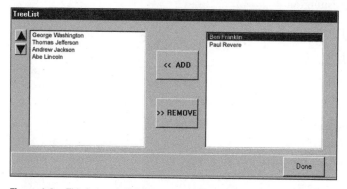

Figure 1.2   This is how build-list-and-reorder questions appear.

Question 4

The calendar year is divided into four seasons:

> Winter
>
> Spring
>
> Summer
>
> Fall

Identify the season when each of the following holidays occurs:

Christmas	Fourth of July
Labor Day	Flag Day
Memorial Day	Washington's Birthday
Thanksgiving	Easter

The correct answer is:

> Winter
>> Christmas
>>
>> Washington's Birthday
>
> Spring
>> Flag Day
>>
>> Memorial Day
>>
>> Easter
>
> Summer
>> Fourth of July
>>
>> Labor Day
>
> Fall
>> Thanksgiving

In this case, all the items in the list were used. However, this may not always be the case.

To move an item from the right list to its appropriate location in the tree, you must first select the appropriate tree node by clicking on it. Then, you select the item to be moved and click on the Add button. If one or more items have been added to a tree node, the node will be displayed with a "+" icon to the left of the node name. You can click on this icon to expand the node and view the item(s) that have been added. If any item has been added to the wrong tree node, you can remove it by selecting it and clicking on the Remove button.

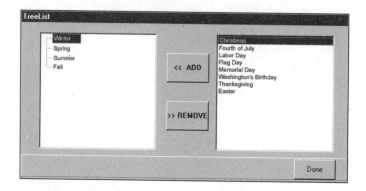

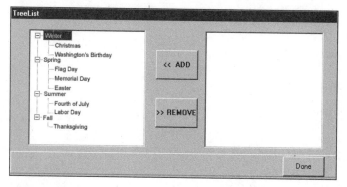

Figure 1.3 This is how create-a-tree questions appear.

Drag-and-Connect Question Format

Questions in the drag-and-connect format present a group of objects and a list of "connections." To answer the question, you must move the appropriate connections between the objects.

This type of question is best described using graphics. Here's an example.

Question 5

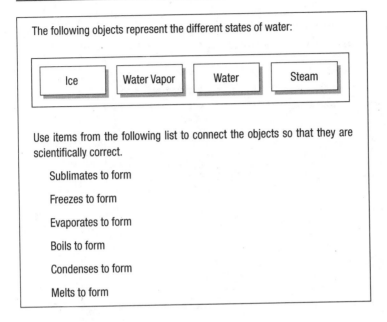

The correct answer is:

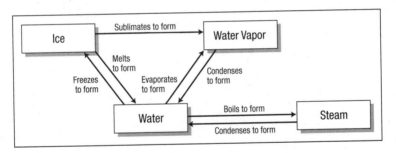

For this type of question, it's not necessary to use every object, and each connection can be used multiple times.

Select-and-Place Question Format

Questions in the select-and-place (drag-and-drop) format present a diagram with blank boxes, and a list of labels that need to be dragged to correctly fill in the blank boxes. To answer the question, you must move the labels to their appropriate positions on the diagram.

This type of question is best described using graphics. Here's an example.

Question 6

Place the items in their proper order, by number, on the following flowchart. Some items may be used more than once, and some items may not be used at all.

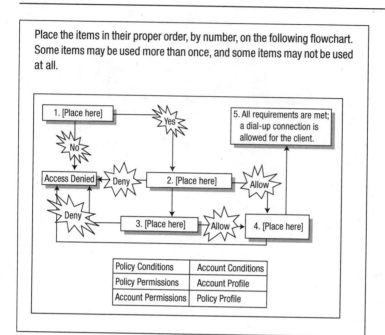

The correct answer is:

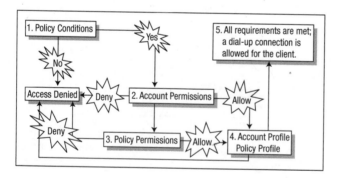

Microsoft's Testing Formats

Currently, Microsoft uses four different testing formats:

➤ Case study

➤ Fixed length

➤ Adaptive

➤ Short form

As we mentioned earlier, the case study approach is used with Microsoft's design exams, and you are unlikely to encounter it on Exam 70-223. Design exams consist of a set of case studies that you must analyze to enable you to answer questions related to the case studies. Such exams include one or more case studies (tabbed topic areas), each of which is followed by 4 to 10 questions. The question types for design exams and for Core Four Windows 2000 exams are multiple choice, build list and reorder, create a tree, drag and connect, and select and place. Depending on the test topic, some exams are totally case-based, whereas others are not.

Other Microsoft exams employ advanced testing capabilities that might not be immediately apparent. Although the questions that appear are primarily multiple choice, the logic that drives them is more complex than older Microsoft tests, which use a fixed sequence of questions, called a *fixed-length test*. Some questions employ a sophisticated user interface, which Microsoft calls a *simulation*, to test your knowledge of the software and systems under consideration in a more or less "live" environment that behaves just like the original. The Testing Innovations link at **www.microsoft.com/trainingandservices/default.asp?PageID=mcp** includes a downloadable practice simulation.

For some exams, Microsoft has turned to a well-known technique, called *adaptive testing*, to establish a test-taker's level of knowledge and product competence. Adaptive exams look the same as fixed-length exams, but they discover the level of difficulty at which an individual test-taker can correctly answer questions. Test-takers with differing levels of knowledge or ability therefore see different sets of questions; individuals with high levels of knowledge or ability are presented with a smaller set of more difficult questions, whereas individuals with lower levels of knowledge are presented with a larger set of easier questions. Two individuals may answer the same percentage of questions correctly, but the test-taker with a higher knowledge or ability level will score higher because his or her questions are worth more.

Also, the lower-level test-taker will probably answer more questions than his or her more-knowledgeable colleague. This explains why adaptive tests use ranges of values to define the number of questions and the amount of time it takes to complete the test.

Adaptive tests work by evaluating the test-taker's most recent answer. A correct answer leads to a more difficult question (and the test software's estimate of the test-taker's knowledge and ability level is raised). An incorrect answer leads to a less difficult question (and the test software's estimate of the test-taker's knowledge and ability level is lowered). This process continues until the test targets the test-taker's true ability level. The exam ends when the test-taker's level of accuracy meets a statistically acceptable value (in other words, when his or her performance demonstrates an acceptable level of knowledge and ability), or when the maximum number of items has been presented (in which case, the test-taker is almost certain to fail).

Microsoft also introduced a short-form test for its most popular tests. This test delivers 25 to 30 questions to its takers, giving them exactly 60 minutes to complete the exam. This type of exam is similar to a fixed-length test, in that it allows readers to jump ahead or return to earlier questions, and to cycle through the questions until the test is done. Microsoft does not use adaptive logic in this test, but claims that statistical analysis of the question pool is such that the 25 to 30 questions delivered during a short-form exam conclusively measure a test-taker's knowledge of the subject matter in much the same way as an adaptive test. You can think of the short-form test as a kind of "greatest hits exam" (that is, the most important questions are covered) version of an adaptive exam on the same topic.

Note: Some of the Microsoft exams can contain a combination of adaptive and fixed-length questions.

Microsoft tests can come in any one of these forms. Whatever you encounter, you must take the test in whichever form it appears; you can't choose one form over another. If anything, it pays more to prepare thoroughly for an adaptive exam than for a fixed-length or a short-form exam: The penalties for answering incorrectly are built into the test itself on an adaptive exam, whereas the layout remains the same for a fixed-length or short-form test, no matter how many questions you answer incorrectly.

 The biggest difference between an adaptive test and a fixed-length or short-form test is that on a fixed-length or short-form test, you can revisit questions after you've read them over one or more times. On an adaptive test, you must answer the question when it's presented and will have no opportunities to revisit that question thereafter.

Strategies for Different Testing Formats

Before you choose a test-taking strategy, you must know if your test is case study based, fixed length, short form, or adaptive. When you begin your exam, you'll know right away if the test is based on case studies. The interface will consist of a tabbed window that allows you to easily navigate through the sections of the case.

If you are taking a test that is not based on case studies, the software will tell you that the test is adaptive, if in fact the version you're taking is an adaptive test. If your introductory materials fail to mention this, you're probably taking a fixed-length test (50 to 70 questions). If the total number of questions involved is 25 to 30, you're taking a short-form test. Some tests announce themselves by indicating that they will start with a set of adaptive questions, followed by fixed-length questions.

You'll be able to tell for sure if you are taking an adaptive, fixed-length, or short-form test by the first question. If it includes a checkbox that lets you mark the question for later review, you're taking a fixed-length or short-form test. If the total number of questions is 25 to 30, it's a short-form test; if more than 30, it's a fixed-length test. Adaptive test questions can be visited (and answered) only once, and they include no such checkbox.

The Case Study Exam Strategy

Most test-takers find that the case study type of test used for the design exams (70-219, 70-220, and 70-221) is the most difficult to master. When it comes to studying for a case study test, your best bet is to approach each case study as a standalone test. The biggest challenge you'll encounter is that you'll feel that you won't have enough time to get through all of the cases that are presented.

Each case provides a lot of material that you'll need to read and study before you can effectively answer the questions that follow. The trick to taking a case study exam is to first scan the case study to get the highlights. Make sure you read the overview section of the case so that you understand the context of the problem at hand. Then, quickly move on and scan the questions.

As you are scanning the questions, make mental notes to yourself so that you'll remember which sections of the case study you should focus on. Some case studies may provide a fair amount of extra information that you don't really need to answer the questions. The goal with this scanning approach is to avoid having to study and analyze material that is not completely relevant.

When studying a case, carefully read the tabbed information. It is important to answer each and every question. You will be able to toggle back and forth from case to questions, and from question to question within a case testlet. However, once you leave the case and move on, you may not be able to return to it. You may want to take notes while reading useful information so you can refer to them when you tackle the test questions. It's hard to go wrong with this strategy when taking any kind of Microsoft certification test.

The Fixed-Length and Short-Form Exam Strategy

A well-known principle when taking fixed-length or short-form exams is to first read over the entire exam from start to finish while answering only those questions you feel absolutely sure of. On subsequent passes, you can dive into more complex questions more deeply, knowing how many such questions you have left.

Fortunately, the Microsoft exam software for fixed-length and short-form tests makes the multiple-visit approach easy to implement. At the top-left corner of each question is a checkbox that permits you to mark that question for a later visit.

Note: Marking questions makes review easier, but you can return to any question by clicking the Forward or Back button repeatedly.

As you read each question, if you answer only those you're sure of and mark for review those that you're not sure of, you can keep working through a decreasing list of questions as you answer the trickier ones in order.

 There's at least one potential benefit to reading the exam over completely before answering the trickier questions: Sometimes, information supplied in later questions sheds more light on earlier questions. At other times, information you read in later questions might jog your memory about Cluster Services facts, figures, or behavior that helps you answer earlier questions. Either way, you'll come out ahead if you defer those questions about which you're not absolutely sure.

Here are some question-handling strategies that apply to fixed-length and short-form tests. Use them if you have the chance:

➤ When returning to a question after your initial read-through, read every word again—otherwise, your mind can fall quickly into a rut. Sometimes, revisiting a question after turning your attention elsewhere lets you see something you missed, but the strong tendency is to see what you've seen before. Try to avoid that tendency at all costs.

➤ If you return to a question more than twice, try to articulate to yourself what you don't understand about the question, why answers don't appear to make sense, or what appears to be missing. If you chew on the subject awhile, your subconscious might provide the details you lack, or you might notice a "trick" that points to the right answer.

As you work your way through the exam, another counter that Microsoft provides will come in handy—the number of questions completed and questions outstanding. For fixed-length and short-form tests, it's wise to budget your time by making sure that you've completed one-quarter of the questions one-quarter of the way through the exam period, and three-quarters of the questions three-quarters of the way through.

If you're not finished when only five minutes remain, use that time to guess your way through any remaining questions. Remember, guessing is potentially more valuable than not answering, because blank answers are always wrong, but a guess may turn out to be right. If you don't have a clue about any of the remaining questions, pick answers at random, or choose all a's, b's, and so on. The important thing is to submit an exam for scoring that has an answer for every question.

 At the very end of your exam period, you're better off guessing than leaving questions unanswered.

The Adaptive Exam Strategy

If there's one principle that applies to taking an adaptive test, it could be summed up as "Get it right the first time." You cannot elect to skip a question and move on to the next one when taking an adaptive test, because the testing software uses your answer to the current question to select whatever question it plans to present next. Nor can you return to a question once you've moved on, because the software gives you only one chance to answer the question. You can, however, take notes, because sometimes information supplied in earlier questions will shed more light on later questions.

Also, when you answer a question correctly, you are presented with a more difficult question next, to help the software gauge your level of skill and ability. When you answer a question incorrectly, you are presented with a less difficult question, and the software lowers its current estimate of your skill and ability. This continues until the program settles into a reasonably accurate estimate of what you know and can do, and takes you on average through somewhere between 15 and 30 questions as you complete the test.

The good news is that if you know your stuff, you'll probably finish most adaptive tests in 30 minutes or so. The bad news is that you must really, really know your stuff to do your best on an adaptive test. That's because some questions are so convoluted, complex, or hard to follow that you're bound to miss one or two, at a minimum, even if you do know your stuff. So the more you know, the better you'll do on an adaptive test, even accounting for the occasionally weird or un-fathomable questions that appear on these exams.

 Because you can't always tell in advance if a test is fixed length, short form, or adaptive, you will be best served by preparing for the exam as if it were adaptive. That way, you should be prepared to pass no matter what kind of test you take. But if you do take a fixed-length or short-form test, remember the tips from the preceding section. They should help you improve on what you could do on an adaptive test.

If you encounter a question on an adaptive test that you can't answer, you must guess an answer immediately. Because of how the software works, you may suffer for your guess on the next question if you guess right, because you'll get a more difficult question next!

Question-Handling Strategies

For those questions that take only a single answer, usually two or three of the answers will be obviously incorrect, and two of the answers will be plausible—of course, only one can be correct. Unless the answer leaps out at you (if it does, reread the question to look for a trick; sometimes those are the ones you're most likely to get wrong), begin the process of answering by eliminating those answers that are most obviously wrong.

Almost always, at least one answer out of the possible choices for a question can be eliminated immediately because it matches one of these conditions:

➤ The answer does not apply to the situation.

➤ The answer describes a nonexistent issue, an invalid option, or an imaginary state.

After you eliminate all answers that are obviously wrong, you can apply your retained knowledge to eliminate further answers. Look for items that sound correct but refer to actions, commands, or features that are not present or not available in the situation that the question describes.

If you're still faced with a blind guess among two or more potentially correct answers, reread the question. Try to picture how each of the possible remaining answers would alter the situation. Be especially sensitive to terminology; sometimes the choice of words ("remove" instead of "disable") can make the difference between a right answer and a wrong one.

Only when you've exhausted your ability to eliminate answers, but remain unclear about which of the remaining possibilities is correct, should you guess at an answer. An unanswered question offers you no points, but guessing gives you at least some chance of getting a question right; just don't be too hasty when making a blind guess.

Note: If you're taking a fixed-length or a short-form test, you can wait until the last round of reviewing marked questions (just as you're about to run out of time, or out of unanswered questions) before you start making guesses. You will have the same option within each case study testlet (but once you leave a testlet, you may not be allowed to return to it). If you're taking an adaptive test, you'll have to guess to move on to the next question if you can't figure out an answer some other way. Either way, guessing should be your technique of last resort!

Numerous questions assume that the default behavior of a particular utility is in effect. If you know the defaults and understand what they mean, this knowledge will help you cut through many Gordian knots.

Mastering the Inner Game

In the final analysis, knowledge breeds confidence, and confidence breeds success. If you study the materials in this book carefully and review all the practice questions at the end of each chapter, you should become aware of those areas where additional learning and study are required.

After you've worked your way through the book, take the practice exam in the back of the book. Taking this test will provide a reality check and help you identify areas to study further. Make sure you follow up and review materials related to the questions you miss on the practice exam before scheduling a real exam. Only when you've covered that ground and feel comfortable with the whole scope of the practice exam should you set an exam appointment. Only if you score 85 percent or better should you proceed to the real thing (otherwise, obtain some additional practice tests so you can keep trying until you hit this magic number).

If you take a practice exam and don't score at least 85 to 90 percent correct, you'll want to practice further. Microsoft provides links to practice exam providers and also offers self-assessment exams at **www.microsoft.com/trainingandservices/**. You should also check out **ExamCram.com** for downloadable practice questions.

Armed with the information in this book and with the determination to augment your knowledge, you should be able to pass the certification exam. However, you need to work at it, or you'll spend the exam fee more than once before you finally pass. If you prepare seriously, you should do well. We are confident that you can do it!

The next section covers other sources you can use to prepare for the Microsoft certification exams.

Additional Resources

A good source of information about Microsoft certification exams comes from Microsoft itself. Because its products and technologies—and the exams that go with them—change frequently, the best place to go for exam-related information is online.

If you haven't already visited the Microsoft Certified Professional site, do so right now. The MCP home page resides at **www.microsoft.com/trainingandservices** (see Figure 1.4).

Note: This page might not be there by the time you read this, or may be replaced by something new and different, because things change regularly on the Microsoft site. Should this happen, please read the sidebar titled "Coping with Change on the Web."

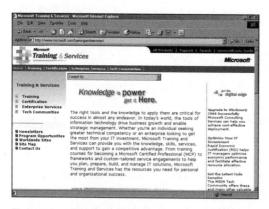

Figure 1.4 The Microsoft Certified Professional home page.

Coping with Change on the Web

Sooner or later, all the information we've shared with you about the Microsoft Certified Professional pages and the other Web-based resources mentioned throughout the rest of this book will go stale or be replaced by newer information. In some cases, the URLs you find here might lead you to their replacements; in other cases, the URLs will go nowhere, leaving you with the dreaded "404 File not found" error message. When that happens, don't give up.

There's always a way to find what you want on the Web if you're willing to invest some time and energy. Most large or complex Web sites—and Microsoft's qualifies on both counts—offer a search engine. On all of Microsoft's Web pages, a Search button appears along the top edge of the page. As long as you can get to Microsoft's site (it should stay at **www.microsoft.com** for a long time), use this tool to help you find what you need.

The more focused you can make a search request, the more likely the results will include information you can use. For example, you can search for the string

```
"training and certification"
```

to produce a lot of data about the subject in general, but if you're looking for the preparation guide for Exam 70-223, "Installing, Configuring, and Administering Microsoft Clustering Services by Using Microsoft Windows 2000 Advanced Server," you'll be more likely to get there quickly if you use a search string similar to the following:

```
"Exam 70-223" AND "preparation guide"
```

Likewise, if you want to find the Training and Certification downloads, try a search string such as this:

```
"training and certification" AND "download page"
```

Finally, feel free to use general search tools—such as **www.search.com**, **www.altavista.com**, and **www.excite.com**—to look for related information. Although Microsoft offers great information about its certification exams online, there are plenty of third-party sources of information and assistance that need not follow Microsoft's party line. Therefore, if you can't find something where the book says it lives, intensify your search.

Overview of Windows 2000 Server Platforms

. . . .

Terms you'll need to understand:

✓ Basic disks

✓ Dynamic disks

✓ RAID 1

✓ RAID 5

✓ Rolling upgrade

Techniques you'll need to master:

✓ Understanding the hardware requirements for the different Windows 2000 Server platforms

✓ Performing a clean install of Windows 2000 Advanced Server

✓ Upgrading from Windows 2000 Server to Windows 2000 Advanced Server

✓ Upgrading from Windows NT Server 4.0 Enterprise Edition to Windows 2000 Advanced Server

✓ Understanding the difference between basic and dynamic disks

✓ Understanding the requirements for performing a rolling upgrade

✓ Upgrading from Windows NT Server 4.0 to Windows 2000 Advanced Server

Overview of Windows 2000 Server Platforms

The Windows 2000 platform is built on the Windows NT technology and includes many new features and enhancements that increase its performance, capabilities, and reliability. The platform that is installed will depend on the needs of the business and the role the server will play, because each platform comes with unique features that make it suitable for different network environments.

The Windows 2000 Server platform includes the following operating systems:

➤ Windows 2000 Server

➤ Windows 2000 Advanced Server

➤ Windows 2000 Datacenter Server

For those businesses running mission-critical applications or services that require a high level of availability, Windows 2000 Advanced Server and Windows 2000 Datacenter Server offer solutions to meet these business needs. Both platforms offer clustering technologies to help avoid server, application, or service downtime. Through network load-balancing and Microsoft Cluster Service, businesses can increase the availability of applications and services and ensure that they remain available to users.

 Cluster Service supports two nodes in Windows 2000 Advanced Server and four nodes in Windows 2000 Datacenter.

The focus of this book will be on the installation, configuration, and administration of Microsoft Cluster Service on Windows 2000 Advanced Server. This chapter will provide a brief introduction to the Windows 2000 Server platforms and a general overview of the installation process for Windows 2000 Advanced Server, with special attention being given to the installation options that pertain to Microsoft Cluster Service. By the end of the chapter, you should be familiar with configuring a computer to run Windows 2000 Advanced Server in preparation for the installation of Cluster Service. You should also be familiar with the requirements for performing a rolling upgrade of cluster nodes running Windows NT Server 4.0 Enterprise Edition. The main topics discussed throughout the chapter include Windows 2000 system requirements, installing Advanced Server, upgrading from previous operating systems, and performing a rolling upgrade.

Windows 2000 System Requirements

Before installing Windows 2000, you need to check the system requirements for running the operating system to ensure that your hardware meets the minimum standards defined by Microsoft. These are the minimum requirements that the operating system needs to run. Obviously, performing this preinstallation task can save time and money—nothing could be worse than beginning the installation of Windows 2000 only to find that your hardware does not meet the minimum requirements. Also keep in mind that the different versions of Windows 2000 have different hardware requirements. Table 2.1 summarizes the minimum hardware requirements for the Windows 2000 Server platforms.

Note: These are the minimum requirements to run the operating systems. You will see the best performance if the hardware requirements surpass these minimums. The hardware requirements will also need to be increased depending on the server's role and the applications it will run.

Installing Windows 2000 Advanced Server

As with the installation of any operating system, you should take certain preliminary steps before performing the setup. These steps may help you avoid problems that could arise during the actual installation process. If you are just installing Advanced Server, all you need to focus on are the requirements needed to run it. If you plan to use the systems in a cluster configuration, they must also meet the requirements of the cluster software. Therefore, when performing the installation of Advanced Server, you must give special attention to the system hardware

Table 2.1   The three Windows 2000 Server platforms and the minimum hardware requirements for each.

Operating System	Minimum Hardware Requirements
Windows 2000 Server	133MHZ or higher Pentium-compatible CPU, 128MB RAM (256MB recommended), and 2GB hard disk with at least 1GB free space. Supports up to four processors and 4GB of memory.
Windows 2000 Advanced Server	133MHZ or higher Pentium-compatible CPU, 128MB RAM (256 recommended), and 2GB hard disk with at least 1GB free space. Supports up to eight processors and 8GB of memory.
Windows 2000 Datacenter Server	Pentium III Xeon processor or higher, 256MB of RAM recommended, and 2GB hard disk with at least 1GB free space. Supports up to 32 processors and 64GB of memory.

and to certain configuration options, because these will later impact the installation of the cluster software.

Here are some preliminary steps you should take before beginning the installation of the operating system. Performing these basic tasks can help you avoid problems that may otherwise arise during that actual installation process:

➤ Verify that the hardware meets the minimum requirements for Advanced Server.

➤ Confirm that the hardware is on the Windows 2000 Hardware Compatibility List (HCL). If the hardware is not on the HCL, contact the manufacturer for a supported driver.

➤ Verify that the system components are also on the HCL for Cluster Service.

Performing a Clean Installation

The installation process for Advanced Server has not changed significantly from Windows NT 4. When you're performing a clean installation of Advanced Server, setup can be initiated from the CD-ROM, setup floppies, or a network share. Cluster Service can be installed during the installation of Windows 2000 Advanced Server, or it can be added after the installation is complete. The installation of Cluster Service is covered in Chapter 5.

Starting a New Installation Directly from the CD-ROM

A new installation of Windows 2000 Advanced Server can be initialized directly from the CD-ROM by performing the following steps:

1. Insert the Windows 2000 Advanced Server CD-ROM.

2. Restart the computer.

3. Wait for the Setup dialog box to appear and follow the onscreen instructions.

Note: In order to start the setup process directly from the CD-ROM, your system must be able to start from the CD-ROM. If your system does not support this feature, the setup process can be started from floppy disks.

Starting a New Installation from Floppy Disks

If your system is not capable of starting from the CD-ROM, you can create setup floppies to initiate the setup process by performing the following steps:

1. On any Windows platform, insert the Windows 2000 Advanced Server CD-ROM, and from the command prompt type "cdrom:\bootdisk\makeboot a:". This will create the four floppies needed to start the installation process (be sure to label them as well).

2. Insert the first setup disk into the A: drive on the computer where you wish to install Advanced Server.

3. Restart the computer.

4. Follow the onscreen instructions.

Starting a New Installation from a Network Share

When installing Windows 2000 Advanced Server across the network, setup can be initiated from a shared CD-ROM drive or from a shared folder. The target system will require network client software to connect to the distribution share. On a network server, the i386 folder will need to be copied into a shared folder or the CD-ROM drive will need to be shared. Here are the steps to follow:

1. Start the computer on which you want to install Advanced Server with the network client software.

2. Connect to the network server containing the installation files.

3. Run Winnt.exe to initiate the setup program.

4. The local computer restarts and the installation of Advanced Server begins.

Note: The nodes in a cluster must be members of the same domain. They can be configured as member servers or domain controllers. You will need to consider whether they will join an existing domain or be configured as domain controllers within their own domain. Domain considerations are discussed further in Chapter 5.

Once setup has been initiated, the installation process is the same for each method and proceeds as follows:

1. Start the installation process using one of the previously listed methods.

2. At the Welcome To Setup screen, press Enter to install Windows 2000 Advanced Server.

3. Press F8 to accept the licensing agreement.

4. Select a partition on which to install Windows 2000 Advanced Server and press Enter.

5. Choose a file system for the partition. The partition can be formatted with File Allocation Table (FAT) or New Technology File System (NTFS). Setup formats the partition with the selected file system and then copies the installation files onto the hard drive.

6. Press Enter to restart the computer. Once the computer restarts, the Graphic User Interface (GUI) mode portion of setup begins.

7. Windows 2000 Server Setup detects and installs devices on the computer. This portion of setup may take several minutes.

8. To change the regional settings, locale, or keyboard layout, click one of the customize buttons. Click Next.

9. Provide your name and the name of your organization or business. Click Next.

10. Select the licensing mode to use. Each client computer requires a Client Access License to connect to computers running Windows 2000 Advanced Server. You can choose Per Server or Per Seat licensing. With Per Server licensing, licenses are purchased on a per-server basis. With Per Seat licensing, licenses are purchased based on the number of client computers. Click Next.

11. Provide a computer name. Type the password for the Administrator account. Click Next.

12. Select any optional components that you want to install. Click Next.

 Cluster Service can be installed along with the operating system at this point in setup by selecting it from the list of optional components. It can also be installed after setup is complete through the Add/Remove Programs icon in the Control Panel.

13. Specify the correct date and time for your computer. Click Next.

14. Select either the Typical or Custom option for the network settings. The Typical option will automatically install Client for Microsoft Networks, File and Print Sharing for Microsoft Networks, and TCP/IP. The Custom option allows you to choose additional network settings to install. Click Next.

15. Specify whether this computer will be a member of a workgroup or a domain. Click Next.

16. Setup installs and configures components, finishes copying files, saves configuration changes, and deletes any temporary files.

Basic vs. Dynamic Disks

The Windows 2000 platforms now offer two types of disk storage: basic storage and dynamic storage. With basic storage, the physical disk can be divided into partitions, extended partitions, and logical drives. It also allows for the creation of volume sets, stripe sets, mirrored sets (RAID 1), and stripe sets with parity

(RAID 5). All new disks that are added to a computer running Windows 2000 are automatically initialized as basic disks.

Dynamic disks are supported only by the Windows 2000 platforms. The physical disk can be divided into volumes, spanned volumes, mirrored volumes (RAID 1), striped volumes, and striped volumes with parity (RAID 5). Dynamic disks extend the capabilities of basic disks by adding the ability to perform disk-management tasks without having to restart the computer and by improving the recovery of damaged storage.

Note: A physical disk can be intialized as either a basic disk or a dynamic disk, but not both.

When determining whether to use basic storage or dynamic storage, keep in mind that Cluster Service cannot read from dynamic disks. This limitation applies to the shared disk that connects the cluster members. The local disks within each computer can be either basic or dynamic, but the shared disk must remain a basic disk.

If the shared disk is converted from basic to dynamic before the installation of Cluster Service, the Configuration Wizard will not be able to detect the shared disk. You will need to quit the wizard and revert the shared disk from dynamic back to basic through Disk Manager. If the disk has already been configured as a cluster disk, the option to convert from basic to dynamic will not be available in Disk Manager.

 Along with being initialized as a basic disk, the shared disk must have all its partitions formatted with the NT file system.

Upgrading from Windows 2000 Server

If your systems are currently running Windows 2000 Server, you will need to upgrade to Windows 2000 Advanced Server to take advantage of clustering technologies. The only way to upgrade your systems to Advanced Server is to perform a clean install of the operating system. There is no upgrade path from Windows 2000 Server to Windows 2000 Advanced Server. A new installation will need to be performed, which means all data will have to be restored from backup and applications will have to be reinstalled under the new operating system. Cluster Service can either be installed during the installation of Windows 2000 Advanced Server or it can be added after using the Add/Remove Programs icon in the Control Panel.

One important point to keep in mind when planning to install Cluster Service is how it is going to affect the applications and services currently on the server. Most applications will not be affected by the installation of Cluster Service and will function within the cluster once they are migrated into it (services such as WINS, DNS, and DHCP will take full advantage of the cluster once they are migrated). There will also be some applications that cannot be migrated into a cluster, and those will have to be uninstalled prior to the installation of Cluster Service and reinstalled afterwards.

Upgrading from Windows NT Server 4.0 Enterprise Edition

If your computer is currently running Windows NT Server 4.0 Enterprise Edition, you can upgrade directly to Windows 2000 Advanced Server. Performing an upgrade instead of a clean install will allow you to maintain all your previous files, applications, and settings. This can make configuration much simpler.

An upgrade can be initiated using one of the methods described in the sections that follow.

Starting an Upgrade from the CD-ROM

The upgrade to Windows 2000 Advanced Server can be initiated directly from the CD-ROM. To start an upgrade from the CD-ROM:

1. Insert the Windows 2000 Advanced Server CD-ROM.

2. Setup displays a dialog box.

3. Follow the onscreen instructions.

Upgrading from a Network Location

The upgrade to Windows 2000 Advanced Server can also be initiated from across the network. To start an upgrade from a network connection:

1. Copy the i386 folder from the Windows 2000 Advanced Server CD-ROM into a shared folder on a distribution server or share the CD-ROM drive containing the Advanced Server CD.

2. From the computer on which you want to install Windows 2000 Advanced Server, connect to the shared folder or CD-ROM drive on the distribution server.

3. Run winnt32.exe.

4. Follow the onscreen instructions.

Rolling Upgrade

A *rolling upgrade* allows you to upgrade your cluster nodes that are running Windows NT 4.0 Enterprise Edition to Windows 2000 Advanced Server in such a way that services and resources remain available to users even throughout the upgrade process. Nodes are upgraded one at a time, ensuring that one cluster node is always available. The only downtime experienced during the upgrade process is the time it takes to move resources from one cluster member to another. Performing a rolling upgrade also minimizes risk—if the upgrade on one node fails, the other node is still available. You can also perform the upgrade at any time, because the resources are still available to clients on the second cluster member.

 Be sure to plan ahead for a rolling upgrade. Windows 2000 Advanced Server does not have an uninstall option. If you need to return to your previous version of Windows, you will need to reinstall the operating system along with all the applications.

In order to perform a rolling upgrade, your cluster nodes must first meet the preliminary requirements. Each cluster node must be running the following software:

➤ Windows NT Server 4.0 Enterprise Edition

➤ SP4 or later

➤ Microsoft Cluster Service

➤ Internet Information Server 4.0, if the cluster has an IIS resource

 When you are preparing the computers for a rolling upgrade, be sure to reapply the service pack after installing IIS 4.0 and Microsoft Cluster Server.

Note: Some resources managed by the cluster might not be supported in a rolling upgrade. A rolling upgrade can still be performed, but those resources will need to be taken offline during the upgrade process.

During the upgrade process, one node in the cluster is paused and its resources are moved to the second node in the cluster. The upgrade to Windows 2000 Advanced Server can then be performed on the first cluster node while the second node continues to handle client requests (the upgrade process can be initiated by running Winnt32.exe from the CD-ROM or from a network share).

The setup program will not only upgrade the operating system, but also will detect the previous version of clustering and automatically upgrade to clustering for Windows 2000 Advanced Server.

Note: A rolling upgrade does not support upgrading from Windows NT Server 4.0 Enterprise Edition to Windows 2000 Datacenter Server. To upgrade to this operating system, a clean install must be performed.

Once the upgrade process has been completed and tested on the first cluster node, the node can be resumed. The upgrade process can then be performed on the second cluster node while the newly upgraded cluster member responds to client requests.

Performing a Rolling Upgrade

Upgrading your cluster nodes to Windows 2000 Advanced Server occurs in four phases (see Table 2.2) during which one node will be paused and upgraded while the other handles the resources groups. Follow these steps to perform a rolling upgrade:

1. Once the cluster nodes are running the required software, point to Start|Programs|Administrative Tools and click on Cluster Administrator. From within Cluster Administrator, you can pause the first node to be upgraded.

2. Once the Cluster Administrator is open, select the node to be paused and choose Pause Node from the File menu. Once the node is paused, the next step will be to move its groups to the second node.

3. To move the groups from the paused node to the active node, click the group you want to move and choose Move Group from the File menu. This step will have to be repeated for each group.

4. Upgrade the paused node to Windows 2000 Advanced Server. During setup, Microsoft Cluster Service will automatically be upgraded to Cluster Service for Windows 2000 Advanced Server.

5. Once the upgrade is complete, the node automatically rejoins the cluster but remains in a paused state.

6. Launch the Cluster Administrator utility again, as outlined in Step 1, and resume the node.

7. Following the steps just outlined, the upgrade process will now be completed on the second cluster member.

Table 2.2	The four phases of performing a rolling upgrade to Windows 2000 Advanced Server.
Phases	**Steps to Complete**
Phase 1	This is basically a preliminary step to ensure that both of the cluster nodes are running the required software.
Phase 2	During phase two, one of the nodes is paused and its groups are moved to the second cluster node while the first node is upgraded to Windows 2000 Advanced Server. The second node handles the resources and services client requests.
Phase 3	During phase three, the upgrade is complete and the first node automatically rejoins the cluster and is resumed. The second node is then paused and the groups are moved to the first node while the second node is upgraded.
Phase 4	During the fourth phase, the upgrade on the second node is complete, and it rejoins the cluster and is resumed. The groups can then be redistributed among the nodes.

For an upgrade to be successful, two requirements must be met. The first, which has already been discussed, is that the systems must be running Windows NT 4.0 Enterprise Edition with Service Pack 4 or later. The second requirement is that all the resources managed by the cluster must support a rolling upgrade. If there are some resources that do not support a rolling upgrade, you can take those resources offline or perform a clean installation of Cluster Service and reconfigure the cluster after the installation is complete.

At some point during the upgrade process, the cluster members will be running in mixed mode: one will be running Windows NT 4.0 Enterprise Edition and the other will be running Windows 2000 Advanced Server. It is important to remember that if you add a resource to the cluster while it is running in mixed mode, it may not be supported by both operating systems. If, while the cluster is running in mixed mode, you add a resource that is supported by Windows 2000 Advanced Server but not by Windows NT 4.0 Enterprise Edition, the resource will not fail over to the node running the down-level operating system. Any of the following resource types added while the cluster is running in mixed mode will not fail over to the node running the down-level operating system:

➤ WINS resource

➤ DHCP resource

➤ Dfs root file share

Although not a requirement for Cluster Service, it is recommended that fault-tolerant RAID (hardware or software) be implemented on the local disks and the shared disk to ensure high availability of the data. Hardware-level RAID is the only option for the shared disk because software RAID cannot be used by Cluster Service. Whether software-level RAID on the local disks will be implemented under Windows 2000 Advanced Server needs to be considered before performing a rolling upgrade. In order to implement software-level RAID under Windows 2000, the disk must be a dynamic disk. Once the upgrade to Advanced Server has been completed, the disk has to be converted from basic to dynamic in order to implement RAID 1 or RAID 5. If you want the local disks to remain as basic disks, software-level RAID will need to be implemented before the upgrade to Advanced Server. Windows 2000 can only implement software-level RAID on a dynamic disk but can support it on a basic disk if it is an upgrade. Otherwise, the local disks will need to be converted to dynamic disks after the upgrade is complete.

 Remember that the local disks on each cluster node can remain as basic disks or be converted to dynamic disks. Only the shared disk managed by Cluster Service must remain a basic disk.

Upgrading from Windows NT Server 4.0

If your system is running Windows NT Server 4.0, there is no upgrade path to Windows 2000 Advanced Server. A clean installation will need to be performed and any applications currently running under Windows NT Server 4.0 will need to be reinstalled after the installation is complete and data is restored from backup.

Practice Questions

Question 1

> You are planning the installation of Windows 2000 Advanced Server. What is the minimum amount of RAM and hard drive space required? [Check all correct answers]
>
> ❑ a. 1GB of hard drive space
>
> ❑ b. 2GB of hard drive space
>
> ❑ c. 64MB of RAM
>
> ❑ d. 128MB of RAM
>
> ❑ e. 256MB of RAM

The correct answers are a and d. The minimum requirements to install Windows 2000 Advanced Server are 1GB of free hard drive space and 128MB of RAM. Answers b, c, and e are incorrect because they do not reflect the minimum requirements for RAM and hard drive space when installing Windows 2000 Advanced Server.

Question 2

> Which of the following operating systems can be upgraded directly to Windows 2000 Advanced Server?
>
> ○ a. Windows NT Server 4.0
>
> ○ b. Windows 2000 Server
>
> ○ c. Windows NT Server 4.0 Enterprise Edition
>
> ○ d. Windows 2000 Datacenter Server

The correct answer is c. Windows NT Server 4.0 Enterprise Edition is the only operating system that can be upgraded directly to Windows 2000 Advanced Server. Windows NT Server 4.0 can be upgraded to Windows 2000 Server, but there is no upgrade path for either operating system to Windows 2000 Advanced Server; therefore, answers a and b are incorrect. Answer d is incorrect because there is also no upgrade path possible from Windows 2000 Datacenter to Windows 2000 Advanced Server.

Question 3

Your company is planning on implementing two new mail servers that will be running Exchange 5.5 Enterprise Edition. The mail servers will become an essential part of the company's day-to-day tasks. Which Windows platforms come with built-in features that would help the company provide a high level of availability for its mail servers? [Check all correct answers]

❑ a. Windows 2000 Professional

❑ b. Windows 2000 Datacenter Server

❑ c. Windows 2000 Server

❑ d. Windows 2000 Advanced Server

❑ e. Windows NT Server 4.0

The correct answers are b and d. Windows 2000 Datacenter Server and Windows 2000 Advanced Server both come with clustering technologies to increase the availability of mission-critical applications, services, and data. Answers a, c, and e are incorrect because none of these operating systems come with clustering technologies.

Question 4

> Your company currently has two servers in a cluster configuration config-
> ured with an IIS resource. You have been assigned the task of upgrading the
> cluster members to Windows 2000 Advanced Server. You are also required
> to minimize downtime during the upgrade process. You decide to perform a
> rolling upgrade of the servers. What software requirements must be met
> before a rolling upgrade of the cluster members is possible? [Check all
> correct answers]
>
> ❑ a. Windows NT Server 4.0
>
> ❑ b. Service Pack 4
>
> ❑ c. Service Pack 3
>
> ❑ d. Internet Information Server 4.0
>
> ❑ e. Windows NT Server 4.0 Enterprise Edition
>
> ❑ f. Index Server
>
> ❑ g. Windows 2000 Server
>
> ❑ h. Microsoft Cluster Server

The correct answers are b, d, e, and h. In order to perform a rolling upgrade, cluster members must be running Windows NT Server 4.0 Enterprise Edition with SP4 or later, Internet Information Server 4.0 because the cluster has an IIS resource, and Microsoft Cluster Server. Answers a and g are incorrect because these two operating systems do not support clustering technologies and cannot be upgraded to Windows 2000 Advanced Server without a clean install being performed. Answer c is incorrect because support for a rolling upgrade was not introduced until SP4. Answer f is incorrect because Index Server is not needed to perform a rolling upgrade.

Question 5

> You have two cluster nodes running Windows NT Server 4.0 Enterprise Edition. You are planning a rolling upgrade of the nodes to Windows 2000 Advanced Server. You would like to implement software-level RAID on the local disks within each computer. Which of the following steps allow you to do this? [Check all correct answers]
>
> ❑ a. Perform the upgrade to Windows 2000 Advanced Server. Once the upgrade is complete, create a new stripe set with parity on the basic disks.
>
> ❑ b. Create a stripe set with parity under Windows NT Server 4.0 Enterprise Edition. Upgrade to Windows 2000 Advanced Server.
>
> ❑ c. Perform the upgrade to Windows 2000 Advanced Server. Convert the local disks from basic to dynamic disks. Create a new striped volume with parity.
>
> ❑ d. Upgrade the operating system to Windows 2000 Advanced Server. Convert the disk from dynamic to basic. Create a new stripe set with parity.

The correct answers are b and c. To implement software-level RAID under Windows 2000, it must already be in place before the upgrade is performed or the disks must be converted to dynamic disks after Windows 2000 is installed. Answer a is incorrect because the disks must be converted to dynamic in order to create any new RAID configurations. Answer d is incorrect because disks are automatically initialized as basic disks after the installation. For a new RAID configuration to be created, these disks would have to be converted from basic to dynamic, not from dynamic to basic.

Question 6

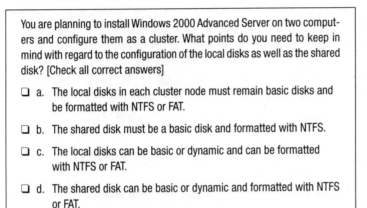

You are planning to install Windows 2000 Advanced Server on two computers and configure them as a cluster. What points do you need to keep in mind with regard to the configuration of the local disks as well as the shared disk? [Check all correct answers]

❑ a. The local disks in each cluster node must remain basic disks and be formatted with NTFS or FAT.

❑ b. The shared disk must be a basic disk and formatted with NTFS.

❑ c. The local disks can be basic or dynamic and can be formatted with NTFS or FAT.

❑ d. The shared disk can be basic or dynamic and formatted with NTFS or FAT.

The correct answers are b and c. The local disks with each cluster member can be basic or dynamic and formatted with either NTFS or FAT. The shared disk managed by Cluster Service must remain a basic disk and must be formatted with NTFS. Answer a is incorrect because the local disks in each node can remain as basic disks or be converted to dynamic disks. Answer d is incorrect because the shared disk must remain a basic disk and be formatted with NTFS.

Question 7

You want to install Windows 2000 Advanced Server on two computers. You would like to perform a network installation. Where should the source files be placed?

○ a. Copy the i486 directory from the Advanced Server CD-ROM into a shared folder on the target computers.

○ b. Copy the i386 directory from the Advanced Server CD-ROM into a shared folder on the distribution server.

○ c. Copy the i486 directory from the Advanced Server CD-ROM into a shared folder on the distribution server.

○ d. Copy the i386 directory from the Advanced Server CD-ROM into a shared folder on the target computers.

The correct answer is b. The i386 directory needs to be copied into a shared folder on the distribution server. From the target computers, connect to the shared folder on the distribution folder and initiate setup. Answers a and c are incorrect because the i386 directory contains the installation files, not the i486 directory. Answer d is incorrect because the i386 directory needs to be copied into a shared directory on a network server, not onto the computers on which you will be installing the operating system.

Question 8

Your company is running several applications that are critical to its day-to-day workload. You have four computers that you want to use in a cluster configuration to ensure the high availability of the applications. Which Windows platform can you use to support this configuration?

○ a. Windows 2000 Professional

○ b. Windows NT Server 4.0

○ c. Windows 2000 Advanced Server

○ d. Windows 2000 Datacenter

The correct answer is d. Windows 2000 Datacenter is the only platform that supports four nodes in a cluster configuration. Windows 2000 Advanced Server only supports two nodes. Therefore, answer c is incorrect. Windows 2000 Professional and Windows NT Server 4.0 do not come with clustering technologies. Therefore, answers a and b are incorrect.

Question 9

> Your computer does not support starting from the CD-ROM. What command
> can you use to create the setup floppies needed to start the installation of
> Windows 2000 Advanced Server?
>
> ○ a. **WINNT /ox**
>
> ○ b. **Makedisk**
>
> ○ c. **Makeboot**
>
> ○ d. **WINNT**

The correct answer is c. The **Makeboot** command can be used to create the setup
floppies needed to start the installation of Advanced Server when the computer
does not support starting from the CD-ROM. Answer a and d are incorrect
because **WINNT /ox** is the command used in Windows NT 4.0 to create the
setup floppies and **WINNT** is used to launch setup. Answer b is incorrect because **Makedisk** is not a valid command.

Need to Know More?

 Libertone, David. *Windows 2000 Cluster Server Guidebook: A Guide to Creating and Managing a Cluster, Second Edition.* Prentice Hall, Upper Saddle River, NJ 2000. ISBN 0130284696. Includes information on the hardware and software for Cluster Service and an overview of performing a rolling upgrade.

 Microsoft Corporation. *Microsoft Windows 2000 Server Deployment Planning Guide.* Microsoft Press, Redmond, WA, 2000. ISBN 1-57231-805-8. Refer to Chapter 19 "Determining Windows 2000 Storage Management Strategies" for detailed information about basic and dynamic disks.

 The following technical white papers provide useful information on installation and rolling upgrades:

Upgrading and Installing on Cluster Nodes. Microsoft Corporation, Redmond, WA, 2000. **www.microsoft.com/technet/win2000/win2ksrv/manuals/asgs/agsch05.asp**.

Windows 2000 Clustering: Performing a Rolling Upgrade. Microsoft Corporation, Redmond, WA, 2000. **www.microsoft.com/WINDOWS2000/library/planning/incremental/rollupgr.asp**.

 Search the Hardware Compatibility List (HCL) for hardware that is supported by Windows 2000 and Cluster Service at **www.microsoft.com/hwtest/hcl**.

 Search TechNet on the Internet at **www.microsoft.com/technet/default.asp** or the TechNet CD for more information on performing a clean installation or upgrade of Windows 2000 Advanced Server.

Cluster Terminology

Terms you'll need to understand:

✓ Cluster

✓ SCSI adapter

✓ SCSI chain

✓ SCSI terminator

✓ Fibre Channel

✓ Cluster resources

✓ Cluster dependencies

✓ Cluster groups

✓ Failover

✓ Failback

✓ Quorum resource

✓ True cluster

✓ Failover cluster

Techniques you'll need to master:

✓ Installing SCSI adaptors, cables, and hard drives

✓ Terminating SCSI Buses

✓ Installing Fibre Channel devices

This chapter presents you with information about the terminology of clustering. Clustering components, devices, and models are covered in this chapter. You will learn what a cluster is and how it functions to provide fault tolerance as well as what devices are used to make a cluster and how they are implemented. You will also be shown the different components that make a cluster and their functions. Finally, you will be taught the different cluster models that can be used and when they would be appropriate to implement.

Definition of a Cluster

A *cluster* is a group of computers working together as if it were a single computer. This allows access to and management of the cluster as a single unit.

Figure 3.1 shows a cluster and its components. Let's look at each component individually.

Each system within the cluster is a node, and all nodes have their individual NetBIOS names. In Figure 3.1, the NetBIOS names are Server1 and Server2. Each cluster has a NetBIOS name, which is the cluster name. In this case, let's say the cluster name is Cluster1.

Each server is a node in the cluster. Each node has a TCP/IP address, as does the cluster as a whole. In the example shown in Figure 3.1, let's assume Server1 has an IP address of 10.0.0.1/8 and Server2 has an IP address of 10.0.0.2/8. If you were to ping Server1, you would get a response (if it were online) from 10.0.0.1. Also, if you were to ping Server2 (if it were online), you would get a response from 10.0.0.2.

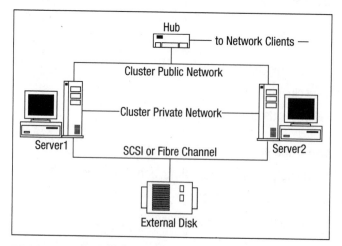

Figure 3.1   Cluster diagram.

Let's also assume that Cluster1 has an IP address of 10.0.0.10/8. If either Server1 or Server2 is unavailable and you issue the command **PING 10.0.0.10** or **PING CLUSTER1**, you would get a response from the cluster. Whichever node is available will respond to the client requests to the cluster name or IP address.

If you ping Server1 and Server1 is offline, but Server2 is online, you would get no response. Messages sent to a specific server go directly to that server, but those sent to the cluster name or cluster address can be responded to by either node that is online. The network clients do not need to know which node is online to be able to access the cluster, as long as they use the cluster name rather than the node name.

The private network is dedicated to communications between cluster nodes. This connection is not used for client access to the cluster nodes. Instead, public connections are used for client access to the cluster nodes.

 It is best for each node to have two network cards. This allows one for private communications and one for client communications. The public connection can be used for private communications between servers in case the private network fails.

There are four types of clusters in the Microsoft world:

➤ *Failover cluster*—This is a cluster made up of two or more nodes. One server is active at a time. If one server fails, the other will assume the responsibilities of the first server.

➤ *Network Load Balancing (NLB)*—Allows certain services to be accessed on up to 32 servers as one TCP/IP virtual server, so that access is load-balanced across the multiple servers. An example of NLB would be multiple Web servers with the same content that are accessed in a way that equals the load on all the servers to provide better performance.

➤ *Component Load Balancing (CLB)*—Used to distribute application services among several servers. This allows for load balancing of access to the services and for fault tolerance of the application as a whole. This is a function of Application Center 2000.

➤ *Distributed partition views*—Used with SQL to distribute a single database across several servers for load balancing. For example, if there are three servers, the database could be split into thirds and each server would manage one third of the database. Because one-third of the database resides on each server, client access would be balanced among them.

Hardware Cluster Components

Clusters of any type require special hardware implementations to operate properly. These requirements will be more than those required for the operating system alone.

Note: The hardware must be installed and functioning with the operating system before Clustering Services can be activated.

Each node, or individual server, in a cluster must be able to communicate with the other node, or nodes, in the cluster. If any node should fail, the other node, or nodes, must be aware when the failure occurs so it is able to assume the responsibilities of the failed node and resume its failed functions.

There are two types of hardware components that allow the nodes to communicate and share information: Small Computer System Interface (SCSI) and Fibre Channel. Both hardware interfaces must be PCI.

Note: Peripheral Component Interconnect (PCI) is a 32- or 64-bit adapter card that provides a faster communication speed between the motherboard and any device attached to the PCI adapter.

Small Computer System Interface (SCSI)

SCSI is a general interface that allows a PC to be connected to many different types of devices.SCSI devices can be either internal or external devices, but all the devices need an interface to communicate with the PC.

SCSI Adapter

The SCSI adapter is a controller card, similar to the IDE or floppy controller that controls IDE hard disks or the floppy drive in a PC. The SCSI adapter controls the SCSI devices attached to it and allows information to pass from the PC bus to the SCSI bus, and vice versa. The SCSI bus is faster and more versatile than IDE.

The SCSI adapter sends signals to the SCSI devices that contain their own controller that carries out the command of the adapter on the device.

SCSI adapters and SCSI devices receive information from each other based on an identification process. The person installing the device on the SCSI bus assigns a SCSI ID to each SCSI device, including the adapter. Each device and adapter will come from the factory preconfigured with a default ID, but these IDs can and usually must be changed before the device or adapter is installed.

Note: The device or adpater with the highest SCSI ID has a higher priority than the devices with lower SCSI IDs.

No two SCSI devices connected to the same adapter, or on the same SCSI bus, can have the same SCSI ID. This would result in a conflict, and the devices will not function properly, if at all, until the conflict is resolved.

The SCSI adapter can support multiple devices, depending on the width of the address bus. The address bus is used to signal which device with the specified SCSI ID is to receive the transmitted commands. The SCSI address bus width and the number of devices supported are shown in Table 3.1.

For example, if you install a SCSI card with a 16-bit address bus, you could have 15 devices connected to the SCSI adapter. The number of supported devices is one less than the address bus width because the adapter also uses a SCSI ID.

SCSI Hard Drive

One of the numerous SCSI devices is the SCSI hard drive. A SCSI hard drive allows for faster performance than a standard IDE hard drive. This is the reason SCSI devices are used for clustering and are standard in most servers. Faster performance helps prevent disk subsystem bottlenecks.

Clusters share a common hard drive or set of hard drives on a SCSI bus to allow for the nodes to share data required to continue services to clients in case of a failure. When a node fails, another node will continue the functions of the failed node by taking control of the shared drive(s) where the data is stored. The shared disk resource where the cluster database is stored is called the *Quorum resource*. In every cluster, there must be at least one Quorum resource.

The shared drives are where the shared applications and folders are located. The shared applications are installed from all nodes to the shared resource, using the same configuration. This will allow for one node to continue the services of another node that has failed.

 The shared resources must have the same drive letters on all nodes. This can be changed in the Computer Management Utility under the Disk Management option.

Table 3.1 Devices supported by SCSI address bus.	
Address Bus Width	Number of Devices
8	7
16	15
32	31

Note: For the shared resources to be fault tolerant, the RAID implementation must be managed by hardware.

SCSI Chain

All SCSI devices managed by a SCSI adapter are on the same SCSI chain or SCSI bus. All these devices communicate to the PC through the SCSI adapter, which is connected to the PC bus.

The SCSI chain can contain both internal and external devices. This allows for greater versatility of the SCSI bus. You do not have to have one SCSI adapter to support all the internal devices and another to support all the external devices.

Note: Not all SCSI adapters have external connectors for external devices. On the other hand, some SCSI adapters are made for specific devices that only have external connectors. However, most SCSI adapters have both internal and external connectors.

The hardest part of using SCSI chains is terminating them. Terminating a SCSI chain is similar to the termination used on a thinnet network: Each end of the network cable must be terminated in order to prevent signals from bouncing back and causing collisions, which prevents communication. The SCSI chain is similar: If the ends are not terminated, the devices on the SCSI chain cannot send or receive signals.

Looking at the first example in Figure 3.2, you can see that the SCSI chain has both internal and external devices. Hard Disk 1 and the scanner must both be terminated in order for all the devices to be able to communicate.

The second example in Figure 3.2 shows a SCSI adapter with three internal hard drives. In this case, Hard Disk 1 and the SCSI adapter must be terminated to allow signals to be transferred properly from and to all the devices.

Finally, the third example in Figure 3.2 shows a SCSI adapter and two external devices on the SCSI chain. The SCSI adapter and external CD-ROM need to be terminated in this case.

There are two places you can terminate the SCSI adaptor: the internal bus and the external bus. Referring again to Figure 3.2, in example 2, the external bus should be terminated, and in example 3, the internal bus should be terminated.

The SCSI adapter that is used to connect to the shared drives and Quorum resource must be dedicated to the shared drives and Quorum resource. Internal SCSI devices should not be connected to the SCSI chain, especially the system disk or boot disk.

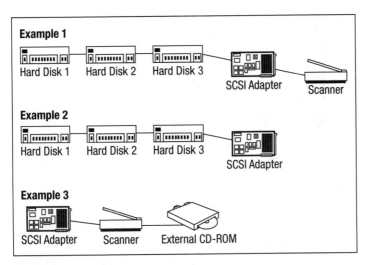

Figure 3.2   SCSI chain examples.

There are two types of termination: active and passive. Both of these termination types can be handled by the BIOS chip on the SCSI adapter card. Termination can be managed in the SCSI BIOS setup to specify whether the termination is enabled or disabled on the internal or external connectors.

Note: Some older SCSI adapters require a physical resistor to be added to terminate the card or to be removed to stop termination on the card.

Active termination is only active when the SCSI adapter has power. This requires the PC to be powered on when a cluster is set up. Passive termination does not require power. Therefore, even if one node in the cluster fails, the chain is still terminated.

When SCSI adapters that use active termination are used, it is best to have SCSI "Y" cables to keep the SCSI chain terminated even when one node is offline. Figure 3.3 shows an example of using a SCSI "Y" cable for termination. With the SCSI adapters being active, when one goes offline, the end of the SCSI chain is no longer terminated and the devices will malfunction. With a SCSI "Y" cable, the ends are always terminated, regardless of the power state of either SCSI adapter.

Fibre Channel

A newer type of connectivity to external devices that has emerged in the last few years is *Fibre Channel*. Fibre Channel is a technology that allows signals to be transmitted to devices over fiber-optic cable. This allows for a faster connection speed to and from the devices as well as the ability to place these devices in

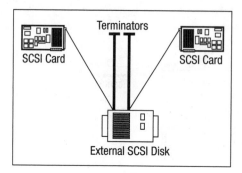

Figure 3.3 A SCSI "Y" cable.

separate buildings in case of a natural disaster. For example, if a fire should destroy one building, the devices in the other building would be spared. The devices that can be separated from the servers and placed in other locations are the server with the hard disks and backup systems.

Note: Fibre Channel allows for the transmission of SCSI commands as well as the transmission of video and network communications.

Fibre Channel depends on Fibre Channel hubs or switches to connect PCs and devices. A Fibre Channel chain can contain 126 devices. Fibre Channel chains are actually loops (like in a ring network) or they can be similar to a star network (with a Fibre Channel hub).

Devices can all be connected to a hub, to a switch, or from device to device. If the devices are all connected to a hub or switch, they can be hot-swapped without disrupting the whole Fibre Channel loop. This isn't the case if the devices are connected from one to another.

There are differences in the SCSI and Fibre Channel set ups. SCSI has cable length limitations of 3 meters, whereas Fibre Channel can have 30 meters between devices (with distances totaling 10 km). Data rates on the SCSI chain can be up to 20MBps whereas Fibre Channel supports up to 1GBps.

Note: Fibre Channel can also use copper cabling or even twisted-pair, with some reduction of functionality.

All Fibre Channel devices have a Gigabit Interface Converter (GBIC), which is a plug-in module specific to the type of cable being plugged into the device (note that there are different types of fiber-optic cable). The GBIC will convert electrical signals to optical signals, and vice versa.

Instead of replacing a hub, switch, or whatever device type, you can replace the GBIC, and this will usually fix a Fibre Channel connection problem.

The specific GBIC required can be placed in a hub, switch, or external device, or even in the Fibre Channel adapter on a server or workstation. This modularization allows for an easier upgrade if the cabling changes. This way, only the module needs replacing, not the device.

Note: Fibre Channel devices are listed in a separate Hardware Compatiblity List (HCL). Search the Microsoft Web site for "Cluster/FibreChannel Adapter."

Operating System Cluster Components

Once the hardware portion of the cluster is implemented (the installation is covered in detail in Chapter 5), the actual components need to be set up in the operating system itself.

This is the portion of the cluster that will make it specific to the requirements and applications used in your setup. These components are the basis of how the applications will be managed by the cluster.

Resources

Resources are logical entities controlled by the cluster. These resources can be active only on a single node of the cluster at a time.

Here are the different types of resources available in Cluster Services:

➤ *DHCP Service*—Enables DHCP on a cluster for fault tolerance if a node fails. Enabling the DHCP Service resource requires the location of the database files and the backup database files.

➤ *Distributed Transaction Coordinator (MS DTC)*—Allows the MS DTC service to be enabled for fault tolerance on a cluster installation. This resource has no configurable parameters.

➤ *File Share*—Allows for the setup of a shared folder on the cluster so that the share is available at all times. The configurable parameter is the path of the share.

File Share permissions are set in Cluster Administrator.

➤ *Generic Application*—Used to specify applications that are not cluster aware but that will be supported as fault tolerant on the cluster. The configurable parameters are the application command line, the current directory, the network name or computer name, and the application's ability to interact with the desktop. If the application is configured to interact with the desktop, the application will actually be run on the node that owns the resource.

➤ *Generic Service*—Used to run services that are not cluster aware so that they will be fault tolerant on the cluster. The configurable parameters are the service name, startup parameters, the network name or computer name, and the path to the directory where the files reside.

➤ *IIS Server Instance*—Allows an instance of IIS to be fault tolerant on the cluster. You can specify the WWW Administrative Web site or another Web site. Also, the FTP Web site can be specified. Configurable parameters are the alias and the permissions on the sites.

➤ *IP Address*—Used to specify an IP address for a group (discussed later in the "Groups" section of this chapter) to allow access to the group by IP address. Parameters specified are the IP address, the subnet mask, and the network name.

➤ *MSMQ Server*—Provides fault tolerance setup for Microsoft Message Queue Server for sending messages to or between applications.

➤ *Network Name*—Used to specify an alternate name for a group to allow access to the group by computer name (virtual server). Parameter configuration requires the computer name to be used.

➤ *NNTP Server Instance*—Enables the clustering of NNTP newsgroups on a cluster. This requires that the NNTP service be running.

➤ *Physical Disk*—Specifies which disk is used by a group. Parameter configuration requires that the drive letter of the disk to be used.

Note: Once the Physical Disk resource is created, the drive letter cannot be changed.

➤ *Print Spooler*—Provides clustering of the print spooler to enable the nodes to service the network printers. If one node goes offline, the network printers will still function. Configurable parameters are the path to the print spooler and job completion timeout for the queued print jobs.

➤ *SMTP Server Instance*—Provides fault-tolerant clustering of the Simple Mail Transport Protocol (SMTP) for mail delivery. Requires the SMTP service to be running.

➤ *Time Service*—Used to maintain a consistent time within the cluster.

➤ *WINS Service*—Enables the WINS service on a cluster for fault tolerance if a node fails. Enabling the WINS Service resource requires the location of the database files and the backup database files.

These resources allow you to keep services or applications available for client use a majority of the time, depending on the cluster type. If a resource fails on one node, you can configure options that allow the resource to fail over to another node so that it can function on that node. Other options allow the resource to be restarted on the same node in case of a resource failure.

For example, the DHCP service could be clustered between Node A and Node B. If DHCP services are active on Node A, but Node A fails for some reason, the DHCP services could be started on Node B or even attempted to be restarted on Node A again. This is discussed in greater detail in Chapter 10.

Dependencies

Dependencies are created when one resource depends on other resources for functionality. If any resource should fail, so will any resource that depends on the failed resource.

Resources and their dependencies are listed in Table 3.2.

For example, if Node A has a print spooler set up on the Physical Disk resource W:, and drive W: fails, the print spooler would no longer be available for client use.

The major resource that fails most often is the Physical Disk resource. For this reason, the external disk(s) should be in an array and use hardware RAID 1 or RAID 5 to prevent such failures.

Groups

A *group* is a collection of resources that will fail over to another node if any resource within the group fails (depending on the failover settings of the group).

A group can be owned by only one node at a time. If one or all resources fail, the group as a whole, not individual resources, will change ownership.

A Physical Disk resource can exist in only one group at a time. If any other resources depend on that resource, they must also be in the same group. For example, if Group 1 contains Physical Disk resource W:, which the DHCP Service resource and the Print Spooler resource depend on, and the DHCP Service resource fails, Group 1 would fail as a whole and be moved with all of the Resources in Group 1 to another active node.

Table 3.2 Resources and their dependencies.	
Resource	**Dependency**
DHCP Service	Physical Disk
	IP address
Distributed Transaction Coordinator	Physical Disk
File Share (DFS)	Network name
File Share (not DFS)	None
Generic Application	Network name
Generic Service	Network name
	IP address
IIS Server Instance	Physical Disk
	Network name
IP Address	None
Message Queue	Physical Disk
	Network name
Network Name	IP address
NNTP Server Instance	IP address
Physical Disk	None
Print Spooler	Physical Disk
	Network name
SMTP Server Instance	IP address
Time Service	None
WINS Service	Physical Disk

Failover

Failover is the process of a group being moved from one node to another when a resource fails within the group.

Groups can be set to retry the failed resource a certain number of times before being moved to the other resource. The actual configuration of the failover is covered in more detail in Chapter 10.

Failback

Failback is the process of a group being failed over to another node in the cluster and, when the original node comes back online, the group being moved back to the original node.

For example, suppose a Print Spooler resource is in the Print group on Node A. If Node A fails and the Print group is failed over to Node B, when Node A comes back online, the Print group will be moved back to Node A.

Failback is used in cases where groups are separated between different nodes to allow for equal processor and memory usage. If one node fails, the other nodes will be more burdened than before. It is best in some cases to enable failback for load balancing between nodes.

Quorum Resource

The *Quorum resource* is the shared disk for the cluster that holds the database of cluster information. The database information contains data necessary to recover the cluster.

The Quorum resource must be a Physical Disk resource. This allows any node to have control of the Quorum resource to update the node's local database in case of corruption. If a node joins a cluster but no other node is active, the node can retrieve the database information and join the cluster instead of making a new cluster.

The Quorum resource is a very important database for the proper function of the cluster. The Quorum resource can be backed up in case of corruption, which is covered in more detail in Chapter 13.

Cluster Models

There are five different configurations of clusters. The model used will depend on the requirements of your organization.

The cluster models have different types of fault tolerance for keeping the resources available for clients. The models also have different hardware requirements to provide better failover capabilities, or they have just enough hardware to provide failover until the original node can be brought back online.

Model A

In this model, each node controls some of the resources. For example, each node has a group for balancing processing loads. Each server should have the same hardware to be able to handle both groups if one node fails. Because both nodes are participating in the ownership of a group, they are both active, making this model an active-active type of cluster.

For example, if Node A is running Group 1 and Node B is running Group 2, in the case of a node failure, each node should be able to handle the processing load of its group and the group of the other node. If Node A fails, Node B should have the processing power to run both Group 1 and Group 2.

This model provides for high availability and is best suited for file and print sharing.

Model B

In this model, one node is a spare in case the other node fails. This model will run all the groups on one node, with the other node sitting idle. This provides one server with a lot of processing power and the other node with just enough to manage the groups that are failed over until the original node comes back online. The second node does not have to have inferior hardware; it can be equal in processing power, depending on how critical the resource is to the organization. This model has one active node and one node on standby that is passive. This makes the model an active-passive type of cluster.

For example, suppose Node A is running a critical SMTP service in Group 1 and Node B is running no groups. If Node A fails, Node B will start Group 1 and run Group 1 until Node A comes back online (if failback is enabled), Node B fails, or Group 1 is moved back to Node A manually.

This model provides an organization with high availability for mission-critical applications.

Model C

In this model, there is one node that runs the groups of resources while the second node sits idle until the first node fails. The first node also runs all the non-cluster-aware applications. Because the first node is running more applications, it's usually a more powerful PC than the second node.

When the first node fails, the cluster-aware applications will fail over to the second node and continue functioning for client access. The non-cluster-aware applications will fail but not fail over, which makes them unavailable for client access.

Model C provides high availability for the cluster-aware applications, but the non-cluster-aware applications will be available normally just like any other application on a nonclustered server.

Model D

This model has only a single node in the cluster. There is no failover ability for the applications. This model provides for ease of administration to manage resources and groups.

Also, with configuration of the groups and resources, if a group or resources fails, the server can attempt to restart the group or resource rather than cause a failover to another node. This model also provides the option of future scalability by adding a second node to provide hardware fault tolerance.

The availability of applications on this model is a little higher than normal, but not much. If the server hardware should fail, all resources are offline to clients.

Model E

This model is a hybrid of all the other models to provide the best options of each.

Each node runs groups with its own resources and also runs non-cluster-aware applications on each node. The other node will also have the ability to provide for the failover of the other node's groups to itself in case of a node failure.

For example, suppose Node A is running Group 1 and one non-cluster-aware application, and Node B is running Group 2 and a non-cluster-aware application. When Node A fails, Node B would be running Group 1, Group 2, and its original non-cluster-aware applications. The non-cluster-aware applications that were running on Node A would no longer be available. This model requires that both servers be of equal processing power and have more processing power than would be required to run their regular loads.

Availability is very high for the cluster-aware applications and normal for the non-cluster-aware applications.

Practice Questions

Question 1

> Which of the following is required for each SCSI device?
>
> ○ a. Terminator
>
> ○ b. SCSI ID
>
> ○ c. SCSI adapter
>
> ○ d. Ribbon cable

The correct answer is b. Each device requires a unique SCSI ID on the SCSI chain. Only two devices require a terminator—those on each end of the SCSI chain. Therefore, answer a is incorrect. The trick of the question is that not every device requires its own SCSI adapter; several devices can share a SCSI adapter, as they can a ribbon cable. Therefore, answers c and d are incorrect.

Question 2

> How many SCSI devices can be placed on a SCSI adapter with a SCSI address bus width of 32?
>
> ○ a. 7
>
> ○ b. 15
>
> ○ c. 31
>
> ○ d. 32

The correct answer is c. The SCSI address bus width specifies how many SCSI IDs can be used on the SCSI bus. One must be subtracted for the SCSI adapter, which also uses a SCSI ID. With a SCSI address bus width of 32, 32 devices can be supported, but one of these will be the SCSI adapter. Therefore, answers a, b, and d incorrect.

Question 3

> Which of the following types of devices can be used to connect the nodes in a cluster to a shared device? [Check all correct answers]
>
> ❑ a. IDE
> ❑ b. SCSI
> ❑ c. EIDE
> ❑ d. Fibre Channel

The correct answers are b and d. The two types of devices that can be used to connect nodes in a cluster together to a Shared Disk resource are SCSI and Fibre Channel. Therefore, answers a and c are incorrect. Choices a and c are used as standard internal hard disk types but not usually on the high-performance servers. They are mainly for workstations but can be used on low-performance servers.

Question 4

> Which of the following cluster types allows an application to perform specific services between the different nodes in a cluster?
>
> ○ a. Failover Cluster
> ○ b. Network Load Balancing
> ○ c. Component Load Balancing
> ○ d. Distributed Partition Views

The correct answer is c. Component Load Balancing spreads an application's services between the nodes of the cluster. Failover allows one node to run a resource and then the other node to run it when the first node fails. Therefore, answer a is incorrect. Network Load Balancing allows multiple servers to be accessed as one service, such as IIS. Therefore, answer b is incorrect. Distributed Partition Views splits portions of a SQL database between servers. Therefore, answer d is incorrect.

Question 5

A workstation connected to a Fibre Channel hub fails to see the other devices on the hub. However, all other devices work fine and can access each other. When the workstation is moved to a different hub port, it works fine. What can be done?

○ a. Replace the GBIC

○ b. Replace the Fibre Channel optic cable between the workstation and the hub

○ c. Replace the Fibre Channel hub

○ d. Replace the workstation

The correct answer is a. It is important to remember that the GBICs are the actual ports on the Fibre Channel devices. The troubleshooting trick is that the GBICs are modular and can be replaced without replacing the whole device. If the workstation works fine when connected to another port, then the optic cable is fine, the Fibre Channel hub is fine, and the workstation is functional. The only option left is to replace the GBIC in the hub. Therefore, answers b, c, and d are incorrect.

Question 6

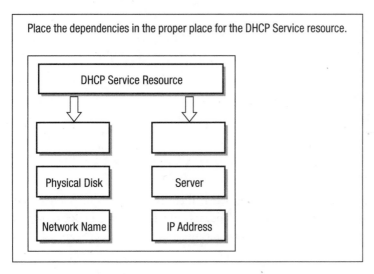

Place the dependencies in the proper place for the DHCP Service resource.

DHCP Service Resource

Physical Disk

Server

Network Name

IP Address

The correct answer is:

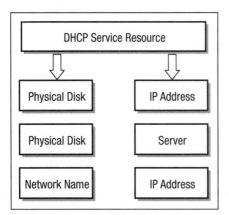

DHCP Service Resource

Physical Disk

IP Address

Physical Disk

Server

Network Name

IP Address

The DHCP Service requires a disk to write to the database that is used by the service, as well as an IP address to be contacted by clients requesting an IP address. The Physical Disk and IP Address do not have to be in the specified spots; they can be switched.

A network name is not required when a DHCP server is contacted for an IP address, and a server is not a resource; therefore those labels are not used.

Question 7

> When a resource fails, what happens to the group it is in?
>
> ○ a. It is renamed.
>
> ○ b. It is deleted.
>
> ○ c. It causes the entire group to fail.
>
> ○ d. It fails back.

The correct answer is c. When one or more resources in a group fails, the group as a whole fails.

Groups are not renamed or deleted when there is a group failure. Therefore, answers a and b are incorrect. Failback occurs only if the original node on which the group operates comes back online and the group is configured to fail back. Therefore, answer d is incorrect.

Question 8

> Which of the following models has only one node?
>
> ○ a. A
>
> ○ b. B
>
> ○ c. C
>
> ○ d. D
>
> ○ e. E

The correct answer is d. Model D has only one node; the rest have two. Therefore, answers a, b, c, and e are incorrect.

Question 9

> What type of card must the SCSI or Fibre Channel adapter be in the cluster servers?
>
> ○ a. Vesa local bus
>
> ○ b. PCI
>
> ○ c. AGP
>
> ○ d. IDE

The correct answer is b. The SCSI and Fibre Channel adapters in the cluster servers must be PCI adapter cards. None of the others are possible card types. Therefore, answers a, c, and d are incorrect.

Question 10

> The first node of a two-node cluster has a NetBIOS name of Server1. The second node's NetBIOS name is Server2. The cluster name is Cluster1. A user pings the name Cluster1 and gets a response, but when he pings Server1, there is no response. What can he expect when he pings Server2?
>
> ○ a. No response
>
> ○ b. Partial response
>
> ○ c. Delayed response
>
> ○ d. A response

The correct answer is d. If the cluster name responds to a ping, one or both nodes are available. If Server1 gives no response, Server2 must give a response; otherwise, when the user pinged the cluster name, there would have been no response. Therefore, answer a is incorrect. Choices b and c are incorrect because there will be no partial or even a delayed response.

Need to Know More?

 Lee, Richard R. *Windows NT Microsoft Cluster Server.* Osborne/ McGraw-Hill, Berkley, CA, 1999. ISBN 0078825008. This book includes information on SCSI, Fibre Channel, and storage solutions.

 Fibre Channel Technology: Understanding Fibre Cabling and Connecting to Building Infrastructure. Compaq Computer Corporation, Houston, TX, 1998. **www5.compaq.com/support/techpubs/whitepapers/ ecg 0030298.html.** This technical white paper discusses Fibre Channel connections and how they can be used.

 Windows 2000 Clustering Technologies: Cluster Server Architecture. Microsoft Corporation, Redmond, WA, 1999. **www.microsoft.com/ WINDOWS2000/library/howitworks/cluster/clusterarch.asp.** This technical white paper discusses the Cluster Server technologies available with Windows 2000.

 Search TechNet on the Internet at **www.microsoft.com/technet/ default.asp** or the TechNet CD for more information on installing SCSI and Fibre Channel on a Windows 2000 Advanced Server PC.

Cluster Services

Terms you'll need to understand:

- ✓ Configuration database
- ✓ Checkpoint Manager
- ✓ Remote Procedure Calls (RPCs)
- ✓ Communications Manager
- ✓ Configuration Database Manager
- ✓ Event Processor
- ✓ Event Log Manager
- ✓ Failover Manager
- ✓ Global Update Manager
- ✓ Log Manager
- ✓ Node Manager
- ✓ Object Manager
- ✓ Resource Monitor
- ✓ Event Log Manager
- ✓ Membership Manager

Techniques you'll need to master:

- ✓ Understanding the capabilities of Cluster Service managers
- ✓ Understanding which Cluster Service managers perform which functions
- ✓ Understanding Resource Monitors

This chapter presents the components that make up the Cluster Service, describing in detail their functionality and capability to control the individual nodes and the cluster as a whole. We also discuss how these components monitor and manage nodes to keep the cluster available.

Cluster Components

The Cluster Service is made up of 10 components that control the whole cluster to keep it available. These components work together very closely to maintain the availability of the cluster. These components are listed in Table 4.1 and will be covered in more detail throughout the chapter.

Checkpoint Manager

The Checkpoint Manager maintains the Quorum log on the Quorum resource. Cluster applications store their information in the Quorum log for use in updating all the nodes within the cluster. The Checkpoint Manager also copies the Registry information on the node that has ownership of the Quorum resource to the Quorum log for recovering cluster database information.

Any changes made to the configuration database will be synchronized to all nodes within the cluster that require the data change. For example, if an IP Address resource is modified on one node, any other node that is a possible owner must also be changed. This way, if the one node fails, the other node will not bring the resource online without the updated change.

Communications Manager

The Communications Manager oversees communication among all the nodes in a cluster. This allows all the nodes to be aware of each other and keeps local databases current by synchronizing the nodes in the cluster.

All communications are done on a private network or mixed network, both of which allow for node-to-node communications. Communication takes place using Remote Procedure Calls (RPCs) between the nodes.

RPCs are used to allow applications or services on one PC to communicate with services on another PC. Messages can be passed from one cluster component on one node to a cluster component on another node.

For example, using the previous example, the nodes that require the update of the IP address resource change will communicate with one another using RPCs so that all nodes are updated with this change.

Table 4.1   Cluster Service components.

Component	Function
Checkpoint Manager	Saves logs on the Quorum resource
Communications Manager	Manages node communication
Configuration Database Manager	Manages the cluster configuration database
Event Processor	Manages all the Cluster Service components
Failover Manager	Manages the failover process
Global Update Manager	Manages cluster updates made by other components
Log Manage	Manages the Recovery log on the Quorum resource
Node Manager	Manages cluster membership
Resource Monitor	Used to check the status of resources on the nodes
Event Log Manager	Synchronizes the Event log between all nodes in a cluster
Membership Manager	Manages the health and membership the nodes within the cluster
Object Manager	Manages the Cluster Services objects

Configuration Database Manager

The Configuration Database Manager handles the changes made to the configuration database and maintains information on all the physical and logical components of the cluster, such as nodes, resources, groups, and their respective properties.

For example, when a change is made to a resource (such as the IP Address resource used in the previous examples), the Configuration Database Manger updates the configuration database on the Quorum resource. Once this change is made, the Checkpoint Manager is triggered to update all the nodes that are possible owners of the changed resource. The specific nodes updated are determined by the Global Update Manager (discussed later in this chapter).

Event Processor

The Event Processor is the heart of the clustering services. It manages the events that occur within the cluster or nodes. For example, the Event Processor manages whether a node is online, offline, or paused. A cluster is offline until the Event Processor calls the Node Manager to start or join a cluster when a node starts.

The Event Processor also passes events from one node to another so that applications and cluster components are aware of events occurring on other nodes. For example, when a node in a cluster is started, the Event Processor calls the Node Manager to start and then cause the node to either join another node that is already online or create the cluster by being the first node online. When any node in a cluster comes back online, the event will be declared to an existing node, which may cause a failed group that was running on the failed node to fail back to the node that just came online.

Failover Manager

The Failover Manager determines which node in a cluster owns a specific group. If a resource within a group fails, the Failover Managers of all nodes determines what to do with the failed resources. The Failover Manager may decide to restart the resources or just fail over the group to another node.

The Failover Manager decides whether to allow for the failback of a failed group. For example, suppose a Physical Disk resource is a member of the Test group on Node A. If the Physical Disk resource fails, the Failover Manager determines whether the group should be moved to Node B or the Physical Disk resource should just be restarted.

Global Update Manager

The Global Update Manager determines which nodes in a cluster will have changes made to their configuration database by the Configuration Database Manager. Any nodes not updated will be forced into an offline state because the databases are not synchronized.

The Global Update Manager calls the Configuration Database Manager to synchronize the databases on all nodes, assuring uniform information between the nodes.

Log Manager

The Log Manager determines whether the cluster database information on each node is current with the recovery database on the Quorum resource.

The Log Manager calls the Checkpoint Manager to perform the actual updates to the databases with the most recent checkpoints. For example, if a resource is changed on Node A, the Log Manager will determine whether the database on Node B and the Quorum resource should also be updated. If the other databases are not updated, the Log Manager calls the Checkpoint Manager to update the other databases.

Node Manager

The Node Manager tracks and determines the membership of the cluster. It tracks current nodes that are part of the cluster and determines whether they are online.

To determine whether the nodes are online, the Node Manager sends out a heartbeat to the other nodes. When it is determined that a node has failed, the Node Manager notifies all other existing nodes, and the process—knows as a regroup event—will start to determine what to do about the groups residing on the failed node.

Note: Heartbeats are covered in more detail in Chapter 7.

For example, if Node B fails, the Node Manager on Node A would detect its failure. Any information in the configuration database about the groups and resources running on Node B is used to restart those resources and groups on Node A if the Failover Manager determines that this is necessary.

Object Manager

The Object Manager handles the state of resources and groups on all nodes in the cluster.

If it is determined that a group is to be moved to another node, the Object Manager stops the group's resources, taking them offline, so that they can be moved to another node and then be brought back online.

For example, if a resource fails on Node A that is part of the Test group, and the Failover Manager determines that the group should be moved to Node B, the Object Manager takes offline any other resources in the Test group as well as the Test group itself. Once the Test group and its resources are moved to Node B, the Object Manager brings the Test group and its resources back online.

Resource Monitor

The Resource Monitor is used on all nodes in a cluster to send messages to resources to determine their status. The Resource Monitor is passive and does not initiate the messages, but sends the messages on behalf of the Cluster Service.

Resource Monitors not only send messages but also monitor the Cluster Service itself for failures. One Resource Monitor will run, by default, on every node to monitor the Cluster Service and the node's resources. Other Resource Monitors can be started for specific resources for fault tolerance of the monitor itself. If the Resource Monitor should fail, no resources on that node can be interacted with by any utility on any other node. Setting up multiple Resource Monitors prevents this from occurring.

Setting up individual monitors prevents one resource failure from affecting other resources. This is similar to running a program in a different memory space.

Event Log Manager

The Event Log Manager is used to keep the Event logs identical among all nodes within a cluster. This component allows an administrator to view the Event logs in Event Viewer on any node within the cluster and see information or errors for any node within the Cluster. This feature is important because any failure on any node can cause a failure of the cluster as whole. An administrator would not be able to sufficiently monitor for errors if he had to view all Event logs on all nodes within the cluster.

Membership Manager

The Membership Manager runs on all nodes and determines which nodes within the Cluster are active. It can determine when a failure has occurred and will remove the failed node from the list of active nodes. When a node comes back online, the Membership Manager will detect its presence and add the node to the list of active nodes.

The list of active nodes is used to determine the placement of groups and their resources. Cluster Administrator uses this list to to determine its own list of active nodes.

Practice Questions

Question 1

Which component can tell a node whether another node is online?

- ○ a. Global Update Manager
- ○ b. Communications Manager
- ○ c. Node Manager
- ○ d. Resource Monitor

The correct answer is c. The Node Manager tracks the membership of a cluster and has an up-to-date list of all the current nodes in that cluster.

The Global Update Manager supervises the updates to the configuration database. Therefore, answer a is incorrect. The Communications Manager oversees the messages being sent between nodes. Therefore, answer b is incorrect. The Resource Monitor is used to send messages to resources to determine their status. Therefore, answer d is incorrect.

Question 2

Which component manages the cluster configuration database?

- ○ a. Configuration Database Manager
- ○ b. Checkpoint Manager
- ○ c. Global Update Manager
- ○ d. Node Manager

The correct answer is a. The Configuration Database Manager manages the configuration database by making changes to it.

The Checkpoint Manager writes updates to the Quorum log. Therefore, answer b is incorrect. The Global Update Manager determines which nodes get updated to synchronize the configuration database. Therefore, answer c is incorrect. The Node Manager tracks the membership of a cluster and has an up-to-date list of all the current nodes in the cluster. Therefore, answer d is incorrect.

Question 3

> If a change is made to a resource on Node A, which component determines that the database on Node B is no longer the same as the database on Node A?
>
> ○ a. Configuration Database Manager
>
> ○ b. Global Update Manager
>
> ○ c. Checkpoint Manager
>
> ○ d. Log Manager

The correct answer is d. The Log Manager determines whether databases are out of sync.

The Configuration Database Manager manages the configuration database by making changes to it. Therefore, answer a is incorrect. The Global Update Manager determines which nodes are updated to synchronize the configuration database. Therefore, answer b is incorrect. The Checkpoint Manager writes updates to the Quorum log. Therefore, answer c is incorrect.

Question 4

> Which component updates the Quorum log?
>
> ○ a. Configuration Database Manager
>
> ○ b. Log Manager
>
> ○ c. Checkpoint Manager
>
> ○ d. Object Manager

The correct answer is c. The Checkpoint Manager writes updates to the Quorum log.

The Configuration Database Manager manages the configuration database by making changes to it. Therefore, answer a is incorrect. The Log Manager determines whether databases are out of sync. Therefore, answer b is incorrect. The Object Manager oversees the state of resources and groups. Therefore, answer d is incorrect.

Question 5

> Which component changes the state of a group if it is to be failed over to another node?
>
> ○ a. Object Manager
>
> ○ b. Failover Manager
>
> ○ c. Communications Manager
>
> ○ d. Event Processor

The correct answer is a. The Object Manager oversees the state of resources and groups.

The Failover Manager determines when to fail a group over to another node, restart the group, or perform a failback of the group. Therefore, answer b is incorrect. The Communications Manager supervises the messages being sent between nodes. Therefore, answer c is incorrect. The Event Processor sends notification of events to applications and services on other nodes. Therefore, answer d is incorrect.

Question 6

> Which function does the Failover Manager provide? [Check all correct answers]
>
> ❑ a. Determines whether a group should be returned back to its original node
>
> ❑ b. Determines whether a node should be notified of a group failure
>
> ❑ c. Determines whether a group or resource should be failed over to another node
>
> ❑ d. Determines whether a failed group should be restarted

The correct answers are a, c, and d. The Failover Manager determines whether a group should be moved to another node (failover), moved to its original node (failback), or whether a failed resource or group should just be restarted.

The Event Processor notifies other nodes in the case of a group failure. Therefore, answer b is incorrect.

Question 7

Which of the following components are used when a resource is modified?
[Check all correct answers]

- ❑ a. Configuration Database Manager
- ❑ b. Checkpoint Manager
- ❑ c. Failover Manager
- ❑ d. Global Update Manager

The correct answers are a, b, and d. When a change is made to a resource, the
Configuration Database Manger updates the configuration database on the Quorum resource. Once this change is made, the Checkpoint Manager is triggered to
update all the nodes that are possible owners of the changed resource. The Global Update Manager determines the specific nodes to be updated.

The Failover Manager determines whether a group should be moved to another
node (failover), moved to its original node (failback), or whether a failed resource
or group should just be restarted. Therefore, answer c is incorrect.

Question 8

Which of the following are advantages to using multiple Resource Monitors? [Check all correct answers]

- ❑ a. Less memory is used
- ❑ b. More processor time is used
- ❑ c. The Cluster Services are more stable
- ❑ d. Less processor time is used

The correct answer is c. When multiple Resource Monitors are used to monitor
resources, the CPU and memory incur more overhead, but all the resources will be
more stable. In other words, one resource failure will not cause all resources to fail.

More memory and processor time are used. Therefore, answers a and d are incorrect. Choice b will occur, but this is a disadvantage, not an advantage.

Question 9

Which of the following is used for communication between nodes?

○ a. LPC

○ b. RPC

○ c. IPX/SPX

○ d. NetBEUI

The correct answer is b. Intracluster communication is accomplished via remote procedure calls (RPCs).

Local procedure calls (LPCs) are used by a PC to communicate with itself. Therefore, answer a is incorrect. IPX/SPX and NetBEUI are not protocols that can be implemented by Cluster Services. Therefore, answers c and d are incorrect.

Question 10

On which node(s) do the Cluster Service components operate?

○ a. The first node to come online

○ b. The second node to come online

○ c. The node that has ownership of the Quorum resource

○ d. All nodes

The correct answer is d. The Cluster Service components operate on all nodes in a cluster to provide for cluster communication and node management.

Because the Cluster Service components operate on all nodes, answers a, b, and c are incorrect.

Need to Know More?

Lee, Richard R. *Windows NT Microsoft Cluster Server.* Osborne/McGraw-Hill, Berkley, CA, 1999. ISBN 0078825008. This book includes information on Cluster Service components and their functions within the cluster.

Windows 2000 Clustering Technologies: Cluster Server Architecture. Microsoft Corporation, Redmond, WA, 2000. **www.microsoft.com. TechNet/Win2000/win2ksrv/technote/clustsrv.asp**. This technical white paper covers many aspects of the Cluster Server, including the managers, as well as a wide range of information about clusters.

Search TechNet on the Internet at **www.microsoft.com/technet/default.asp** or the TechNet CD for more information on Cluster Service components and their abilities.

Cluster Installation

Terms you'll need to know:

✓ SCSI bus

✓ Fibre Channel bus

✓ Shared disk

✓ Private disk

✓ Node-to-node communication

✓ Client-to-cluster communication

✓ Cluster name

✓ Cluster IP address resource

Techniques you'll need to master:

✓ Identifying the preinstallation tasks that need to be performed before the configuration of Cluster Service

✓ Identifying the hardware requirements needed for Cluster Service to run

✓ Configuring SCSI bus and Fibre Channel bus

✓ Configuring a shared disk in preparation to install Cluster Service

✓ Identifying the software requirements of Cluster Service

✓ Installing and configuring Cluster Service on two nodes

✓ Automating deployment

✓ Verifying a successful installation of Cluster Service

✓ Identifying single points of failure

This chapter discusses the installation of Cluster Service on systems running Windows 2000 Advanced Server. Attention is given to the pre-installation tasks that need to be completed before the actual installation of Cluster Service. Step-by-step instructions for installing Cluster Service are also included in the chapter. You should be familiar with both the pre-installation tasks as well as the actual installation process before braving the exam.

To successfully install Cluster Service, you must have a thorough understanding of certain elements. The following topics are covered throughout the chapter to assist in your understanding of the cluster-installation process: hardware, security rights, software, configuration, automated deployment, installation verification, and points of failure. When working through the chapter, also keep in mind the terms you'll need to know and the techniques you'll need to master that are shown on the first page of this chapter.

Hardware

When looking at the hardware requirements, you have basically two considerations. First, because Cluster Service runs on Advanced Server, the hardware must meet the requirements for the operating system (refer to Chapter 2 for the minimum hardware requirements and check the Hardware Compatibility List [HCL] for hardware compatibility). Second, Cluster Service has specific hardware requirements that must be met as well. These will be discussed in detail in the following sections.

Here's a list of the specific hardware requirements for Cluster Service that must be met by both computers:

➤ Each computer requires a minimum of two disk controllers, one of which must be SCSI or Fibre Channel.

➤ Each computer must have at least one private disk for the Advanced Server installation.

➤ There must be at least one external disk (shared disk) that connects to both computers.

➤ A SCSI or Fibre Channel bus is needed to access the shared disk.

➤ Each computer requires at least one network adapter, but two or more is recommended.

Disk Controllers

Each of the computers in the cluster requires at least two disk controllers (adapters). One of the disk controllers will be used for the internal private disk, whereas the other controller will be used for the external shared disk. Cluster Service cannot use the storage device and controller that serves the Advanced Server installation. Therefore, two controllers are necessary—one for Advanced Server and one for Cluster Service. The disk controllers will be connected to the external disk using a SCSI or Fibre Channel bus (refer to Chapter 3 for more information on SCSI adapters, cables, and Fibre Channel devices).

Private Disks and Shared Disks

Each node in the cluster requires at least one internal private disk for the installation of Advanced Server (the private internal disk also requires a separate disk controller). Between the two nodes, there must also be at least one shared hard drive or multiple shared hard disks; the installation or configuration of Cluster Service will fail if there is not at least one shared disk. The shared disk will contain shared applications and shared data, thereby increasing their availability, because if one node fails, the other can take control of the shared disk and continue to service client requests.

It is recommended that the shared disk have at least two partitions, using one small partition dedicated to the Quorum resource (discussed in Chapter 3). If possible, though, you should use a separate disk for the Quorum resource.

Before proceeding with the installation of Cluster Service, you will need to verify that the shared disk(s) has been assigned the same drive letter on both cluster nodes. This can be done by booting each system one at a time and using the Disk Management utility. Keep in mind that Cluster Service supports only NT File System (NTFS), so the shared disk must be formatted using this file system. Also, the shared disk cannot be dynamic; it must remain a basic disk.

To verify the drive letter assignment of the shared disk, follow these steps:

1. Open Start|Programs|Administrative Tools and click Computer Management.

2. From within the Computer Management snap-in, expand Storage and click Disk Management.

3. Drive letter assignments will be displayed in the details pane, as shown in Figure 5.1.

Network Adapters

Each cluster member needs at least one PCI network adapter. The recommended configuration is to have two network adapters per node to connect to the network, because using one network adapter per node creates a single point of failure. One network adapter will be used to connect the cluster members to the public network (client-to-cluster communication). This adapter carries the client-to-cluster traffic. The second network adapter will be used to connect the cluster members to a

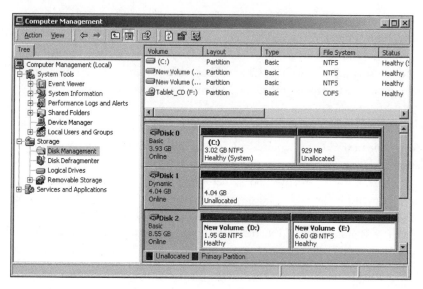

Figure 5.1   The Computer Management snap-in can verify that the shared disk has been assigned the same drive letter on each of the nodes.

private network (node-to-node communication). The private network consists of only the cluster members, and the adapters on the private network carry traffic only between the two cluster members, as shown in Figure 5.2.

 Make sure TCP/IP is bound to the network adapters because it is the only protocol supported by Cluster Service.

You will need to determine how IP addresses will be assigned to the cluster nodes. A DHCP server can assign the IP addresses, or they can be static. Keep in mind that if you use a DHCP server to assign IP addresses to your cluster nodes and the DHCP server becomes unavailable, the nodes will self-assign themselves an IP address in the range of 169.254.0.0 (Automatic Private IP Addressing). To eliminate this possibility, consider assigning each of the network adapters a static IP address.

Use the following steps to configure the network adapters under Advanced Server:

1. Right-click My Network Places and choose Properties.

2. Right-click the LAN connection you want to configure and choose Properties.

3. Click the TCP/IP protocol and click the Properties button.

4. The resulting dialog box allows you to configure the IP address for the network adapter, as shown in Figure 5.3.

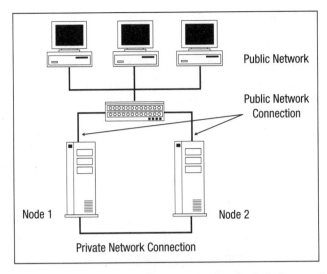

Figure 5.2 One adapter should be used for client-to-cluster communication; the other adapter should be used for node-to-node communication.

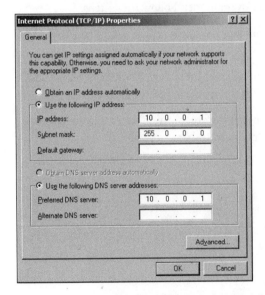

Figure 5.3 To assign a static IP address, select the option Use The Following IP Address and type in an IP address and subnet mask.

Once you've configured the IP addresses for each of the network adapters, consider changing the name of the LAN connections so that they are more easily recognizable.

Security Rights

Before configuring Cluster Service to run, you must make sure a domain user account exists for the service to run under. Once the domain user account is created, it must also be granted specific user rights. This can be accomplished by simply making the cluster user account a member of the Administrators group. The cluster user account also requires three other user rights that are not granted to the Administrators group:

➤ Log on as a service

➤ Lock pages in memory

➤ Act as part of the operating system

These three user rights do not need to be specifically granted to the user account. During the installation and configuration of Cluster Service, the user account is automatically assigned these user rights.

Use the Active Directory Users And Computers snap-in to create a domain user account that the Cluster Service can run under. Follow these steps:

1. Open Start|Programs|Administrative Tools. Click the Users And Computers snap-in.

2. Expand the domain in which you want to create the domain user account. This would be the domain that the cluster nodes are members of.

3. Right-click the Users container or the organizational unit in which you want to create the new user account, point to New, and click User.

4. From the New Object-User dialog box, fill in the name for the user account and click the Next button, as shown in Figure 5.4.

5. Choose a password for the user account. Make sure to select the User Cannot Change Password and Password Never Expires options in the dialog box, as shown in Figure 5.5.

Software

Before configuring Cluster Service to run, specific software needs to be set up. Here is a list of the software needed to run Cluster Service:

➤ Advanced Server or Datacenter Server, both systems configured in one of the following server roles:

➤ Member servers

➤ Domain controllers

➤ Name Resolution (any of the following methods):

  ➤ DNS

  ➤ WINS

  ➤ Hosts

Because Cluster Service runs on Advanced Server and Datacenter Server, you will need one of these platforms installed on both computers designated as cluster nodes.

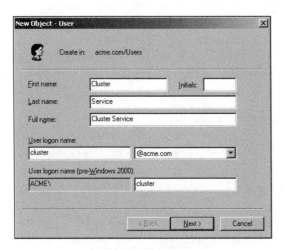

Figure 5.4   The New Object-User dialog box.

Figure 5.5   Once you have chosen a password for the user account, be sure to select the User Cannot Change Password and the Password Never Expires options.

Once the operating system has been installed, the computers will be configured as member servers. You will need to consider the roles the cluster nodes will be configured for. You have the option of configuring your two servers as domain controllers or having them remain as member servers within an existing domain. Regardless of which option you use, the cluster nodes must be members of the same domain. Keep in mind that if you choose to configure the nodes as member servers within an existing domain, the availability of the cluster nodes becomes dependent on the availability of a domain controller. This creates a single point of failure. If you choose this option, make sure there is more than one domain controller on the network that is accessible to the cluster nodes. Also keep in mind that if the cluster nodes are configured as member servers, they become dependent on an external resource for authentication. In order for authentication to occur, the network must always be available. This, in turn, creates another point of failure.

The second option is to configure both cluster nodes as domain controllers. Doing so eliminates the need for the cluster nodes to be authenticated by an external source, thus eliminating the network as a single point of failure. The cluster nodes can be configured as domain controllers within an existing domain or as domain controllers within their own domain. If the nodes are configured to be in their own domain, make sure it is a domain in the existing corporate forest. This allows you to take advantage of the two-way transitive trust relationships that are automatically created between domains in the same forest. If the domain is in a different forest, one-way trusts will have to be manually set up. When establishing domains in a forest, it is always recommended that you use as few domains as possible. The preferred option when setting up the systems would be to configure them as domain controllers within an existing domain.

You can use the **DCPROMO** command to promote a member server running Windows 2000 to a domain controller.

Configuring the nodes as domain controllers within their own domain means the nodes do not have to provide authentication services to network clients, only to the Cluster Service and any other services running on the nodes.

Once the server roles and domain membership has been determined, you will also need to provide the systems with some form of name resolution. Name resolution is the process of mapping a computer name to an IP address. In order for clients to locate resources on the network, including resources in a server cluster, there must be some form of name resolution. Name resolution is also used during the configuration of Cluster Service when the second node joins the first. The cluster nodes must be configured to use DNS, WINS, or static HOSTS files, so that names can be mapped to IP addresses.

Once these preliminary steps have been completed, you are now ready to start the installation and configuration of Cluster Service.

Configuration

The installation of Cluster Service is done one node at a time. When performing the installation of Cluster Service on the first node, make sure that the second node is powered off and that the shared disk is powered on.

If Cluster Service was installed during the installation of Advanced Server, you will be ready to launch the Cluster Service Configuration Wizard. If Cluster Service was not added during the installation of the operating system, it can be added through the Control Panel. Here are the steps to follow:

1. Open Start|Settings and click Control Panel.

2. Double-click the Add/Remove Programs icon.

3. Double-click the Add/Remove Windows Components option.

4. Select Cluster Service from the list of components, as shown in Figure 5.6, and click Next.

5. The required files will be located in the i386 folder. Insert the Advanced Server CD-ROM or provide the path to a network share. Click OK.

6. Click Next.

7. The Cluster Service Configuration Wizard appears. Click Next. Click I Understand to accept Microsoft's warning that hardware not listed on the HCL is not supported by Cluster Service (see Figure 5.7).

8. The next dialog box gives you the option of creating or joining a cluster (see Figure 5.8). If you are installing on the first node, select the first option (that the server is the first node in the cluster). If a cluster node already exists and you are installing on the second node, choose the second option (the installation of Cluster Service on the second node will be covered in the next section). Click Next.

9. All nodes are grouped under a shared name that can be used when accessing or administering the cluster. Enter a NetBIOS name for the cluster. It can be a maximum of 15 characters (see Figure 5.9). Click Next.

Figure 5.6 Via the Add/Remove Programs icon in the Control Panel, Cluster Service can be installed if it was not installed with the operating system.

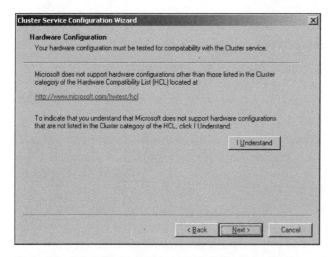

Figure 5.7 Select I Understand to accept that Cluster Service does not support hardware that is not on the HCL.

10. Provide the username and password for the Cluster Service account that was created during the pre-installation tasks (see Figure 5.10). Then provide the domain name and click Next.

11. The username and password are validated. Click Next.

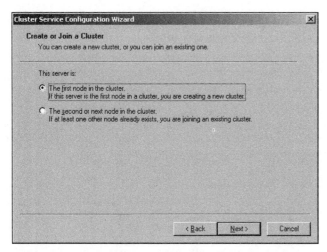

Figure 5.8 If you are configuring Cluster Service on the first node, select the first option in the list.

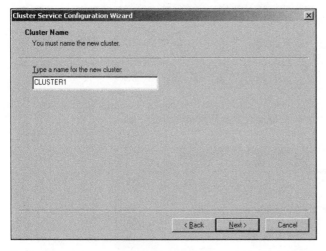

Figure 5.9 Provide a name for the new cluster, using a maximum of 15 characters.

12. At this point in the configuration, Cluster Service will detect all disks on all SCSI buses (except the bus that contains the disk that Advanced Server is installed on). Remove any disks you do not want to be managed by the cluster (see Figure 5.11). Click Next.

13. The next dialog box that appears will prompt you to select a location for the Quorum resource. You can dedicate an entire disk to the Quorum resource or choose a partition with at least 5MB of free space (see Figure 5.12). Keep in mind that the recommended partition size for the Quorum Resource is 100MB.

Note: The next dialog box that appears will depend on the configuration of the network. If the cluster nodes are configured with multiple network adapter cards, you will be presented with two dialog boxes, allowing you to configure each adapter for use (what type of traffic will be carried). It is recommended that each node have at least two network cards because using only one creates a sinlge point of failure. For the purpose of this example, each node is configured with only one network card, but as already stated, this is not the recommended configuration.

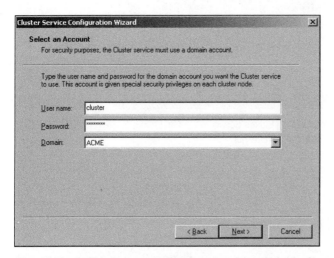

Figure 5.10 Provide the username, password, and domain for the Cluster Service user account that was created during the preinstallation tasks.

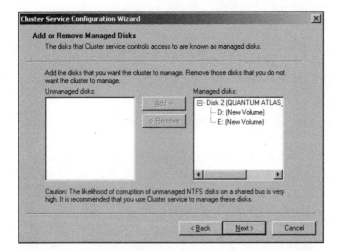

Figure 5.11 From this dialog box, you can choose which disks you want the cluster to manage.

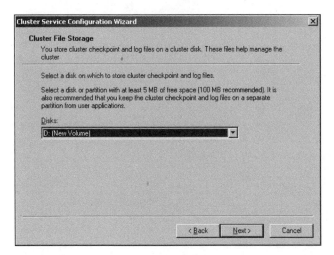

Figure 5.12   Choose a disk or a partition that is at least 5MB in size
for the location of the Quorum resource.

14. The next step in configuring the cluster is to begin the detection of the
    network adapters and configure the network. Click Next to begin configur-
    ing the network adapters for use.

15. A dialog box will appear for each network adapter card, allowing you to
    configure its use and the type of traffic it will carry (see Figure 5.13). Be sure
    to check the option Enable This Network For Cluster Use. The role that this
    network will play can then be selected. Click Next.

*Note: Because there is only one network card in each of the cluster nodes, the last
option is selected to enable all communications across this network. If there were two
network cards per node, one could be configured for client access only (public network)
and the other could be configured for internal cluster communication only (private
network). For fault tolerance, one network card can be configured for the cluster-to-
cluster communication only and the second one can be configured for all
communications. This way, if the private connection fails, the other one can still be
used for cluster-to-cluster communication.*

16. The last step is to assign a static IP address and a subnet mask to the cluster.
    This becomes known as the *IP Address resource* (see Figure 5.14). Adminis-
    trators can then connect to and manage the cluster using the IP address.
    Click Next.

17. Click Finish to complete the installation process and restart the computer.

Once Cluster Service has been installed and configured on the first node, you
can begin the installation process on the second node. For the installation to be

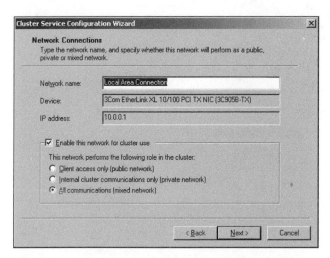

Figure 5.13 The Network Connections dialog box allows the network adapter to be configured to carry certain traffic.

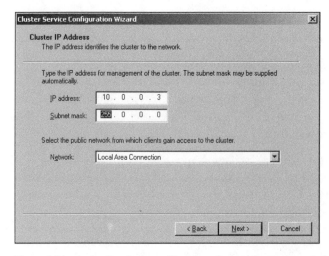

Figure 5.14 Assign the cluster an IP address that can be used by administrators to connect to and manage the cluster.

completed, the first cluster node and the shared disk must both be turned on. If Cluster Service has not been installed on the second node, follow Steps 1 through 7 to first install the service and begin the Cluster Service Configuration Wizard.

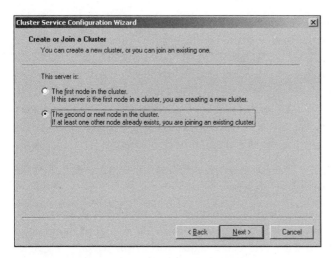

Figure 5.15   When installing Cluster Service on the second node, select the second option in the Create Or Join A Cluster dialog box.

At this point, the configuration of the Cluster Service will vary from that of the first node. Here are the steps to follow:

1. When the option to create or join a cluster appears, as shown in Figure 5.15, select the second option, because this node will be the second node in the cluster. Click Next.

2. Provide the name of the cluster that you want this node to join. Click Next.

3. Provide the password for the Cluster Service account. Click Next.

4. Click Finish to complete the installation on the second node.

Note: Refer to the section titled "Verifying Installation," later in this chapter, to help you determine whether the installation and configuration of Cluster Service was successful.

Automated Deployment

The installation of Cluster Service can be automated along with the installation of Windows 2000 Advanced Server. If the hardware is not identical between the systems, you can automate the installation process by setting up a distribution server and creating an unattend.txt file. The text file is used to supply the answers that would otherwise need to be entered manually during the setup process. Windows 2000 comes with a default unattend.txt file that can be edited to meet your installation requirements, or a new answer file can be created. You can use Setup Manager to create an answer file, or you can use a text editor such as Notepad. Once the answer file is created, it is specified using the **Winnt** command.

In order to automate the installation of Cluster Service using an unattend.txt file, you will need to add specific information to the text file. The Cluster component within the text file will need to be set to "On." This will install Cluster Service as well as the Administration components. Placing the cluscfg.exe parameter under the GUIRUNONCE section of the text file will automatically launch the Cluster Service Configuration Wizard at first startup. You will also need to include a [Cluster] section within the answer file, specifying parameters such as the NetBIOS name assigned to the cluster and the IP address.

Note: The GUIRUNONCE section of an answer file specifies commands that should be run after setup completes and the system restarts.

Windows 2000 also comes with the System Preparation tool (Sysprep), which can be used in conjunction with third-party software to create a disk image of your installation. This tool can be used to create an image that will be deployed onto computers with similar hardware (the master computer and the target computers must have the same Hardware Abstraction Layers and mass storage devices). To deploy Cluster Service using this method, install Advanced Server onto a test computer and then install Cluster Service either during the installation of the operating system or by using the Windows Components Wizard via the Add/Remove Programs icon in the Control Panel. The Sysprep tool can be used to duplicate the system. Using third-party software, you can then deploy the image onto the computers that will become cluster nodes. Once the image has been deployed, the Cluster Service Configuration Wizard can either be run manually or run automatically by placing the cluscfg.exe utility in the GUIRUNONCE section of the Sysprep.inf file.

Verifying Installation

Once the installation and configuration of Cluster Service are complete, there are several ways to verify whether the installation was successful:

➤ Open up the Registry on the cluster node and verify that the "Cluster" key has been created under the HKEY_LOCAL_MACHINE subtree, as shown in Figure 5.16.

➤ Under the Administrative Tools, open the Cluster Administrator to verify that the cluster disks are online. If the status of the disks is "online," it means that the Cluster Service has been configured correctly and is working properly.

➤ Once the Cluster Service has been installed on both nodes, use the Cluster Administrator utility to verify that both nodes are present. If both nodes are present, the cluster is running and operational, as shown in Figure 5.17.

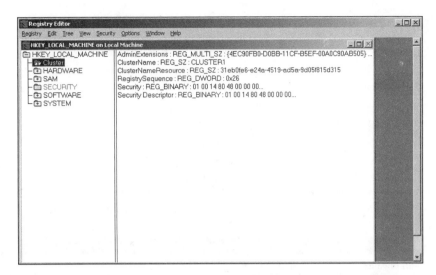

Figure 5.16   To verify the successful installation and configuration of Cluster Service, use the Registry editor to see whether the Cluster key has been created.

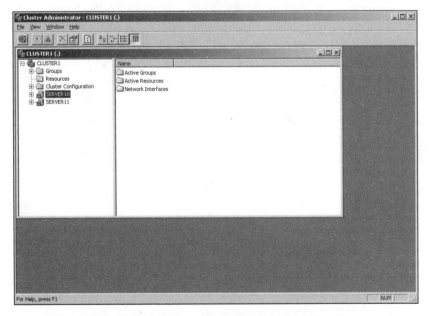

Figure 5.17   To verify that Cluster Service is correctly installed on both nodes, open up the Cluster Administrator utility. If both nodes are present, Cluster Service was successfully installed.

Points of Failure

Clusters are designed to provide high availability for network resources, applications, and services. If one cluster node fails, the other node will continue to service client requests. They are not capable of protecting all components. The availability of the cluster will also be dependent on the configuration of the network environment. In order to provide maximum availability of the cluster and its resources, you should identify all single points of failure in your network environment. A single point of failure can include both software and hardware. For example, if IP addresses are dynamically assigned to cluster nodes, their availability depends on the availability of a DHCP server. Table 5.1 lists some of the common single points of failure and their recommended solutions.

Table 5.1 Some single points of failure and recommended solutions.	
Point of Failure	**Solution**
DHCP	Assign static IP addresses to all interfaces on the cluster nodes.
Disks	Implement hardware- or software-level RAID for the private disks. Use hardware-level RAID on the shared disk(s).
Hardware failure	Always ensure there are spare parts on hand, such as controller cards and drives.
Power outages	Use UPS devices to provide power in case of power failures.
Routers, hubs, etc.	Have spare components on hand. Implement redundant routes.
Network cards	Configure each cluster node with at least two network cards.
Authentication	Make the cluster nodes domain controllers in an existing domain or in their own domain so that they do not become dependent on an external server for authentication.

Practice Questions

Question 1

You are the administrator of a network and are responsible for the planning and deployment of a cluster. The cluster nodes are configured as domain controllers on their own subnet. You want to isolate the internal cluster communication and also eliminate the possibility of this becoming a single point of failure. How should the network adapters on the cluster nodes be configured during the installation and configuration of Cluster Service? [Check the two best answers]

❑ a. Configure the private network adapters for All Communications.

❑ b. Configure the public network adapters for All Communications.

❑ c. Configure the private network for Client Access Only.

❑ d. Configure the public network for Client Access Only.

❑ e. Configure the private network for Internal
        Cluster Communication Only.

The correct answers are b and e. The network adapters used for the private network should be configured for Internal Cluster Communication Only, thereby isolating the cluster traffic between nodes. The network adapters used for the public network should be configured for All Communications. By doing so, if the private network becomes unavailable, cluster-to-cluster communication can still take place over the adapters connected to the private network. Answer a is incorrect, because setting the private adapter for all communications doesn't isolate internal cluster communication. Answer c is incorrect because the private network is used for internal cluster communication, not client-to-cluster communication. Answer d is incorrect, because cluster nodes will not be able to use the public network as a backup should the private network fail if it is set for client access only.

Question 2

You are preparing for the installation of Cluster Service. While performing the preliminary steps, you create a domain user account under which the service can run. Once the user account is created, you add it to the Administrators group on each cluster node. What other step should you complete to grant the Cluster Service account the appropriate user rights necessary for it to function correctly?

○ a. Add the Cluster Service account to the Server Operators group on each node.

○ b. No further steps are required. The wizard will automatically grant the user rights to the service account.

○ c. Add the Cluster Service account to the Cluster Operators group on each node.

○ d. Open the local security policy to grant the service account the appropriate user rights.

The correct answer is b. During the installation and configuration of Cluster Service, the service account is automatically granted the necessary user rights for it to function correctly. Answer a is incorrect because adding the account to the Server Operators group would not give the account the necessary user rights. Answer c is incorrect because there is no group called Cluster Operators. Answer d is incorrect because the user rights do not need to be manually assigned to the user account.

Question 3

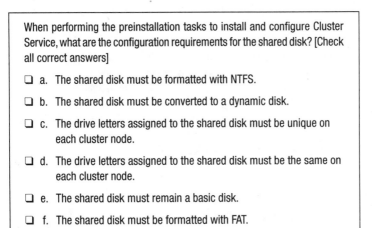

When performing the preinstallation tasks to install and configure Cluster Service, what are the configuration requirements for the shared disk? [Check all correct answers]

❑ a. The shared disk must be formatted with NTFS.

❑ b. The shared disk must be converted to a dynamic disk.

❑ c. The drive letters assigned to the shared disk must be unique on each cluster node.

❑ d. The drive letters assigned to the shared disk must be the same on each cluster node.

❑ e. The shared disk must remain a basic disk.

❑ f. The shared disk must be formatted with FAT.

The correct answers are a, d, and e. The shared disk must be a basic disk and be formatted with NTFS. The drive letters assigned to the shared disk must be the same on each cluster node. This can be verified using the Computer Management snap-in. Answer b is incorrect because the shared disk must remain a basic disk, not be converted to a dynamic one. Answer c is incorrect because the drive letter assignment for the shared drive must be the same on each node. Answer f is incorrect because the shared disk must be formatted with NTFS.

Question 4

What requirements must be met to begin the installation and configuration of Cluster Service on the second node? [Check all correct answers]

❑ a. The first node must be powered off.

❑ b. The shared disk must be powered on.

❑ c. The first node must be powered on.

❑ d. The shared disk must be powered off.

The correct answers are b and c. To begin the installation and configuration of Cluster Service on the second node, the shared disk and the first cluster node must both be powered on. Answer a is incorrect because if the first node is not powered on, the second node will not be able to join the cluster. Answer d is incorrect because if the shared disk is powered off, neither node will be able to access it.

Question 5

You are responsible for designing and implementing a cluster configuration for your company, which is running several mission-critical applications that must maintain a high availability. Because the availability of the cluster is dependent on the configuration of the network, you plan to eliminate as many points of failure as possible. Your company has also expressed its expectations for the cluster.

Required result:

➤ Eliminate the cluster hardware as a single point of failure.

Optional results:

➤ Eliminate domain membership as a point of failure.

➤ Eliminate IP addressing as a single point of failure.

Proposed solution:

➤ Implement hardware-level RAID on the shared disks; implement software-level RAID on the private disks in each node.

➤ Configure each node with two network adapters—one for Internal Cluster Communication and the other for All Communications.

➤ Assign static IP addresses to all adapters on each cluster node.

➤ Configure the nodes as member servers in an existing domain with one domain controller.

Which of the following statements best describes the proposed solution?

○ a. It meets the required result and both optional results.

○ b. It meets the required result and one optional result.

○ c. It meets only the required result.

○ d. It meets neither the required result nor the optional results.

The correct answer is b. The proposed solution meets the required results and one of the optional results. Implementing hardware-level RAID on the nodes eliminates hardware failure as a single point of failure, and configuring each node with two adapters ensures there is a second network available for cluster communication. Configuring each node with static IP addresses eliminates IP addressing as a point of failure. Configuring the cluster nodes as member servers in an existing domain makes them dependent on the network for authentication. To eliminate this as a point of failure, the cluster nodes should be configured as domain controllers within an existing domain or as domain controllers within their own domain in the existing corporate forest.

Question 6

> Which of the following are considered to be software requirements to run
> Cluster Service? [Check all correct answers]
>
> ❏ a. DHCP for IP addressing
>
> ❏ b. Name resolution, such as DNS or WINS
>
> ❏ c. Windows 2000 Server
>
> ❏ d. Index Server
>
> ❏ e. Windows 2000 Advanced Server

The correct answers are b and e. Cluster Service requires Advanced Server (or
Datacenter Server) to run as well as some form of name resolution, such as DNS
or WINS. Cluster Service does not require DHCP, thus making answer a incorrect. Answer c is incorrect because Windows 2000 Server does not support Cluster Service. Finally, Cluster Server does not require Index Server, thus making
answer d incorrect.

Question 7

> Two servers running Windows 2000 Advanced Server need to be config-
> ured in a cluster. Each node is configured with two network adapters; the
> adapters for the private network will be used for cluster-to-cluster commu-
> nication, and the adapters for the public network will be used for client-to-
> cluster communication. You assign static IP addresses to each adapter on
> both nodes and then install and configure Cluster Service. How many IP
> addresses will be assigned?
>
> ○ a. 2
>
> ○ b. 3
>
> ○ c. 4
>
> ○ d. 5

The correct answer is d. Each network adapter is manually assigned an IP address. Also, during the installation and configuration of Cluster Service on the
first node, the cluster itself is also assigned an IP address that can be used by
administrators to connect to and manage the cluster.

Question 8

> You just installed Cluster Service on cluster nodes Server10 and Server11.
> You run Cluster Administrator on both nodes to verify the installation. On
> Server10, Server11 is listed as being offline, and on Server11, Server10 is
> listed as being offline. Each one is configured with two network adapter
> cards—one for the private network and one for the public network. Which
> of the following is the probable cause?
>
> ○ a. The private connection between the nodes has failed.
>
> ○ b. The public connection has failed.
>
> ○ c. Cluster Service has failed to start.
>
> ○ d. The IP addresses assigned to the cluster nodes are incorrect.

The correct answer is a. If the private connection becomes unavailable, each node
will not know whether the other is online. Answer b is incorrect because if the
public connection becomes unavailable, it will not impact communication between the cluster nodes because they are configured with a private network connection for cluster-to-cluster communication. If the cluster service has failed to
start, Cluster Administrator would not be available, thus making answer c incorrect. Answer d is incorrect because if the IP addresses assigned to the cluster were
incorrect, the installation of Cluster Service would not be successful.

Question 9

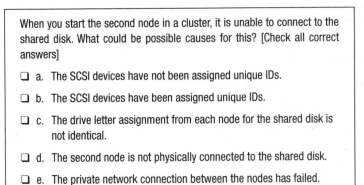

When you start the second node in a cluster, it is unable to connect to the shared disk. What could be possible causes for this? [Check all correct answers]

❏ a. The SCSI devices have not been assigned unique IDs.

❏ b. The SCSI devices have been assigned unique IDs.

❏ c. The drive letter assignment from each node for the shared disk is not identical.

❏ d. The second node is not physically connected to the shared disk.

❏ e. The private network connection between the nodes has failed.

The correct answers are a, c, and d. Each SCSI device needs to be assigned a unique ID, thus making answer a correct and answer b incorrect. Answer c is correct because the drive letter assignment for the shared disk must be the same. Use the Computer Management snap-in to verify that the drive letter assignment for the shared disk is the same for both nodes. If the second node is not physically attached to the shared disk, it will not be able to establish a connection, thus making answer d correct. Answer e is incorrect because the private network connection between two nodes will not impact whether the second node can connect to the shared disk.

Question 10

> Place the following tasks in the order that they would occur during the installation of Cluster Service on two nodes.
>
> Power on the shared disk.
>
> Install Cluster Service on the first node.
>
> Power off the second node.
>
> Power on the second node.
>
> Power on the first node.
>
> Install Cluster Service on the second node.

Correct answer is:

Power on the shared disk.

Power off the second node.

Power on the first node.

Install Cluster Service on the first node.

Power on the second node.

Install Cluster Service on the second node.

Need to Know More?

 Libertone, David. *Windows 2000 Cluster Server Guidebook: A Guide to Creating and Managing a Cluster, Second Edition.* Prentice Hall. Upper Saddle River, NJ. 2000. ISBN 0130284696. Includes information on the installation and configuration of Cluster Service.

 Search TechNet on the Internet at **www.microsoft.com/technet/ default.asp** or the TechNet CD for more information on installing and configuring Cluster Service.

 Step-by-Step Guide to Installing Cluster Service. Microsoft Corporation, Redmond, WA, 2000. **www.microsoft.com/windows2000/library/ planning/server/clustersteps.asp.** This online documentation provides step-by-step instructions on installing and configuring Cluster Service on two nodes.

 Windows 2000 Deployment Planning Guide. Microsoft Corporation, Redmond, WA, 2000. **www.microsoft.com/WINDOWS2000/library/ resources/reskit/dpg/default.asp.** Refer to Chapter 18, "Ensuring the Availability of Applications and Services" for detailed information on planning and deploying Cluster Service.

For more information on the installation of Cluster Service, use the Microsoft Windows 2000 Help. Click Start and then choose Help. Under the list of contents, choose Windows Clustering.

6

Network Load Balancing

. . . .

Terms you'll need to understand:

✓ Network Load Balancing (NLB)

✓ Port rules

✓ Convergence

✓ Client affinity

✓ Unicast mode

✓ Multicast mode

✓ Statistical Mapping Algorithm

✓ Host priority

Techniques you'll need to master:

✓ Installing the Network Load Balancing service

✓ Configuring the Network Load Balancing service

✓ Understanding when to use Network Load Balancing

This chapter covers Network Load Balancing (NLB) for Windows 2000 Advanced Server and Windows 2000 Datacenter Server. The installation and configuration of Network Load Balancing is also covered in this chapter. You will learn how Network Load Balancing functions to provide fault tolerance and high accessibility as well as what is required to make Network Load Balancing function in your organization.

Network Load Balancing is the Windows 2000 version of the Windows Load Balancing service for Windows NT 4. When upgraded from Windows NT 4.0 Enterprise Server, the Windows Load Balancing service will be upgraded automatically to Network Load Balancing in Windows 2000. The only requirement of the upgrade is that all Windows NT 4 servers in the load-balanced cluster must be upgraded. Windows 2000 Network Load Balancing will not function with Windows NT 4 Windows Load Balancing in the same cluster.

What Is Network Load Balancing?

Network Load Balancing provides the capability to cluster 32 servers to act as one server. This type of clustering is not the same as the clustering covered in Chapter 2. With Network Load Balancing, there are multiple servers with the same services installed. These servers can be accessed by a large number of clients that are then balanced among the multiple servers.

The services used with Network Load Balancing include Web services (WWW and FTP), Terminal services, Streaming Media services, Virtual Private Network (VPN) services and other mission-critical applications. Multiple servers can be used to offer these resources to clients. The servers can offer the clients the best service by connecting them to a different server, depending on the configuration.

For example, if a company has 32 servers running its Internet site (each server has a copy of the same Web pages), when a large number of users on the Internet access the company's Web site, these users will be directed to different servers which will answer their requests for Web pages. This allows all the clients to have fast answers to their Web page requests, because they are not waiting for one overburdened server to fill their requests.

Load balancing was originally managed by Round Robin DNS. Round Robin DNS uses a list of servers on a Domain Naming Service (DNS) database. The DNS database has a list of hosts with the same DNS name but different IP addresses, which are the IP addresses of each individual server. When a client requests a name resolution to an IP address, the DNS server responds with the IP address of the first host. When another client requests a name resolution, the client is given the IP address of the next server in the database with the same DNS name. Round Robin DNS does pose a problem: if there are five servers listed with a single name and clients are accessing them by the "cluster name," when one node fails, every fifth person to access the "cluster" is not able to connect because the server is offline. Round Robin DNS access has no ability to determine a server failure. Load balancing, on the other hand, determines a failure and still gives access to the clients accordingly. When a network load balancing node fails, it takes 10 seconds for the load to be redistributed from the failed node.

Note: Check licensing issues with software manufacturers to determine licensing requirements for running applications on a cluster.

Network Load Balancing Installation

The Network Load Balancing service is available only on Windows 2000 Advanced Server and Windows 2000 Datacenter Server for applications using TCP or UDP data ports. The server must be running the TCP/IP protocol and be connected to Fiber Distributed Data Interface (FDDI), Ethernet, or Gigabit Ethernet. The servers also require 1.5MB of free hard drive space and around 4MB of RAM to run the service, and possibly more depending on the network load placed on each server.

The Network Load Balancing cluster services should not be run on a cluster server. These services enable different types of clustering capabilities, but not on the same server. Windows 2000 Network Load Balancing cannot run with other servers in the same cluster that are running Windows NT 4.0 Windows Load Balancing.

Note: It is recommended that the Network Load Balanced servers have an additional Network Interface Card (NIC) to allow for communication between the servers in the cluster. This is not required, but it is recommended to cut down on network traffic on the subnet that clients access.

To install the Network Load Balancing service if it has been removed, you must go to the Properties dialog box for the LAN connection to which you are going to add the Network Load Balancing service. On the General tab, select Install, as shown in Figure 6.1. (Note that if Network Load Balancing is already installed, you will see the dialog box shown in Figure 6.4.)

Note: The Network Load Balancing service is installed by default, but not enabled. In most cases, installing the service will not be necessary.

Once you select Install, you will be presented with another screen of options, as shown in Figure 6.2. In this dialog box, you can select the network component type of service and then click Add.

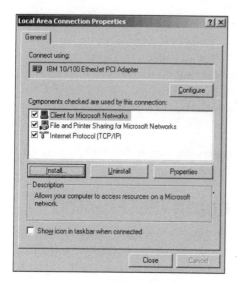

Figure 6.1 The Local Area Connection Properties dialog box with the NLB service not installed.

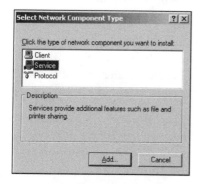

Figure 6.2 Network component type.

Next, you are shown the Select Network Service dialog box (see Figure 6.3). Here, you can select the appropriate network service to add to the server. In this case, you would select Network Load Balancing and then click OK. At this point, you will be taken back to the Local Area Connection Properties dialog box, as shown in Figure 6.4. As you can see, the Network Load Balancing service is installed but not enabled.

Once the Network Load Balancing service is installed, you just have to check the box beside the service to enable it, as depicted in Figure 6.5.

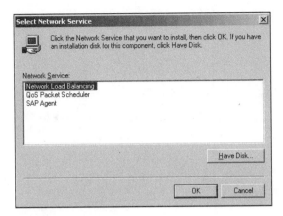

Figure 6.3   Network services.

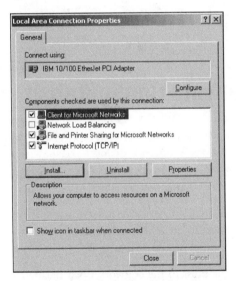

Figure 6.4   The Local Area Connection Properties dialog box with the NLB service installed.

At this point, the Network Load Balancing service is installed and enabled. Installing and enabling the Network Load Balancing service does not require the server to be rebooted. The operating system will shut down the NIC drivers and restart them with the Network Load Balancing service enabled. It does this when the service is enabled and after every configuration change made to the service.

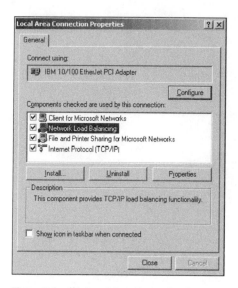

Figure 6.5 The Local Area Connection Properties dialog box with the NLB service enabled.

Network Load Balancing Configuration

Once the Network Load Balancing service is enabled, you will need to configure it to the needs of your organization. To configure the Network Load Balancing service, go to the Local Area Connections Properties dialog box (shown in Figure 6.5), select Network Load Balancing, and then click Properties. This brings up the Network Load Balancing Properties dialog box, as shown in Figure 6.6.

The options listed on this screen are explained further in the following list. These options are for the cluster as a whole. In order for a node to join the cluster, these settings must match the settings on the other nodes:

➤ *Primary IP Address*—This is the IP address of the Network Load Balancing cluster.

➤ *Subnet Mask*—This is the subnet mask used by the cluster with the primary IP address to signify to which subnet the Network Load Balanced cluster belongs.

➤ *Full Internet Name*—This is the fully qualified domain name for the Network Load Balanced cluster for access by clients.

➤ *Network Address*—This is the Media Access Control (MAC) address for the Network Load Balanced cluster. The cluster will ensure that this address is unique.

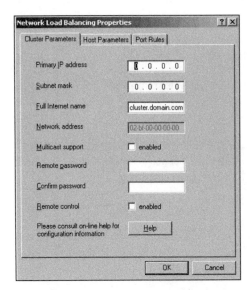

Figure 6.6   The Network Load Balancing Properties dialog box, with the Cluster Parameters tab selected.

Note: Some NICs do not allow their MAC addresses to be overwritten in the packets they send out to the network. If your NIC does not support this option, you must try a different brand or model of network card.

➤ *Multicast Support*—This is a check box that enables or disables multicast support.

Note: Multicasting allows all nodes to operate by working with multicast packets. This allows all nodes to receive the same packets from all clients. It also allows them to communicate with one another using a single network adapter and still communicate with the clients. With multicasting, the NIC's MAC address is retained for packets sent to individual servers, and the cluster address is used for client-to-cluster activity. When using this mode, make sure your routers support multicast addresses in their ARP table.

Unicasting uses the cluster's IP address only when sending packets to clients. In this mode, nodes cannot communicate with other nodes unless there is a second network card. This is the default setting.

➤ *Remote Password*—This option allows password security to request a password from a client trying to remotely administer the Network Load Balanced cluster by using the Windows Load Balancing Services (WLBS) utility. If a password is set and Remote Control is enabled, the user administering the cluster remotely will be queried for a password.

➤ *Confirm Password*—This option verifies the password entered in the Remote Password option box. If the passwords do not match, you will be prompted to reenter the passwords until they are identical. The password is case sensitive.

➤ *Remote Control*—This option enables or disables remote control capability by remote administrators using the WLBS utility.

A Help button is available at the bottom of the Network Load Balancing dialog box in case you forget what an option is for. The Help screen that appears is only for Network Load Balancing help.

Once the Cluster Parameters tab is configured, there are two more tabs that can be configured—the Host Parameters tab and the Port Rules tab. These tabs contain more options for how the individual node will function in the cluster.

The Host Parameters tab allows more individual configuration of a node in the Network Load Balanced cluster. These options are shown in Figure 6.7.

The options for the Host Parameters tab are explained in the following list:

➤ *Priority (Unique Host ID)*—This is the host ID for the node in the cluster. Each node must have a unique ID; it will not function in the cluster until the ID is unique (however, the rest of the cluster will continue to function). Host ID 1 has the highest priority, meaning it will manage all the default traffic for the cluster. The default traffic is the traffic not covered by any of the port rules (discussed later in this chapter).

Note: If the node with the unique ID of 1 should fail or go offline for any reason, the next highest unique host ID will take its place by managing the default traffic.

➤ *Initial Cluster State*—This option enables the Network Load Balancing service to automatically start and let the node join the cluster without intervention.

➤ *Dedicated IP Address*—This is the node's IP address that a client uses to access an individual server. This is the same IP address assigned in the TCP/IP Properties dialog box. This address cannot be assigned by a DHCP server and must be static.

Note: This IP address will not be disabled if Network Load Balancing is disabled. It should be the same IP address originally assigned when TCP/IP was installed on the server.

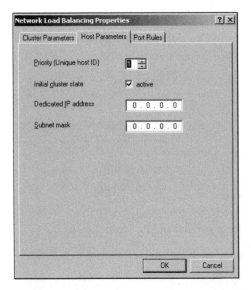

Figure 6.7   The Host Parameters tab of the Network Load Balancing Properties dialog box.

➤ *Subnet Mask*—This is the subnet mask of the dedicated IP address for the server to specify the subnet on which it operates.

These are all the options available for configuring the individual node. The next tab is the Port Rules tab, where you configure how the node functions on the network and within the cluster. The Port Rules tab is shown in Figure 6.8 and explained in the subsequent list:

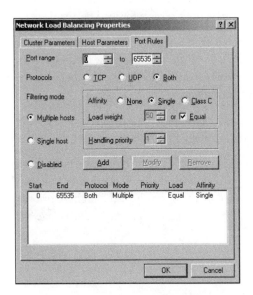

Figure 6.8   The Port Rules tab of the Network Load Balancing Properties dialog box.

➤ *Port Range*—This setting allows you to specify the start and end port numbers for the range of addresses that will be managed by a server or servers, or ignored. The range is from 0 to 65,535, with the default being 1 to 65,535.

Note: To specify one port address only, enter the same port number for the start and end of the range.

➤ *Protocols*—This specifies which TCP/IP protocol to accept or reject—TCP or UDP (or both).

➤ *Filtering Mode: Multiple Hosts*—This specifies that multiple nodes in the Network Load Balanced cluster will manage packets from the selected ports.

➤ *Filtering Mode: Single Host*—This specifies that a single node in the Network Load Balanced cluster will manage packets from the selected ports.

➤ *Filtering Mode: Disabled*—This specifies that all packets for the specified port range will be blocked and not processed. This is, in essence, a firewall for your Network Load Balanced cluster.

➤ *Affinity: None*—With this setting, clients will not be directed to the same server if they send multiple requests to the cluster.

➤ *Affinity: Single*—With this setting, clients will be directed to the same node when they send multiple requests to the cluster. This is the default setting.

➤ *Affinity*—This setting ensures that all clients that have a class C address will be directed back to the same node. This is useful when the clients on an intranet are class C and will be directed back to the same server for internal use, but external users will be sent to various servers for load balancing.

➤ *Load Weight*—This is the percentage of the Network Load Balanced traffic that will be managed by the node. If there are multiple nodes managing the same port range, the value listed here will be divided by the number of nodes to specify the load weight actual percentage.

➤ *Equal Load Distribution*—This check box allows the network load to be balanced equally among all nodes that manage the same port range.

➤ *Handling Priority*—This setting allows for priorities to be placed on the nodes that handle the same port rule. The node with the highest priority (or lowest value) will manage the traffic covered by the port rule. If the highest-priority node goes offline, the node with the next highest priority will manage the traffic covered by the port rule.

After setting the port rules, click the Add button to add the rules to the node.

If a port rule no longer applies, you can select the rule from the list and then click the Remove button. This will delete the selected port rule.

You can modify a port rule by selecting the rule from the list. This shows the settings at the top of the dialog box. These settings can then be changed. Click the Modify button to change the rule with the updates you made.

Because Network Load Balancing only functions with TCP/IP, you can filter specific servers to manage specific functions with a port rule. For example, you can have three nodes manage the FTP site and five nodes manage the HTTP site. The most common ports are listed in Table 6.1.

How Load Balancing Works

When a client accesses a Network Load Balanced cluster, each node receives the packet being sent from the client. Each node compares the incoming packet to its port rules and determines whether it should accept or reject the packet based on the rule. Once a node has accepted a packet, it must then determine whether another node has the same port rule set and whether that node is online. If the node is the only node with the port rule or the only one with the port rule that is online, it processes and responds to the packet sent by the client. If the node is not the only node online with the required port rule to accept the packet, the node with the highest handling priority (or the lowest value) will process and respond to the packet.

Now, if all nodes are set for Multiple Hosts Filtering mode, when traffic comes from the client, each node runs an algorithm based on the client IP address, the port the packet is destined for, and other information to determine which node will manage the packet. The algorithm used to determine which node will manage the client request is called the *Statistical Mapping Algorithm*.

Table 6.1 Common ports.	
Port Type	Port Number(s)
FTP	20, 21, 535, 1024–1065
Telnet	23
SMTP	25
TFTP	69
HTTP	80
NNTP	119
SNMP	161
HTTPS	443
Terminal Services	3389

All nodes of the Network Load Balanced cluster will communicate with one another through multicasting or broadcasting to the cluster name. All nodes receive the packet, and they will determine which nodes are online or offline as well as which nodes have been added to or have left the cluster. Once this has been established, a unique ID is determined for each node to see if the priorities have changed. This determines whether a different node is now supposed to be managing all the default traffic. When all the nodes agree, this is called *convergence*. Once convergence has been achieved, an entry with an event ID of 29 will be written to the event log on each node in the system log. On the other hand, when one node needs to communicate with another specific node, they communicate directly (unicast) with one another.

A problem with Network Load Balancing is that a smart hub (one that acts like a switch) will keep track of the IP address of the PC attached to the physical ports of the hub. This way, it can send a packet destined for an IP address to its specific port on the hub. This causes problems with nodes that are using only one network adapter, because the hub will track only one address and will not be able to manage the same IP address on multiple hub ports. You will have to make sure that your hub supports multiple addresses on one individual hub port and one IP address on multiple hub ports.

Planning for Network Load Balancing

When planning for Network Load Balancing, you need to determine how many clients can access a server with the services and be able to run the applications with little or no access problems. Then you need to determine your anticipated number of clients and divide the number of anticipated clients by the number of clients that can access a single server with no problems. Round this number up, and that will be the number of nodes you need in your Network Load Balancing cluster. If the number of clients anticipated becomes greater, you should add servers to keep the cluster performance at an acceptable level.

Also, always make sure the nodes can handle the extra load placed on them when one server fails.

 If possible, add an extra sever. Having an extra node will ensure performance after a node failure.

If your network subnet runs out of IP addresses before you add this extra node, you can create another Network Load Balanced cluster on another subnet and use Round Robin DNS to alternate traffic between the two clusters using the cluster names. This will work better than using Round Robin DNS for individual servers, unless a whole Network Load Balancing cluster should fail.

N-Tier Clustering

N-tier clustering actually combines server clustering (discussed in Chapter 3) with Network Load Balancing to provide for an n-tier, e-commerce application.

For example, N-tier works by using load balancing to manage client requests from the Internet. As the clients access the Web site, they may need to obtain information that is in a company database, or even place an order for a product.

The database that manages the client orders and client or product information could be located on a server cluster that is running SQL. This type of configuration can be seen in Figure 6.9.

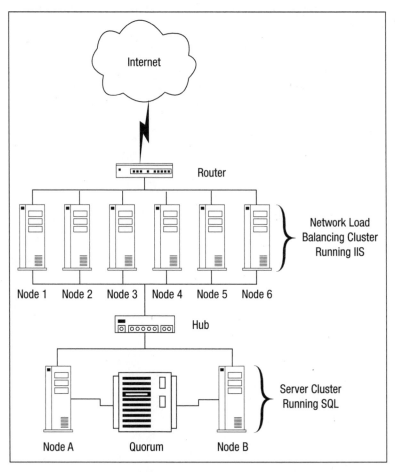

Figure 6.9   Network Load Balancing and a server cluster combined.

This example shows a company with an Internet connection. The Internet connection, such as an ISDN line, is plugged directly into a router and the router is connected to the Network Load Balancing cluster of six nodes. The six nodes are all running IIS with the organization's Web site, which is a shop-online service.

When a user requests information about a product or an order, the IIS node contacts the SQL database—either Node A or Node B of the server cluster. Node A and Node B allow for fault tolerance of the database, which is required for clients to be able to place orders and check existing orders.

This configuration of Network Load Balancing and a server cluster allows for a higher degree of fault tolerance and reliability for the clients. This also allows the organization to be online continually. Downtime can be damaging to many organizations, even if for only 30 minutes, or for some, even less. This configuration can provide uptime of over 99.7 percent. It is a given that other options must be implemented, such as providing for power failure, natural disasters, and the like, but this configuration will provide for no loss due to a server failure.

This configuration also provides for scalability by allowing 26 more nodes to be added to the Network Load Balancing cluster. What's more, upgrading the server cluster to Windows 2000 Datacenter Server allows for two additional nodes.

Practice Questions

Question 1

What is the maximum number of servers that can operate in a Network Load Balanced cluster?

○ a. 2

○ b. 4

○ c. 16

○ d. 32

The correct answer is d. A Network Load Balanced cluster can have a maximum of 32 nodes operating for client access.

A standard cluster server can have a maximum of two nodes if the operating system is Windows 2000 Advanced Server and four nodes if the operating system is Windows 2000 Datacenter Server. Therefore, answers a, b and c are incorrect.

Question 2

Which of the following protocols can be used for Network Load Balancing?

○ a. IPX/SPX

○ b. NetBEUI

○ c. TCP/IP

○ d. AppleTalk

The correct answer is c. The only protocol that can be used for Network Load Balancing is TCP/IP. The nodes of the Network Load Balanced cluster can run other protocols with TCP/IP, but the packets received that are not TCP/IP will not be load balanced. Therefore, answers a, b, and d are incorrect.

Question 3

Which of the following services can be load balanced among five nodes?
[Check all correct answers]

❑ a. Terminal services

❑ b. Exchange services

❑ c. IIS services

❑ d. SQL services

The correct answers are a and c. Terminal Services and IIS services can be network load balanced. These two services do not have data that changes, which means that all the nodes do not need to be constantly updated.

SQL databases constantly change and need updating, and Exchange services do not work well due to the changing content of mailboxes. Therefore, answers b and d are incorrect.

All these services could be load balanced on a single node, but Exchange and SQL can be load balanced *only* on one node.

Question 4

What is the significance of the Primary Address option?

○ a. It specifies the IP address of a single node.

○ b. It specifies the IP address of all nodes in the cluster.

○ c. It specifies the address that is replaced in outgoing packets from a node.

○ d. It specifies the address that is identical to the default node.

The correct answer is b. The primary IP address is the address for the cluster as a whole to be used by clients when accessing the cluster.

The dedicated IP address is the IP address of an individual node. Therefore, answer a is incorrect. An address that is replaced in the outgoing packets from a node is the MAC address of the cluster. Therefore, answer c is incorrect. The dedicated IP address of the default node should be used only for the individual node. IP addresses should not be duplicated, except for the primary address. Therefore, answer d is incorrect.

Question 5

When would a user be asked for the remote password? [Check all correct answers]

❏ a. When administering the node locally

❏ b. When administering the node remotely

❏ c. When using Cluster Manager

❏ d. When using WLBS.EXE

The correct answers are b and d. The only time a user is asked for the remote password is when he or she is administering the cluster remotely using WLBS.EXE. Therefore, answers a and c are incorrect.

Question 6

What happens if two nodes have identical unique host IDs?

○ a. The cluster will fail.

○ b. The nodes with identical IDs will both fail.

○ c. The whole network will fail.

○ d. The node with the duplicate ID will fail when joining the cluster.

The correct answer is d. The node with a duplicate IP address that tries to join the cluster will be unable to due to another node already having the ID. The ID must be changed on the node that failed to join the cluster. This ID must be unique. This situation is similar to a TCP/IP network where any two PCs with the same IP address will not cause the whole network to fail and will not cause either computer to fail. The second PC with the identical IP address will not be allowed to initialize the TCP/IP protocol and will not be able to communicate on the network. Therefore, answers a, b, and c are correct.

Question 7

> Which of the following Affinity options should be set if you want clients to have their packets redirected back to the same node every time they access the cluster?
>
> ○ a. None
>
> ○ b. Single
>
> ○ c. Multiple
>
> ○ d. Class C

The correct answer is b. The Single Affinity setting redirects clients back to the same node (this is the default setting).

The None setting redirects the clients' requests to different nodes each time. Therefore, answer a is incorrect. Multiple is not a valid Affinity setting. Therefore, answer c is incorrect. Answer d is incorrect because the class C setting redirects clients with a class C IP address to the same node.

Question 8

> If a port rule is set to allow FTP access to five different nodes, which filter mode must be set on the selected nodes?
>
> ○ a. No Hosts
>
> ○ b. Single Host
>
> ○ c. Multiple Hosts
>
> ○ d. Disabled

The correct answer is c. Multiple Hosts filtering mode signifies that multiple nodes can accept requests on a specific port rule.

No Hosts is not a valid filtering mode. Therefore, answer a is incorrect. Single Host specifies that a single node is managing the network traffic covered by a specific port rule. Therefore, answer b is incorrect. Disabled will make the node reject the packet that is covered by the port rule. Therefore, answer d is incorrect.

Question 9

What term is used to specify that the nodes of the cluster all have an up-dated list of the cluster members?

- ○ a. Statistical Mapping Algorithm
- ○ b. Broadcast update
- ○ c. Multicast update
- ○ d. Convergence

The correct answer is d. When all nodes in the cluster communicate with one another, they determine whether any nodes are offline and whether nodes have left or joined the cluster. Once all nodes have an updated list of the cluster membership, this is known as *convergence*.

The Statistical Mapping Algorithm determines which node a client is referred to in the NLB, so answer a is incorrect. Unicast and multicast updates are how the nodes communicate with one another, either by communicating with one other node (unicast) or a group of other nodes (multicast); therefore answers b and c are incorrect.

Question 10

When convergence occurs, which log can an administrator consult to deter-mine whether convergence is complete?

- ○ a. Application log
- ○ b. Security log
- ○ c. System log
- ○ d. Replication log

The correct answer is c. Convergence messages are written to the System log in Event Viewer.

The Application log will track the errors created by applications on the system. The Security log tracks auditing of resources to determine resource usage. The Replication log is used to show when the servers have replicated Active Directory data. Therefore, answers a, b and d incorrect.

Need to Know More?

 Lee, Richard R. *Windows NT Microsoft Cluster Server.* Osborne/ McGraw-Hill, Berkley, CA, 1999. ISBN 0078825008. This book includes information on Network Load Balancing.

 Microsoft Corporation. *Microsoft Windows 2000 Server Deployment Planning Guide.* Microsoft Corporation. Redmond, WA, 2000. ISBN 1-57231-805-8. This book covers topics on installing and configuring Network Load Balancing services.

 Introducing Windows 2000 Advanced Server. Microsoft Corporation, Redmond, WA, 2000. **www.microsoft.com/windows2000/guide/ server/solutions/overview/advanced.asp**. This white paper covers the abilities of the Windows 2000 Advanced Server, including clustering and network load balancing.

 Search TechNet on the Internet at **www.microsoft.com/technet/ default.asp** or the TechNet CD for more information about Network Load Balancing on a Windows 2000 Advanced Server PC.

Cluster Communication

Terms you'll need to understand:

✓ Remote procedure call (RPC)

✓ Heartbeats

✓ Network Monitor

✓ Node Manager

✓ Resource Manager

✓ Resource Monitor

✓ User Datagram Protocol (UDP)

Techniques you'll need to master:

✓ Understanding node-to-node communication

✓ Configuring the private network to optimize cluster communication

✓ Monitoring heartbeat traffic using Network Monitor

✓ Verifying heartbeat traffic using Network Monitor

✓ Verifying RPC connectivity between nodes using Network Monitor

In a cluster configuration, the nodes can detect one another's status and availability. This is one of the most important features of Cluster Service. The communication between cluster nodes is crucial to the availability of the resources. This chapter covers cluster communication between cluster nodes. You will learn how the cluster nodes communicate to monitor each other's status and the status of cluster resources. You will also learn how to monitor the cluster nodes using Network Monitor. When working through the chapter, keep in mind the terms you'll need to know and the techniques you'll need to master, which are listed on the chapter title page. To assist in your understanding of how cluster nodes communicate, this chapter covers RPC, heartbeats, and monitoring with Network Monitor.

Cluster Communication

The ongoing communication that occurs between two cluster nodes is crucial to the overall availability of the resources. The ongoing communication between the nodes allows the Cluster Service to monitor the status and availability of the nodes as well as the status of cluster resources. The Cluster Service uses this information to determine when resources need to fail over to another cluster member. The following section discusses how the private network can be optimized for node-to-node communication as well as the mechanisms that Cluster Service uses for this ongoing node-to-node communication.

Recommended Private Network Configuration

As discussed in Chapter 5, the recommended configuration for cluster nodes is to configure each node with two network adapters and establish them on a private network. The private network can then be used for node-to-node communication and to monitor the status of each node. In order to optimize the private network for cluster communication and eliminate any communication problems, the following configuration changes should be made to the private adapter on each cluster node:

➤ Disable NetBIOS over TCP/IP for the private network

➤ Set the correct binding order

➤ Choose the actual network adapter speed and setting

➤ Set the cluster communication order in the Cluster Administrator utility

To disable NetBIOS over TCP/IP for the private network (see Figure 7.1), take these steps:

1. Open Start|Settings and select the Control Panel option.

2. Open the Network and Dial-up Connection icon, right-click the network connection used for the private cluster network, and choose Properties.

3. Select Internet Protocol (TCP/IP) and choose Properties.

4. From the Internet Protocol (TCP/IP) Properties dialog box, choose the Advanced option, and select the WINS tab.

5. Select the option Disable NetBIOS over TCP/IP.

Follow these steps to set the correct binding order:

1. Open the Network and Dial-up Connection icon. From the Advanced menu, select the Advanced Settings option.

2. From the Adapters and Bindings tab, check to make sure the public connection is listed first, followed by the private connection and the RAS connection.

3. From the list of connections, select the private network connection to ensure that TCP/IP is the only protocol bound. All other protocols can be disabled.

Next, you should choose the actual network adapter speed and setting instead of using the default value (see Figure 7.2). The default setting for the network adapter is Auto-select. The network adapter will determine the speed of the network; however, packets may be dropped in the process. To eliminate this, set the net-

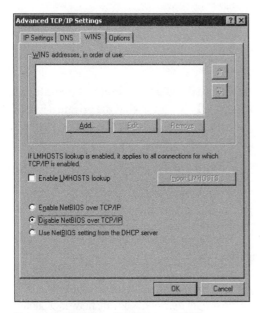

Figure 7.1   Disabling NetBIOS over TCP/IP.

3Com EtherLink XL 10/100 PCI TX NIC (3C905B-TX) Properties ? X

General | Advanced | Driver | Resources

The following properties are available for this network adapter. Click the property you want to change on the left, and then select its value on the right.

Property:
- 802.1p Support
- Duplex Mode
- Flow Control
- Media Type
- Network Address
- Rx Checksum Offload
- Tx Checksum Offload

Value:
Hardware Default ▼
- 100BaseTx
- 10BaseTx
- Auto Select
- Hardware Default

[OK]   [Cancel]

Figure 7.2   Setting the network adapter speed.

work adapter speed to the actual speed of the network instead of using the default settings. Follow these steps:

1. Open the Network and Dial-up Connection icon. Right-click the private network connection and choose Properties.

2. From the dialog box that appears, select the Configure option.

3. Choose the Advanced tab. The dialog box that appears will allow you to set the adapter speed.

Now, set the cluster communication order in the Cluster Administrator utility so that Private Adapter is at the top of the list. This ensures that the private network will always be used for node-to-node communication and the public one will only be used as a backup (see Figure 7.3). Follow these steps:

1. Open Start|Programs|Administrative Tools and select the Cluster Administrator.

2. Select the name of the cluster. From the File menu, choose Properties.

3. From the cluster's Properties dialog box, select the Network Priority tab. Verify that Private Network is listed first.

The public network must be configured for all communications if it is to be used as a backup for the private network. A private network cannot call over to a public network that is configured for client access only.

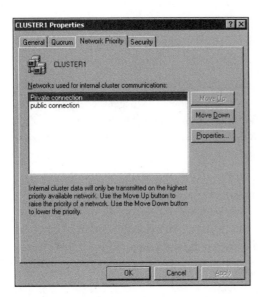

Figure 7.3 Setting the network priority.

RPC

A *remote procedure call* (RPC) is a communication mechanism by which applications can make a call on a remote computer. This is also the mechanism by which cluster nodes communicate. It uses Interprocess Communications (IPC) mechanisms to call program functions on remote computers. RPC is synchronous in nature, which means there must be a reliable high-speed network connection between the two computers. When a call is made on a remote system, a response is required. With RPC, a server can act as a client and make a remote procedure call on another network server. Due to the synchronous nature of RPC, the client will then wait for a reply containing the results of the procedure's execution. Cluster Service uses RPCs for node-to node communication and to monitor the status of cluster resources. It allows a cluster component on one node to make a call to a cluster component on another node.

Resource Monitor

One of the most important functions of Cluster Service is its ability to monitor the status of cluster resources. At least one resource monitor resides on each cluster node and is responsible for monitoring the status of each cluster resource using remote procedure calls (RPCs). The resource monitor tracks resource status by polling the cluster resources at certain intervals. Through RPCs, the resource monitor checks the status of resources using two different polling intervals: LooksAlive poll intervals and IsAlive poll intervals.

LooksAlive poll intervals are simple checks that the resource manager performs on a resource to determine whether it is still running. IsAlive poll intervals are more thorough checks used to determine the status of a resource (online or offline).

The resource monitor passes the information to the Resource Manager (the Resource Manager is covered in Chapter 4). The Resource Manager then uses the information to initiate certain actions, such as restart or failover. The RPC service on each cluster node needs to be running so the status of each resource can be monitored.

Heartbeats

Cluster Service is constantly monitoring the health of the network and the nodes by sending heartbeat messages to other nodes in the cluster. Heartbeat messages generated by the Node Manager on each cluster member are used to monitor the online status of cluster members. Heartbeat messages are exchanged between the cluster nodes at regular intervals of 1.2 seconds. The heartbeat messages are exchanged using User Datagram Protocol (UDP) port 3343.

Node Manager

Cluster Service is composed of several components that are each known as managers. One of these components is the Node Manager (the different managers are discussed in Chapter 4). The primary responsibility of the Node Manager is to track the status of other nodes in the cluster, and it passes the information on to the Resource Manager. The Node Manager runs on each cluster member and maintains a list of all other nodes within the cluster. The Node Managers on each cluster member communicate with each other through heartbeat messages. The Node Manager on each node tracks the status of the other cluster members by generating heartbeat messages and waiting for replies. The Node Manager is also responsible for responding to any heartbeat messages it receives from the other cluster members. If the Node Manager on one of the cluster members fails to respond to a heartbeat message, it is assumed to be offline.

A cluster node can be in one of three states:

➤ *Offline*—A node that is in an offline state might not be running, the Cluster Service itself might not be started, or the service might have failed on startup and is not responding to heartbeat messages.

➤ *Online*—A node that is on an online state is a fully functional member of the cluster. It can own groups and resources and is producing or responding to heartbeat messages.

➤ *Paused*—A node that is in a paused state is still a functioning member of the cluster. The only difference between a node that is online and one that is paused is that a paused node cannot own any resource groups. A node that is in a paused state still responds to and generates heartbeat messages.

Network Monitor

It is important to monitor the communication between cluster nodes to ensure RPC connectivity and that regular heartbeat messages are being sent between them. Network Monitor is a graphical tool that can be used to monitor network traffic coming to and from a computer. It allows you to monitor the traffic being sent between the cluster nodes. The version of Network Monitor that comes with Windows 2000 allows you to capture traffic to and from the computer on which it is installed. In terms of cluster communication, Network Monitor can be installed on each of the nodes to monitor the node-to-node communication. Traffic to and from each node can be captured and analyzed to ensure that regular heartbeat messages are being sent between the nodes.

Network Monitor consists of two components: Network Monitor Driver and Network Monitor Tools. Install Network Monitor Driver on the system for which you want to capture data. Installing the driver only allows data to be captured. To view the captured data, Network Monitor Tools has to be installed.

To capture traffic on each node and view that captured data with a graphical utility, you must install Network Monitor Tools and Agent on each of the nodes. (Network Monitor Tools and Agent installs the driver needed to capture the packets and the tool used to view the captured data.) The second option would be to install Network Monitor Driver on each of the nodes and install Network Monitor Tools on another system and view the captured data from across the network.

To install Network Monitor Driver, follow these steps:

1. Open Start|Settings|Control Panel.

2. Open the Network and Dial-up Connection icon. Right-click the LAN connection and choose Properties.

3. From the dialog box that appears, select Install. From the Select Network Component Type dialog box, select Protocol and then select Add.

4. Select Network Monitor Driver and choose OK.

To install Network Monitor Tools, follow these steps:

1. Open Start|Settings|Control Panel.

2. Open the Add/Remove Programs icon and select Add/Remove Windows Components. Click Next when the Windows Component Wizard appears.

3. From the list of components, select Management and Monitoring Tools and then click Details.

4. Select the checkbox next to Network Monitoring Tools and click OK.

Once Network Monitor has been installed, it can be used to monitor traffic on the private network. To start a capture using Network Monitor, follow these steps:

1. OpenStart|Programs|Administrative Tools Network Monitor.

2. Once Network Monitor appears on the screen, select Capture and choose Start. Network Monitor begins the capture of packets coming to and from the network card. Be sure to select the network adapter connected to the private network when starting the capture to monitor the traffic going between the cluster nodes.

3. To stop and view the captured data, select Capture and choose Stop and View from the menu. Network Monitor then displays the packets that were captured.

4. Cluster Service uses UDP port 3343 to send and receive heartbeat messages. Use the captured data to verify that each of the nodes is receiving heartbeat messages, as shown in Figure 7.4.

 Once you have captured the data, you can set up a filter to only display UDP traffic. To verify heartbeat messages are being sent, you will be looking for UDP port 3343.

Network Monitor can also be used to verify RPC communication between the cluster nodes. To verify RPC connectivity, start a new capture using Network Monitor and create a new group or resource on one of the cluster nodes. This should result in RPC traffic being sent between the nodes that can be verified with the captured data, as shown in Figure 7.5.

 Along with Network Monitor, the RPCping utility can also be used to verify RPC connectivity between cluster nodes. The utility verifies whether the services on one node are responding to calls made by the second node in the cluster. This utility is available for download from Microsoft's Web site and can also be found on the Exchange Server CD.

System Monitor

System Monitor with Windows 2000 can be used to monitor the realtime performance of a computer. It contains different objects, each with a set of counters for monitoring different aspects of system performance. System Monitor comes with built-in objects and counters, and other objects and counters may be added with the installation of certain applications or services.

RPC requires a relatively fast network connection. You can use System Monitor to monitor the speed of the network for RPC connectivity. By monitoring the

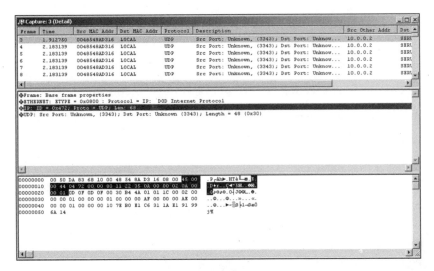

Figure 7.4   Using Network Monitor to verify heartbeat traffic.

Figure 7.5   Using Network Monitor to verify RPC connectivity.

Redirector object and some of the specific counters available with this object, you can test the network connectivity between cluster nodes as well as the speed of the network. The following counters available with the Redirector object should be added to monitor RPC performance between cluster nodes:

➤ Bytes Transmitted/Sec

➤ Bytes Received/Sec

➤ Bytes Total/Sec

Use the following steps to open System Monitor to monitor the performance of a system:

1. Open Start|Programs|Administrative Tools|Performance.

2. From within the Performance console, select System Monitor.

3. Right-click anywhere in the right pane and choose the Add Counter option.

4. In the Performance Object drop-down list, select Redirector.

5. Select the option Select Counter From List.

6. Select the counter from the list and click the Add button. Repeat this step for each counter you want to monitor (see Figure 7.6).

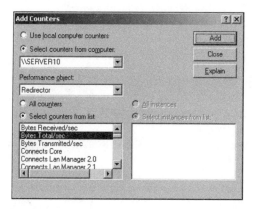

Figure 7.6 Using System Monitor to monitor the speed of the network for RPC connectivity.

Practice Questions

Question 1

What mechanism do cluster nodes use to communicate with one another?

○ a. LPC

○ b. SMTP

○ c. RPC

○ d. IPX/SPX

The correct answer is c. RPC allows a cluster component on one node to make a call to a cluster component on another node. Answer a incorrect because LPC is used within a single system so it can communicate with itself. Answer b is incorrect because SMTP is used to transfer mail. Answer d is incorrect because Cluster Service does not support IPX/SPX, only TCP/IP.

Question 2

Heartbeat messages are sent between cluster nodes using which protocol and port number?

○ a. UDP port 3343

○ b. TCP port 3433

○ c. UDP port 3433

○ d. TCP port 3343

The correct answer is a. Cluster Service uses UDP port 3343 to send and receive heartbeat messages. Therefore, answers b, c, and d are incorrect. Port 3433 is an unassigned port number.

Question 3

> What tool can you use to capture and view heartbeat traffic between cluster nodes?
>
> ○ a. Performance Monitor
>
> ○ b. Network Monitor
>
> ○ c. Network Analyzer
>
> ○ d. Event Viewer

The correct answer is b. Network Monitor allows you to capture and view network traffic coming to and from a system. Answer a is incorrect because Performance Monitor allows you to monitor the realtime performance of a system. You can use it to monitor a network interface, but you cannot view the packets once the data is collected. Answer c is incorrect because there is no such tool available with Windows 2000. Answer d is incorrect because Event Viewer can be used to view messages generated by the operating system, services, and applications but cannot be used to capture and view data on the network.

Question 4

> You have two systems in a cluster configuration. Each node is configured with two network adapters—one for the private network and one for the public network. How can you set the priority so that the private network is always used for node-to-node communication unless the connection fails?
>
> ○ a. Use the Bindings tab under the properties of TCP/IP.
>
> ○ b. From within Cluster Administrator, use the Network Priority tab under the properties for the node you want to configure.
>
> ○ c. Open the Network and Dial-up Connection icon and use the Advanced Settings option to set the binding order.
>
> ○ d. From within Cluster Administrator, use the Network Priority tab under the properties for the cluster.

The correct answer is d. From the Properties dialog box for the cluster, use the Network Priority tab to ensure that Private Network is listed first. Answer a is incorrect because there is no Bindings tab under the properties of TCP/IP. Answer b is incorrect because to change the network priority, you must use the properties of the cluster, not a specific node. Answer c is incorrect because setting the binding order does not determine which adapter will be preferred for node-to-node communication.

Question 5

What function do heartbeat messages provide?

- ○ a. They determine whether clients can access the cluster.
- ○ b. They monitor the online status of cluster resources.
- ○ c. They monitor the status of cluster nodes.
- ○ d. They monitor the status of the Quorum resource.

The correct answer is c. Heartbeat messages are generated to monitor the online status of nodes in the cluster. Therefore, answers a, b, and d are incorrect.

Question 6

What component of Cluster Service is responsible for generating heartbeat messages sent between cluster nodes?

- ○ a. Resource Monitor
- ○ b. Node Manager
- ○ c. Cluster Manager
- ○ d. Resource Manager

The correct answer is b. The Node Manager resides on each cluster node. It is responsible for generating and responding to heartbeat messages. Answer a is incorrect because the Resource Monitor is responsible for monitoring the status of cluster resources. Answer c is incorrect because there is no such component known as the *Cluster Manager*. Answer d is incorrect because the Resource Manager receives information from the Node Manager and Resource Monitor and initiates certain actions based on this information.

Question 7

> What mechanisms does the Resource Monitor use to monitor the status of cluster resources? [Check all correct answers]
>
> ❏ a. By using heartbeat messages
> ❏ b. By using LooksAlive polling
> ❏ c. By using the ping utility
> ❏ d. By using IsAlive polling

The correct answers are b and d. The Resource Monitor uses LooksAlive polling intervals and IsAlive polling intervals to monitor and determine the online status of cluster resources. Answer a is incorrect because heartbeat messages are generated by the Node Manager to monitor the status of cluster nodes. Answer c is incorrect because the ping utility is used to verify TCP/IP connectivity.

Question 8

> What tools can you use to verify RPC connectivity between cluster nodes? [Check all correct answers]
>
> ❏ a. Performance Monitor
> ❏ b. Resource Monitor
> ❏ c. Network Monitor
> ❏ d. RPCping

The correct answers are c and d. Network Monitor and RPCping can be used to verify RPC connectivity between cluster nodes. Answer a is incorrect because Performance Monitor can be used to monitor the realtime performance of system components. Answer b is incorrect because the Resource Monitor uses RPCs to monitor the status of cluster resources.

Question 9

Cluster nodes communicate using RPC, which requires a relatively fast network connection between nodes. What tool can you use to monitor the speed of the network between the cluster nodes?

- O a. Performance Monitor
- O b. Network Monitor
- O c. System Monitor
- O d. Ping utility

The correct answer is c. System Monitor can be used to monitor the speed of the network between the cluster nodes. Answer a is incorrect because Performance Monitor is the monitoring tool that came with Windows NT. Answer b is incorrect because Network Monitor is used to capture and view packets coming to and from a system. Answer d is incorrect because the ping utility is only used to verify TCP/IP connectivity.

Question 10

The Node Manager on each cluster node generates heartbeat messages. How often are heartbeat messages generated?

- O a. Every 1 second
- O b. Every 1.2 seconds
- O c. Every 2 seconds
- O d. Every 1.5 seconds

The correct answer is b. The Node Manager generates heartbeat messages every 1.2 seconds. Therefore, answers a, c, and d are incorrect.

Need to Know More

Libertone, David. *Windows 2000 Cluster Server Guidebook: A Guide to Creating and Managing a Cluster, Second Edition*. Prentice Hall, Upper Saddle River, NJ, 2000. ISBN 0130284696. This book includes some useful information on cluster components and cluster communication.

Search TechNet on·the Internet at **www.microsoft.com/technet/ default.asp** or the TechNet CD for more information cluster communication.

For more information on cluster communication, use the Microsoft Windows 2000 Help. Click Start and then choose Help. Under the list of contents, choose Windows Clustering.

Cluster Groups and Resources

Terms you'll need to understand:

✓ Quorum resource
✓ Resource dependencies
✓ Resource properties
✓ Resource owner
✓ Group
✓ Preferred node
✓ Failover policy
✓ Failback and failover timing
✓ Preferred node
✓ Virtual server

Techniques you'll need to master:

✓ Creating a resource and group
✓ Deleting a resource and group
✓ Moving a resource between groups
✓ Causing resource and group failure
✓ Taking resources and groups offline and online
✓ Setting resource dependencies
✓ Configuring resource and group properties
✓ Configuring failover policies

This chapter covers cluster resource and group creation and configuration in more detail than Chapter 3. The resources of a cluster comprise the basis for client functionality. Groups allow resources to be managed together as a single unit.

Group and resource administration is the heart of what makes a cluster work for an organization and allows the cluster to scale to meet the organization's needs. Without groups and resources, the cluster would not be able to do what it is meant to do—to keep the resources active for client use at all times.

Groups

Groups are sets of resources that belong to a single node. A group and all its resources can be owned by a single node only. The owner of a group is where the resources are currently active and running, if they are online.

For example, suppose Node A owns Group 1, and Group 1 contains the resources File Share, Physical Disk, Network Name, and IP Address. If Node A fails due to a hardware failure, this will cause Group 1 to fail as a whole and be moved to Node B. Once on Node B, Group 1 and all its resources will be restarted. This allows the file share to be available to clients even while Node A is offline.

Once a group fails, it will be moved to the other node in the cluster (in the case of Datacenter Server, there can be other nodes if more than two nodes are set up). The group must be moved to another node as a whole, not in part. Individual resources cannot be moved, only the group and all its resources can be moved as a whole.

Adding a Group

When adding a group to a node in a cluster, you must open the Cluster Administrator. The Cluster Administrator is opened by going to Start|Programs|Administrative Tools and then selecting Cluster Administrator.

Once Cluster Administrator is opened, you can add a group by selecting File|New and then Group, which will start the New Group Wizard.

 A shortcut to adding groups or resources is to right-click in the left or right pane, select New, and then select either Group or Resource.

When the New Group Wizard starts, the window shown in Figure 8.1 will be displayed. This window requires you to enter the name of the new group. You may also enter an optional description. Click the Next button when done.

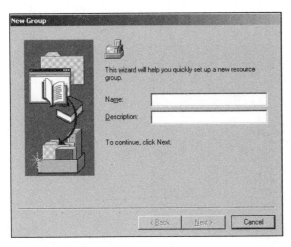

Figure 8.1 The New Group Wizard.

The next screen in the New Group Wizard is Preferred Owners. This screen allows you to specify which nodes in the cluster can be possible owners of the group and in which order the ownership will pass from one node to another if a node fails. In a cluster of three or four nodes, the group will not fail to the next node in the list but rather to the first online node in the list. The Preferred Owners screen is shown in Figure 8.2. You select the nodes in the left pane and then click the Add button to add them to the Preferred Owners list in the right pane. Once multiple nodes are added to the Preferred Owners pane, they can be listed according to the priority of ownership by selecting a node and then selecting the Move Up or Move Down button to reorder the list. If a node needs to be removed from the Preferred Owners list, you simply select the node and then click the Remove button. Finally, click the Finish button. This will create the group, which will be offline and must be brought online to be activated. Groups that are not online are listed with a yellow triangle, as shown in Figure 8.3 for the Test group.

To bring an offline group online, right-click the group and select Bring Online. If all resources in the group are functional, the group should be brought online, causing the yellow triangle to disappear.

When you're creating a group, there will be no resources in the Group. Resources must be added. This topic is covered later in this chapter in the sections "Resources" and "Adding Resources."

Deleting a Group

When a group is no longer needed, it can be taken offline or deleted. A group should be taken offline if the group and its resources will be used again later, but if the group and its resources are no longer needed, they can be deleted.

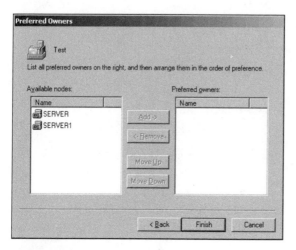

Figure 8.2   Group Wizard–Preferred Owners Tab.

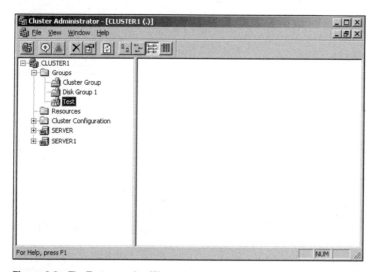

Figure 8.3   The Test group is offline.

To take a group and its resources offline, select the group and then select File|Take Offline. This will take all the resources in the group offline as well and place a yellow triangle next to the group and its resources. A clock will appear temporarily next to the group and resource icons, showing that they are being taken offline. Once the group and its resources are actually offline, yellow triangles will appear next to them. When the group is needed again, just select the group and then select File|Bring Online.

Here's a shortcut to bring a group online or take it offline: Just right-click the group in Cluster Administrator and then select Bring Online or Take Offline, respectively, from the menu that appears.

To actually remove a group completely, all the resources within the group must be removed. A group cannot be deleted until it contains no resources. Once the group contains no resources, you can delete it by selecting the group and then selecting File|Delete.

 Another way to delete a group is to right-click the group and select Delete from the menu that appears.

Renaming a Group

Once a group is created, its name can be changed at any time. Changing the group name does not require the group be taken offline.

To rename a group, open Cluster Administrator and select the group to rename. Next, select File|Rename. The group name is highlighted, and you are able to use the arrow keys and type in letters and numbers to change the name of the group as you would a folder or file in Windows Explorer.

 A shortcut to renaming a group is to right-click the group to be re-named and then select Rename from the menu that appears.

Moving a Group

Once a group is created, it can be moved to other nodes in the cluster at any time (given that the other clusters are online). Moving the group does not require the group be taken offline.

To move the group, open Cluster Administrator and select the group to move. Then, select File|Move Group. The group's resources will be taken offline; then the group itself will be taken offline and moved to the next node on its Preferred list. Once moved, the group will come back online and then all the resources will come back online.

Here's a shortcut to moving a group: Simply right-click the group to be moved and select Move Group from the menu that appears.

Group Properties

With most items in Windows, you can view and change their properties—whether they are files, folders, hardware, or whatever. With clusters, you can get the properties of a group and change its behavior in the cluster.

In Cluster Administrator, select the group for which you want to obtain properties and then select File|Properties. This causes the group's Properties window to appear, as shown in Figure 8.4.

 You can also right-click the group and select Properties from the shortcut menu.

General Group Properties

The General tab of a group's Properties window shows you a lot of information about the group.

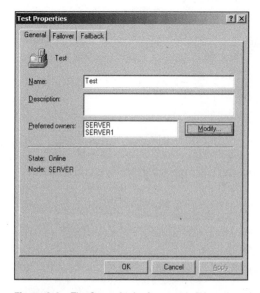

Figure 8.4   The General tab of a group's Properties window.

From the General tab, you can change the name of the group by selecting the Name box and changing the group's name. The description can be changed here as well.

In the Preferred Owners box, you can select Modify and then change the order of the preferred owners. You can even add and remove nodes. An example of this is shown in Figure 8.5.

In the Modify Preferred Owners window, you can change which servers are able to own the group as well as the order in which they are selected when a failover occurs.

The lower portion of the General tab of the Properties window shows the state of the group. The group states are explained in Table 8.1. The Node option shows which node the group is currently running (or was running, if the group is not online).

Failover Group Properties

The Failover tab, shown in Figure 8.6, allows you to configure the failover properties of the group and its resources.

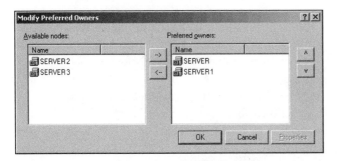

Figure 8.5   Modifying the preferred owners of a group.

Table 8.1 Group states.	
State	**Description**
Online	The group and all its resources are online and functional.
Partially Online	The group and one or more of its resources are online, but some resources are offline.
Offline	The group and all its resources are offline and not accessible.
Pending	One or more resources are coming online or going offline.
Failed	The group has failed because one or more resources cannot be brought online or taken offline in the set allowed time.
Unknown	The state of the group cannot be determined.

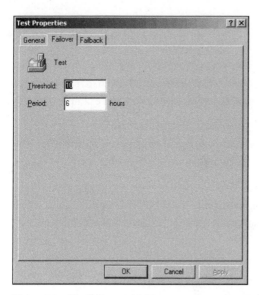

Figure 8.6   The Failover tab of a group's Properties window.

There are two configurable options on this tab to set the options for the failover policy: Threshold and Period. The Threshold option specifies the number of times, in a given period, that a group can be failed over before it is put in a Failed state. The Period option specifies the time in hours in which the group can be failed over before it is placed in a Failed state. The default is that a group can fail 10 times in any six-hour period before it is put in a Failed state.

Failback Group Properties

The Failback tab of the Properties window lets you specify how a group will act after its preferred node has failed and come back online (see Figure 8.7).

By default, groups are set for no failback, which will prevent them from automatically returning to their preferred nodes.

For example, suppose a cluster has two nodes and Node A is Group 1's preferred node. If Node A fails, Group 1 would be moved and started on Node B. When Node A comes back online, Group 1 would not automatically be moved back to Node A.

To configure a group to fail back when its preferred node comes back online, you have to select the option Allow Failback. The default, then, is for the group to return to its preferred node as soon as the preferred node is detected as being online.

The other option is to specify a time period in which the group can be failed back over to the preferred node. The time is entered in 24-hour notation, or values 0 through 23. The times can be set to any value from 0 to 23, but they cannot be the same.

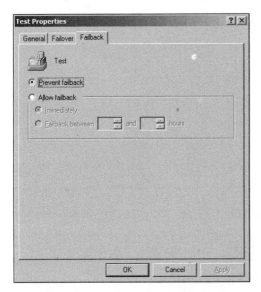

Figure 8.7   The Failback tab of a group's Properties window.

Note: If the first number is greater than the second, the time for failover will be the time specified, plus 24 hours. For example, suppose it is 1:00 P.M. and the preferred node comes back online. The failback time is set between 15 and 14 (or 3:00 P.M. and 2:00 P.M.). This means the failback would not occur until after 3:00 P.M. the next day.

Group Administration

Groups on a cluster are displayed in two places in the Cluster Administrator. Groups are displayed under the Groups folder within the cluster itself or under the Cluster heading. They are also displayed under the node on which they reside, online or offline.

Figure 8.8 shows that Cluster 1 and the node named Server are running the online groups Cluster Group and Disk Group 1 as well as an offline group named Test. These are the only groups listed as being on the cluster, so Node Server 1 would have no groups currently residing on the node, whether the groups are online or offline.

Default Groups

When a cluster is formed, a group is created called a *Cluster Group*. This group contains the disk resource that serves as the Quorum resource for the cluster. It also contains two other resources: the Network Name and IP Address.

The Network Name resource is the resource that creates the network name for the cluster itself, which is the cluster name that network clients use to access the cluster.

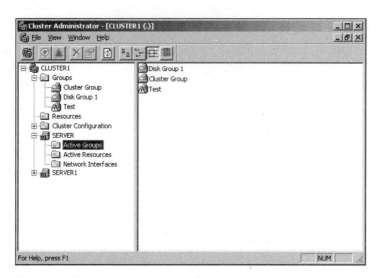

Figure 8.8 Cluster Administrator-Active Groups location.

The IP Address resource is the IP address assigned to the cluster as a whole. This is the IP address that can be used to communicate with the cluster as a whole.

For example, suppose there's a cluster named Cluster1 with two nodes called Server and Server1. The two nodes have IP addresses of 10.0.0.1/8 and 10.0.0.2/8, respectively. Cluster1 has an IP address of 10.0.0.100/8. The Quorum resource is on drive W:. There is also another shared SCSI drive, which is drive X:.

The default groups created are Cluster Group and Disk Group 1. Cluster Group contains the following resources:

➤ Network Name, with a value of Cluster1 (the cluster's name)

➤ IP Address, with a value of 10.0.0.100/8 (the cluster's IP address)

➤ Physical disk drive W: (the Quorum resource)

Disk Group 1 contains the following:

➤ Physical disk X:

For every disk drive that is on the shared bus between the nodes, a disk group will be created for that Physical Disk resource.

Resources

Resources are the entities controlled by a single node in a cluster that provide the access and functionality to the clients accessing the cluster. Resources are fault-tolerant entities that are kept online in case of failure.

The resources available are listed in Table 8.2. These resources will be used in varying degrees, based on the needs of the organization deploying a cluster.

Virtual Server

Before getting into the topic of adding specific resources, we will discuss the combining of two resources to make a virtual server, which is not a resource that is selectable in the New Resource Wizard but is required by most resources to be created first.

A virtual server is another NetBIOS name and IP address for a group. When created, the resources within the group can be accessed by clients as the network name or IP address of the virtual server.

For example, suppose a virtual server is created with a network name of FileServer and an IP address of 10.0.0.200/8, and all File Share resources are created within the same group. This would allow the file shares to be accessed by the UNC path \\FileServer\sharename or \\10.0.0.200\sharename or even by the name or IP address of the cluster or node on which the file share resides. The server's physical location is transparent to the clients.

Creating a Virtual Server

The quickest way to create a virtual server is to select File|Configure Application from the menu bar in Cluster Administrator. This will start the Cluster Application Wizard.

> You can also right-click in either the left or right pane of the Cluster Administrator and select Configure Application from the shortcut menu.

This wizard takes you through the process of using an existing virtual server to add resources or creating a virtual server and adding other optional resources with the virtual server you create. Here are the steps to follow:

- 1. The first screen you are shown is a welcome screen. Select Next to start the wizard and continue to create a virtual server or select Cancel to exit the wizard.

- 2. The second screen, shown in Figure 8.9, allows you to specify whether to create a new virtual server or to use an existing one. If you are adding resources to an existing virtual server, select Use An Existing Virtual Server and then select the group that contains the virtual server. Otherwise, choose Create A New Virtual Server and click Next.

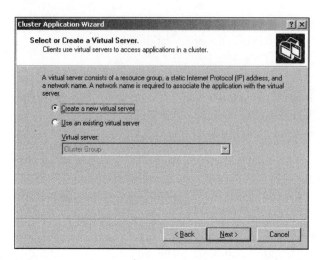

Figure 8.9   The Cluster Application Wizard's Select Or Create A Virtual Server screen.

3. The third screen, shown in Figure 8.10, allows you to create a new group in which to create the virtual server or to use an existing group to which to add a virtual server. Once an option is selected, click Next to continue.

4. The fourth screen, shown in Figure 8.11, allows you to rename the selected group from Step 3. Alternatively, if a new group was selected, you must specify the name of the new group to create. A description for the group can be added or edited, as needed, but this is optional. Select Next when done.

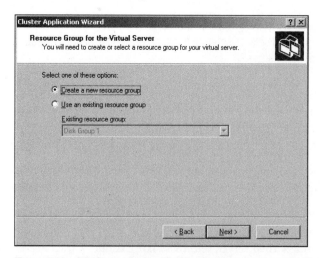

Figure 8.10   The Cluster Application Wizard's Resource Group For The Virtual Server screen.

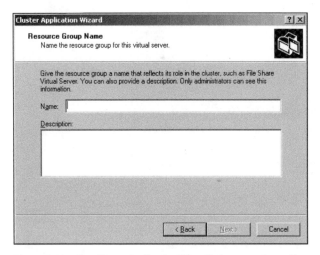

Figure 8.11   The Cluster Application Wizard's Resource Group Name screen.

5. The fifth screen of the wizard allows you to configure the network name and IP address of the virtual server, as shown in Figure 8.12. The network name is the name of the server, and the IP address is the address used to connect to the server. When done, click Next.

6. The sixth screen, shown in Figure 8.13, allows you to configure the properties of the virtual server's resources. Selecting a category and then Advanced Properties allows you to change the properties of the selected category. This is the same as right-clicking the resource in Cluster Administrator and selecting Properties. When done, click Next.

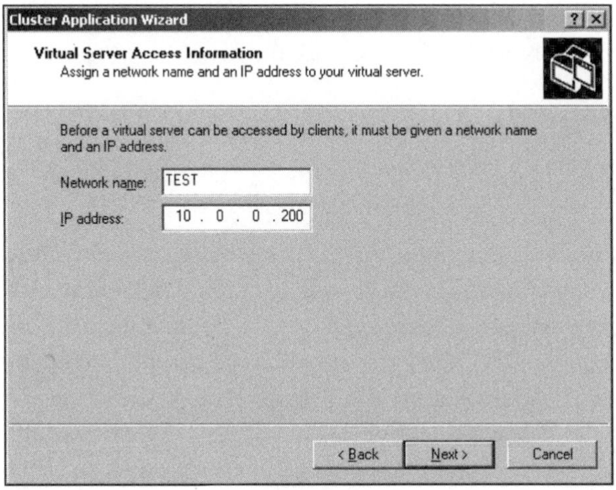

Figure 8.12   The Cluster Application Wizard's Virtual Server Access Information screen.

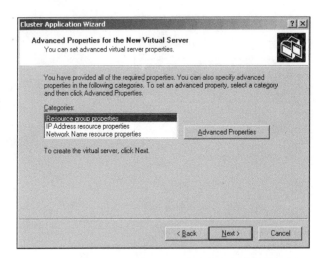

Figure 8.13   The Cluster Application Wizard's Advanced Properties For
The New Virtual Server screen.

7. The seventh screen allows you to create other resources within the same
   group in which the virtual server was just created, as shown in Figure 8.14.
   You can choose Yes, Create A Cluster Resource For My Application Now,
   which will take you through the Add A Resource Wizard, or you can select
   No, I'll Create A Cluster Resource For My Application Later. If you select
   No, you will be shown one more screen that lists all the choices you have
   made, and then you click Finish. This takes you back to the Cluster Administrator, where you will have to bring the newly created resources online.

These steps create the virtual server for you without you having to create the Network Name and IP Address resources manually and individually. It also creates a
new group or uses an existing group in which to place the virtual server resource.

Deleting a Virtual Server

Deleting a virtual server when it is no longer needed is just a matter of deleting
two resources: the IP Address resource and the Network Name resource.

In Cluster Administrator, open the group that contains the virtual server you
want to delete. Resources must be offline to be deleted. Right-click the IP Address resource of the virtual server and select Take Offline. Because the Network
Name resource depends on the IP Address resource, this will take both resources
offline. Next, right-click IP Address again and select Delete. You will then be
asked whether you want to delete the IP Address resource and its dependency,
the Network Name resource. Selecting Yes will delete both resources, and then
the virtual server will be deleted as well as its DNS entry, if DNS is configured to
be dynamically updated.

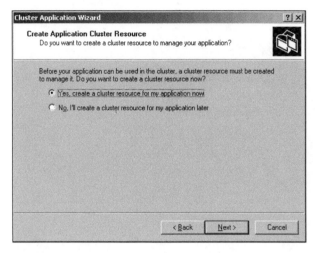

Figure 8.14 The Cluster Application Wizard's Create Application Cluster Resource screen.

If this is done in the opposite order (that is, starting with the Network Name resource instead of the IP Address resource), you will have to perform both operations on each resource.

Adding Resources

For resources to be made fault tolerant, they must first be added to groups. An organization can add resources and their parameters and dependencies as needed.

 Before adding a resource, make sure the group to which you will be adding the resource has all the required dependencies for the new resource. The dependencies must be created first. The dependencies are listed in Table 3.2 of Chapter 3.

All resources are added using the same basic steps. To add a resource:

1. From Cluster Administrator, select File|New|Resource. This will start the New Resource Wizard, as shown in Figure 8.15.

 You can accomplish the same task by right-clicking in the left or right pane and selecting New|Resource from the shortcut menu.

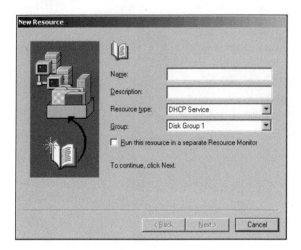

Figure 8.15 The New Resource Wizard.

2. In the Name box, type a name for the new resource. In the Description box, type a description for the resource. This information will appear in the properties of the resource for use when managing the resource.

3. Select a resource type from the Resource Type drop-down list. These are all the available resource types, as shown in Table 8.2; some may require extra services running on the nodes, but they will still appear.

4. Select the group that the resource will belong to once it is created.

 If a group is already highlighted in Cluster Administrator, that Group will be the default group selected when you create a new resource.

5. The Run This Resource In A Separate Resource Monitor checkbox allows you to run the resource in a separate resource monitor for debugging. Click Next.

6. The Possible Owners window appears next. This window allows you to select which of the cluster nodes can be possible owners of the resource in case of failure. Add and remove owners as needed and click Next when done.

7. The Dependencies window appears. Here you can select the dependencies for the resource. Refer back to Table 8.2 for the appropriate dependency for each resource.

Table 8.2 Resources and their dependencies.	
Resource	**Dependency**
DHCP service	Physical disk
	IP address
Distributed Transaction Coordinator	Physical disk
File Share (DFS)	Network name
File Share (not DFS)	None
Generic Application	Network name
Generic Service	Network name
IIS Server Instance	Physical disk
	Network name
IP Address	None
Message Queue	Physical disk
	Network name
Network Name	IP address
NNTP Server Instance	IP address
Physical Disk	None
Print Spooler	Physical disk
	Network name
SMTP Server Instance	IP address
Time Service	None
WINS Service	Physical disk

8. Click Finish. The resource will be created in the group specified in Step 4. Once created, the resource will default to being offline and must be brought online.

9. The group to which the resource belongs should then be moved to each participating node to ensure the resource will function on all nodes in the cluster.

These steps may vary slightly from resource to resource. The following sections briefly discuss specific resources and their requirements.

Dynamic Host Control Protocol (DHCP) Resource

The DHCP resource allows a node in a cluster to run the DHCP services to offer IP addresses to DHCP clients on the network. If the node should fail on which the DHCP resource is running, the resource will be started on the other node and cause no interruption in IP address management for the network.

After you select the dependencies for the resource in Step 7, click Next. The DHCP Service Parameters window (see Figure 8.16) appears. Here you specify the location of the DHCP databases that must be located on the Physical Disk resource selected in Step 7.

Here are descriptions of the fields that appear in this window:

➤ *Database Path*—This is the location of the DHCP database of IP addresses.

➤ *Audit File Path*—This is the directory location of the DHCP Audit Log.

➤ *Backup Path*—This is the directory where the DHCP database is copied for backup purposes.

Once the resource is created, the DHCP service will be modified on the node to reflect the database entries set in Step 8.

To ensure that the resource will function on all nodes in the cluster, all nodes must be running the DHCP service when the group to which the DHCP resource belongs is moved to each participating node.

Distributed Transaction Coordinator Resource

Distributed Transaction Coordinator (DTC) is the service that handles transactions for the Microsoft Message Queue (MSMQ) and SQL Server services. The Distributed Transaction Coordinator is installed when either MSMQ or SQL is installed.

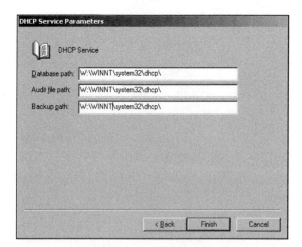

Figure 8.16 The DHCP Service Parameters window, where you can specify the location of the DHCP databases.

File Share

File shares allow for the redundancy of accessing shared folders on a cluster server. The file share must be placed on a shared disk for all nodes in the cluster to be able to service the resource.

After you select the dependencies in Step 7, click Next. The File Share Parameters window appears (see Figure 8.17).

The following list describes the options you can set on the File Share Parameters tab and their purpose:

➤ The Share Name box is for the share name you want the network users to access the share with when typing in a UNC pathname or browsing the network.

➤ The Path box specifies the physical path to the folder that will be shared (for example, W:\Share).

➤ The Comment box is optional. Here, you can provide a comment about the share.

➤ The User Limit area is used just like when creating a normal share; you can let all users connect to the share who try to connect, or you can limit the number of connections to a specified number of users. This is useful if you have an application with a specified number of licenses. This option can be set to allow the number of users who can connect to the share to be equal to the number of licenses that have been purchased.

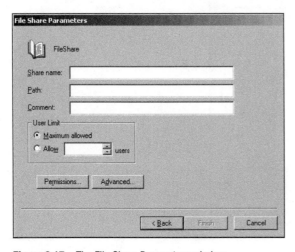

Figure 8.17   The File Share Parameters window.

➤ The Permissions button brings up the window shown in Figure 8.18. This window allows you to set permissions through the Cluster Administrator.

> Permissions on file shares are set through Cluster Administrator, not through the standard procedure of setting shared folder permissions.

➤ The Advanced button on the File Share Parameters window opens the Advanced file share properties page (shown in Figure 8.19). Here, you can set the type of file share to be implemented. The file share types are described in Table 8.3.

The DFS root will be considered a stand-alone share. Even if either of the cluster nodes are domain controllers, the DFS share will not be automatically replicated in Active Directory and must be replicated manually using some type of copy utility. Only one DFS root can exist on the nodes in the cluster. If any other DFS Root share already exists, it must be removed before the DFS File Share resource can be added.

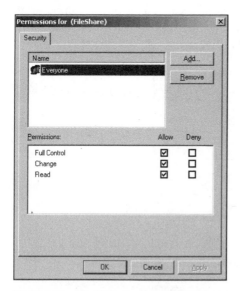

Figure 8.18   File Share Permissions settings screen.

Figure 8.19   Advanced File Share Properties Window.

Links and link replicas can be created as normal in the DFS Manager utility in the Administrative Tools menu. In order for configuration changes to be seen by all nodes, the DFS Root must be moved to all nodes in the cluster so that the configuration data is updated on all nodes.

Any changes made in Cluster Administrator will override the settings made in the DFS Manager utility in Administrative Tools. For example, if you delete the DFS root in DFS Manager, the Cluster Services will cause the File Share resource to fail, and the DFS root will be recreated without any link information.

Generic Application

The Generic Application resource allows you to install an application on a cluster that was not written to be "cluster aware." This means that even though the application was not meant to run on a cluster, it can still function on the cluster and take advantage of failover if it meets the following requirements:

Table 8.3 File share types.	
File Share	**Description**
Normal Share	This file share option shares the folder itself and allows access to all subfolders and their files.
DFS Root	This file share option shares the folder and allows it to participate as a Distributed File System (Dfs) root.
Shared Subdirectories	This file share option shares the folder as noted in Normal Share, but it also shares all subdirectories individually, so every subdirectory is also a share. This is useful if you are setting the users' personal folders on a cluster server. You can create the users' folders and share them with this option. When the users' personal folders are created under Users, they will also be shared.
Hide Subdirectory Shares	When using the Shared Subdirectories option, you can choose to hide all the subdirectories that are also shared. This prevents the shares from being found by users when browsing. This is accomplished by adding '$' to the share name on the subdirectories.

➤ Network clients must be able to use TCP/IP to access the application.

➤ In case of a node failure, the network clients must be able to reconnect to the application.

➤ The application must be able to store its data in a specified location that can be set by the administrator.

If the application meets all these requirements, it can be installed as a Generic Application resource so that it will be fault tolerant for network client access.

After choosing dependencies in Step 7, click Next. The Generic Application Parameters window appears, as shown in Figure 8.20. Here are descriptions of the options you can set for the Generic Application resource:

➤ The command-line entry starts the application, including the path to the application. This line can also include parameters that need to be passed to the application when started.

➤ Current Directory is the directory that contains the data files for the application. The application will "think" it is running in this directory. This directory will be the place for the location of temporary files created by the application.

➤ If you check the next option, Allow Application To Interact With Desktop, the application itself will be running on the cluster node. This option runs the application, and its interface will appear on the Node monitor and taskbar, which is useful if the application is a performance monitor that keeps statistics on the network. The performance monitor will be fault tolerant and show its statistics on the Node screen.

➤ You can check Use Network Name For Computer Name if you want to pass the name of the virtual server on which the Generic Application resource is running to the program itself. This allows the application to show that the application is running on the virtual server instead of the cluster node name.

Once these items are entered, click Next.

The Registry Replication window appears, as shown in Figure 8.21. If the application uses Registry entries in the HKEY_LOCAL_MACHINE key, these can be replicated to all the nodes on the Possible Owners list. Click Add to specify the Registry subkeys that should be replicated to the other nodes, click Modify to change an existing replication key, or click Remove to remove a replicated key.

Generic Service

The Generic Service resource allows you to make a Windows 2000 service fault tolerant. This means that even though a service was not meant to run on a cluster, it can still function on a cluster and take advantage of failover.

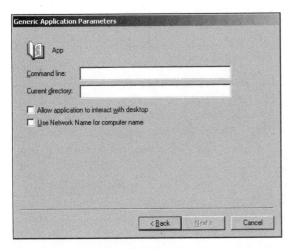

Figure 8.20 The Generic Application Parameters window.

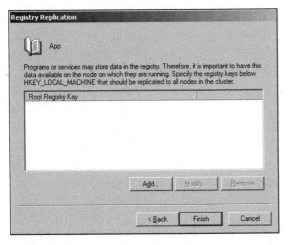

Figure 8.21 The Registry Replication window.

After you select dependencies in Step 7, click Next. The Generic Service Parameters window appears, as shown in Figure 8.22. This window requires the following:

➤ You will provide the name of the service to be started, but not the path to the service. For example, to use the Telnet service, go to Control Panel|Administrative Tools|Services. Open the Properties window for the desired service, and its file name will be shown under Path To Executable. Use the file name without the extension or path.

➤ The Start Parameters option requires the parameters used when starting the service, if any.

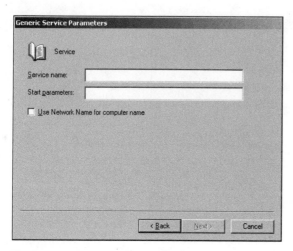

Figure 8.22   The Generic Service Parameters window.

➤ Select the Use Network Name For Computer Name checkbox if you want to pass the name of the virtual server on which the Generic Service is running. This allows the service to show the name of the virtual server on which it is running instead of the cluster node name.

Once these items are entered, click Next. The Registry Replication window appears, as shown previously in Figure 8.21. If the application uses Registry entries in the HKEY_LOCAL_MACHINE key, these can be replicated to all nodes on the Possible Owners list. Click Add to specify the Registry subkeys that should be replicated to the other nodes, click Modify to change an existing replication key, or click Remove to remove a replicated key.

IIS Server Instance

The IIS Server Instance resource allows you to make a WWW or FTP sites fault tolerant.

The Parameters window appears during the creation of the IIS Server Instance Resource, as shown in Figure 8.23. Here, you can set the following options:

➤ Choose which service of IIS to use for the resource.

➤ Once FTP or WWW is selected, you can choose which site to use for this new resource. For example, if you select WWW, the drop-down box will list all the WWW sites hosted on the server.

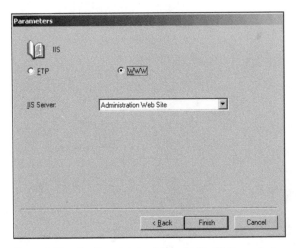

Figure 8.23   The Parameters window for the IIS Server Instance resource.

IP Address

The IP Address resource allows you to make an IP address fault tolerant. The IP Address resource is included in a group to allow all other resources within the group to be accessed by the IP address defined in the IP Address resource. This is half of the procedure to create a Virtual Server resource, as previously covered in this chapter.

After selecting dependencies, the TCP/IP Address Parameters window appears, as shown in Figure 8.24. You will see the following options:

➤ The IP Address field allows you to specify the IP address for the resource. The Address box is for the IP address that this resource will be accessed as by clients.

➤ The Subnet Mask field specifies the subnet in which the IP address exists.

➤ The Network box allows you to choose which network card this IP address will be associated with.

➤ The checkbox Enable NetBIOS For This Address specifies whether the IP address can be accessed by NetBIOS clients, if enabled.

Message Queuing

The Message Queuing resource allows you to make a message queue fault tolerant. The Message Queuing resource allows for the fault tolerance of the Microsoft Message Queue Service.

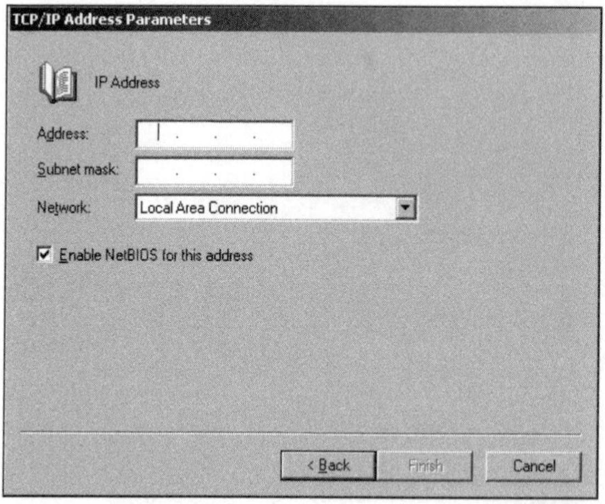

Figure 8.24   The TCP/IP Address Parameters window.

Network Name

The Network Name resource allows you to make a network name fault tolerant. The Network Name resource is included in a group to allow all other resources within that group to be accessed by the network name defined in the Network Name resource. This is half of the procedure to create a Virtual Server resource, as previously covered in this chapter.

After you specify the dependencies, click Next and the Network Name Parameters window appears, as shown in Figure 8.25. The Network Name Parameters window allows you to specify a name the resource.

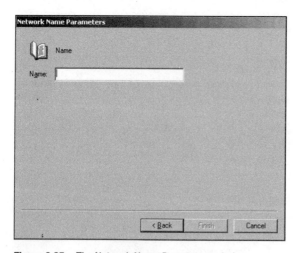

Figure 8.25   The Network Name Parameters window.

NNTP Server Instance

The NNTP Server Instance resource allows you to make a Network News Transfer Protocol service fault tolerant. When you are prompted with the Parameters window, as shown in Figure 8.26, you are allowed to select the NNTP Server instance with which to create the Resource.

Physical Disk

The Physical Disk resource allows you to add a disk to a group that will be used by its resources. When a node fails, the Physical Disk resource will be moved with the group to the next possible owner in the group properties.

The Disk Parameters window, as shown in Figure 8.27, allows you to select the drive letter for the physical disk that will be the new resource.

Note: The disks listed will be those available (that is, those not already used by other Physical Disk resources). Care needs to be taken because sometimes IDE drives can show up. These can be selected, but the resource will never start.

Note: Sometimes when a new Physical Disk resource is created and moved to another node for the first time, the other node will perform Scandisk on the Physical Disk resource before the group and all its resources are restarted on the new node. If this happens in a production environment, this can cause a delay of a few minutes for Scandisk to complete, depending on the size of the physical disk.

Print Spooler

The Print Spooler resource allows you to add a fault-tolerant print spooler to a node to allow clients to print to the printers even in the case of a server failure.

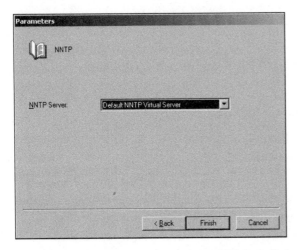

Figure 8.26 The Parameters window for the NNTP Server Instance resource.

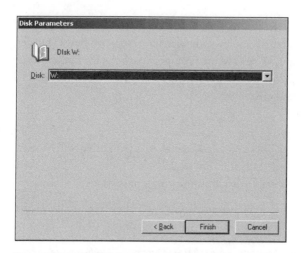

Figure 8.27   The Disk Parameters window.

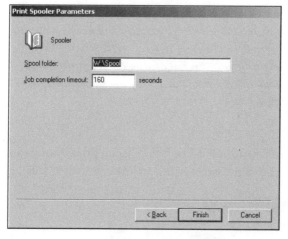

Figure 8.28   The Print Spooler Parameters window.

When setting options in the Print Spooler Parameters window, as shown in Figure 8.28, you can specify the following:

➤ The directory on the Physical Disk resource to use to place the spooled print jobs.

➤ The Job Completion Timeout setting in seconds. This value is used to specify how long to wait for the print jobs to be sent to the print device. If the print jobs are in the spool longer than the time specified, the resource will go offline and be sent to another node.

Simple Mail Transport Protocol (SMTP) Server Instance

The SMTP Server Instance resource allows you to add a fault-tolerant SMTP service to a node to allow clients to send mail.

The SMTP Parameters window is shown in Figure 8.29. This window allows you to select the SMTP server instance that will be used as the resource.

Time Service

The Time Service resource allows you to specify a node (the one that is the time server) to be used to synchronize the time on all the other nodes.

WINS Service

The WINS Service resource allows you to add a WINS database for name resolution and have it be fault tolerant.

The WINS Service Parameters window appears, as shown in Figure 8.30. This window allows you to specify two options:

➤ The database path to the WINS database, which should be located on the Physical Disk dependency.

➤ The backup path for the database so that if the database gets corrupted, the backup files can be copied over the regular database files to restore the WINS database.

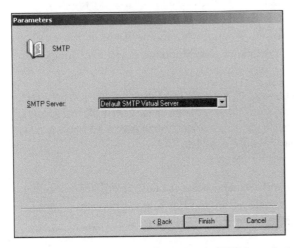

Figure 8.29 The Parameters window for the SMTP Server Instance resource.

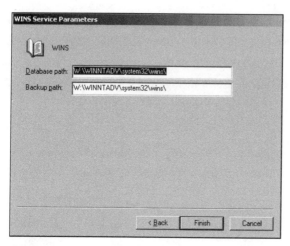

Figure 8.30 The WINS Service Parameters window.

Deleting a Resource

Resources can be removed when they are no longer needed or may be moved to another cluster server entirely. If a resource will be needed later, it can be taken offline, as discussed in this section, to reduce the administrative time to re-create the resource.

To take a resource offline, simply select the resource to be taken offline and then select File|Take Offline. This places a yellow triangle next to the resource as well as a red circle with a white X in it next to the group in which the resource resides. The red X shows that part of the group is not running. To bring it back online again when it is needed, select the resource again and then select File|Bring Online.

 A shortcut to the Take Offline and Bring Online options is to right-click the resource and select the appropriate option from menu that appears. Another shortcut for bringing a resource (or resources) online is to bring the group online in which it resides.

Deleting a resource is almost the same process as taking it offline or bringing it online, except that you select delete from the File menu. Resources do not have to be offline to delete them, as is required with groups.

 Another way to delete a resource is to right-click the resource and select Delete from the shortcut menu.

Renaming a Resource

Any created resource can have its name changed at any time. Changing the name of a resource requires it to be offline.

To rename a resource, select it and then select File|Rename. The resource name is highlighted, and you are able to use the arrow keys and type in letters and numbers to change or edit the name of the resource as you would a folder or file in Windows Explorer.

You can also right-click the resource to be renamed and select Rename from the shortcut menu.

Moving a Resource

After a resource is created, it can be moved to other groups at any time. Moving the resource does not require that the resource be taken offline.

To move a resource, select it and then select File|Change Group. You will then see an extended list of available groups in which to move the resource. You will be given a prompt to verify that the resource should be moved. If the resource being moved has dependencies, a list of the dependencies and the resource itself will be shown, and you will be prompted again for verification before all the dependencies are moved. The selected resource will then be moved to the group that was selected.

You can also move a resource by right-clicking it, selecting Change Group, and then selecting a group from the extended list.

Resource Properties

Just like groups, resources have properties that determine their behavior in the cluster. To get to these properties, in Cluster Administrator, select a resource and then select File|Properties. This brings up the resource's Properties window, as shown in Figure 8.31.

You can also right-click the appropriate resource and select Properties from the shortcut menu.

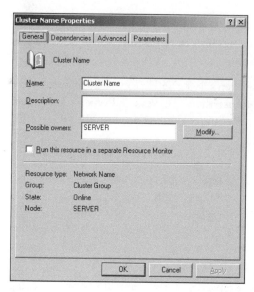

Figure 8.31 The General tab of a resource's Properties window.

General

The General tab of the resource's Properties window shows you a lot of information about the resource and allows you to control this resource. From the General tab, you can change the name of the resource by selecting the Name box and changing the resource's name. The description can also be changed here as well.

In the Possible Owners window, you can change which servers are able to own the resource as well as the order in which they are selected when a failover occurs.

The lower portion of the General tab shows the state of the resource. The state of a resource is the same as the state of a group, which was explained previously in Table 8.1. The Node option shows which node the resource is currently running on (or was running on, if the resource is not online).

Dependencies

The Dependencies tab, shown in Figure 8.32, allows you to configure the dependencies for the resource.

This Dependencies tab lists the current dependencies for the selected resource. The table of dependencies will vary, depending on the resource being examined. If you select a resource, you can then select the Properties button to get the properties for that resource.

You can also select the Modify button to select other resources to add or remove as dependencies. The only dependencies you can add are those that already exist

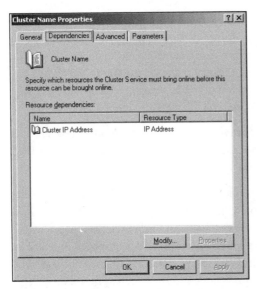

Figure 8.32   The Dependencies tab of a resource's Properties window.

within the group in which the current resource resides. The only resources you can remove are those that are current dependencies.

Advanced

The Advanced tab lets you specify how a resource will act in case of failure. The options are shown in Figure 8.33.

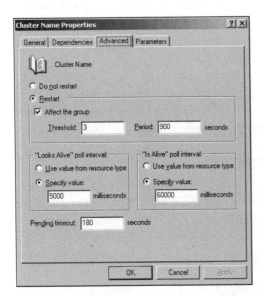

Figure 8.33   The Advanced tab of a resource's Properties window.

The first option specifies whether the resource will automatically restart in case of a failure when the resource goes offline. When you select the option to restart the resource when it fails, you are given many more options to choose from. The Affect The Group checkbox forces the group as a whole to fail over when the resource fails. If the resource is very important to your organization, this option should be selected so that the resource will fail over and remain online.

The Threshold and Period entries are the same as those for groups. The Threshold setting is the number of times a resource can be restarted within the specified period of time before it will fail over to another node.

The other two options are not dependent on the setting of whether to restart the resource in case of failure. The Looks Alive Poll Interval setting determines how often the cluster managers (discussed in Chapter 4) will check the resource to see whether it is online or has gone offline and needs to be brought back online. The same is true for the Is Alive Poll Interval setting, but they differ in one way: The Looks Alive test is a quick test, but it is not entirely accurate. The Is Alive test is a more thorough test, but it requires more time and server resources to determine the resource state.

Both of these settings are set in milliseconds, and there is an option to let the value be determined by the type of resource being checked. Otherwise, the defaults are 5,000 milliseconds for the Looks Alive Poll Interval setting and 60,000 milliseconds for the Is Alive Poll Interval setting.

The last option on the tab is Pending Timeout. This option is used to specify how long a resource can either be online pending or offline pending before it is put in a Failed state.

Parameters

The Parameters tab is used to modify various parameters for a resource. The contents of the tab will vary depending on the type of resource being viewed. The options here resemble the parameters set when the resource was created. These parameters are covered in this chapter under the name of the specific resource.

Resource Administration

Resources on a cluster are displayed in two places, just the same as groups. Select the group, and the resources within the group are listed in the right pane of the Cluster Administrator. All the administrative tasks can be done in either place within the Cluster Administrator under the Groups or Resources folder under the cluster or the Groups or Resources folder under the node on which the resource is running.

Practice Questions

Question 1

Which of the following services must be installed on a node to allow its resource type to be added? [Check all correct answers]

☐ a. DHCP

☐ b. WINS

☐ c. DNS

☐ d. SMTP

The correct answers are a, b, and d. The services that must be installed are DHCP, DTC, IIS, MSMQ, NNTP, SMTP, and WINS. DNS is not an option because it is not a resource type. Therefore, answer c is incorrect.

Question 2

Which of the following, if deleted, will also delete the Network Name resource?

○ a. Time Server resource

○ b. IP Address resource

○ c. File Share resource

○ d. Physical Disk resource

The correct answer is b. The Network Name resource is dependent on the IP Address resource. If there is no IP Address resource, the Network Name resource cannot exist. None of the other choices are directly dependent on the IP Address resource. Therefore, answers a, c, and d are incorrect.

Question 3

How many resource owners can a group have on a Datacenter Server?

○ a. Two

○ b. Three

○ c. Four

○ d. Five

The correct answer is c. On a Datacenter Server, because there can be four nodes in a cluster, all four nodes can be possible owners of a resource. On an Advanced Server, there can only be two nodes, so in this case, there can be two possible owners of a resource group. Therefore, answers a, b, and d are incorrect.

Question 4

What is the difference between failover and failback? [Check all correct answers]

❑ a. In a failover situation, when a node fails, its groups and their resources are moved over to another node.

❑ b. In a failover situation, when a failed node comes back online, its groups and their resources are returned to the original node.

❑ c. In a failback situation, when a node fails, its groups and their resources are moved over to another node.

❑ d. In a failback situation, when a failed node comes back online, its groups and their resources are returned to the original node.

The correct answers are a and d. Failover occurs when the groups and resources are moved to an available node because the current node has failed. Failback occurs when the groups and resources are moved back to the original node on which the resource was running when the original node comes back online. Answers b and c are incorrect because the explanations are reversed for Failback and Failover.

Question 5

Which resources are required to create a virtual server? [Check all correct answers]

- ❑ a. Physical Disk
- ❑ b. IP Address
- ❑ c. Time Server
- ❑ d. Network Name

The correct answers are b and d. A virtual server is a group that contains the IP Address and Network Name resources to emulate a completely different server for clients to access the resources within the group containing the virtual server. A Physical Disk resource and a Time Service resource are not required to create a virtual server; therefore, a and c are incorrect.

Question 6

In Cluster Administrator, when deleting a resource, what must you do first?

- ○ a. Move the resource to another group
- ○ b. Take the resource offline
- ○ c. Bring the resource online
- ○ d. Nothing

The correct answer is d. Any resource to be deleted can be deleted regardless of whether it is online, offline, or has been moved to another group. Therefore, answers a, b, and c are incorrect.

Question 7

In Cluster Administrator, when you're deleting a group, what must be done first?

○ a. The group must be failed over to the node on which it was created.

○ b. The group must be taken offline.

○ c. The group must be put online if it is offline.

○ d. You must verify that the group contains no resources.

The correct answer is d. When you delete a group, it does not matter whether it is online, offline, or even on its original node. The group must contain no resources to be deleted. Therefore, answers a, b, and c are incorrect.

Question 8

Which setting is used to specify the number of times a group can fail over before it is taken offline?

○ a. Threshold

○ b. Period

○ c. Is Alive

○ d. Looks Alive

The correct answer is a. The Threshold setting is used to specify how many times a group can fail before it is taken offline. The Period setting specifies the amount of time (the threshold) after which the group will be taken offline. Therefore, answer b is incorrect. The Is Alive setting determines whether the resource is online. Therefore, answer c is incorrect. The Looks Alive setting determines whether the resource appears to be online. Therefore, answer d is incorrect.

Question 9

What does the Pending Timeout value for a resource indicate?

○ a. The amount of time before the node checks to see whether a resource is alive

○ b. The amount of time before the node checks to see whether a resource looks alive

○ c. The amount of time a resource can be in a Pending state before it is put in an Offline state

○ d. The amount of time a resource can be in a Pending state before it is put in a Failed state

The correct answer is d. The Pending Timeout setting is used to specify the amount of time a resource can be in a Pending state before it is put in a Failed state, not an Offline state. Therefore, answer c is incorrect. The Looks Alive and Is Alive times are specified in the Looks Alive Poll Interval and Is Alive Poll Interval settings. Therefore, answers a and b are incorrect.

Question 10

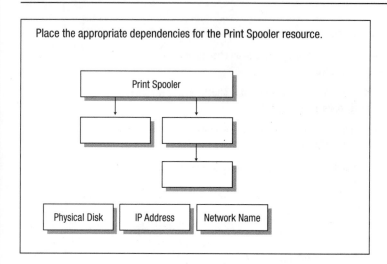

The correct answer is:

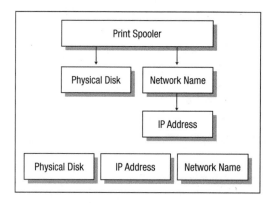

The Physical Disk resource is placed by itself because it doesn't depend on other resources. The Network Name dependency is placed above the IP Address dependency because Network Name is dependent on the IP Address.

Need to Know More?

 Lee, Richard R. *Windows NT Microsoft Cluster Server*. Osborne/ McGraw-Hill, Berkley, CA, 1999. ISBN 0078825008. This book includes information on the configuration and settings for resources and groups.

 Microsoft Corporation. *Windows 2000 Server Resource Kit Deployment Planning Guide*. Microsoft Press, Redmond, WA, 2000. ISBN:157231 8058. This book covers various resources and their settings as well as group 5and resource administration.

 Search TechNet on the Internet at **www.microsoft.com/technet/ default.asp** or the TechNet CD for more information about resource and group administration in Windows 2000 Advanced Server.

 Introducing Windows 2000 Advanced Server. Microsoft Corporation. Redmond, WA, 2000. This technical paper, found at **www.microsoft.com/WINDOWS2000/guide/server/solutions/over- view/advanced.asp**, provides a good general overview of cluster ser- vices and the uses of groups and resources.

Cluster Administration

Terms you'll need to understand:

✓ Cluster Administrator
✓ Cluster.exe
✓ **Cluster Node** command
✓ **Cluster Group** command
✓ **Cluster Resource** command
✓ **Cluster Network** command
✓ Scripting
✓ Preferred owner

Techniques you'll need to master:

✓ Administering a cluster using Cluadmin.exe
✓ Administering a cluster using the Cluster.exe command-line utility
✓ Using the commands and options available with the Cluster.exe command-line utility
✓ Evicting a node from a cluster using Cluadmin.exe and Cluster.exe
✓ Renaming a cluster using Cluadmin.exe and Cluster.exe
✓ Adding a node to a cluster
✓ Setting a preferred owner for a group

Once a cluster is operational, it will be necessary at times to perform maintenance and administrative tasks on the cluster and its members. This chapter introduces the tools available for administering a cluster. It also covers the details involved in performing some common administrative tasks. It is essential for the exam to be familiar with the different tools and how to use them. When working through the chapter, keep in mind the terms you'll need to know and the techniques you'll need to master because they are important for successfully administering a cluster as well as achieving success on the exam.

There are basically three different ways to administer a cluster—via a GUI, the command line, and scripts. The chapter will discuss how to administer a cluster from within the GUI and from the command line, and will include a short discussion on script-based administration.

GUI-Based Administration

The main tool used to administer a cluster is the Cluster Administrator (Cluadmin.exe). This is the GUI-based tool installed by default when Cluster Service is installed, and it is used to perform administrative tasks on the cluster. Keep in mind when you are performing administrative tasks on the cluster that the Cluster Administrator utility can be installed onto your desktop so that the tasks can be performed from across the network; you do not need to be physically sitting at the cluster members to perform the tasks. The utility can be installed on any desktop running one of the following operating systems:

➤ Windows 2000 Server

➤ Windows 2000 Advanced Server

➤ Windows NT Enterprise Edition

➤ Windows NT 4.0 (with Service Pack 3 or later)

The Cluster Administrator utility is installed by default into the %systemroot%/ Cluster folder and can be launched from Administrative Tools, located off the Start menu. When you start the Cluster Administrator tool, any connections that were open from the previous session are restored by default. If there were no open sessions, a dialog box will be displayed prompting you to specify which cluster you want to administer, as shown in Figure 9.1.

 When the Open Connection To Cluster dialog box appears, you can connect to the cluster by specifying either the cluster name or the cluster IP address. You can also connect to a specific node by specifying the node name or IP address.

Figure 9.1   The Open Connection To Cluster dialog box. From here you can specifiy
which cluster or cluster node you want to connect to.

Once Cluster Administrator is open, you will see a window similar to the one
shown in Figure 9.2. From within this window, most administrative tasks can be
performed on the cluster.

Cluster Properties

After the installation of Cluster Service is complete, some of the general cluster
properties initially set during the installation can be modified through the Cluster Administrator utility (these changes can also be made using a command-line
utility that will be discussed further into the chapter in the "Command-Line
Administration" section). Accessing the properties of the cluster is very easy to
do within the Cluster Administrator—simply select the cluster name listed in
the left pane and choose File|Properties.

The cluster's Properties dialog box that appears displays four tabs: General, Quorum, Network Priority, and Security.

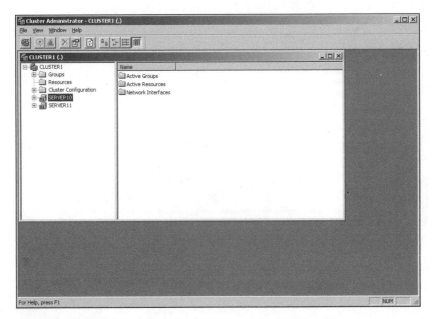

Figure 9.2   The graphical user interface of the Cluster Administrator utility.

The General tab of the Cluster Properties dialog box allows you to change the name of the cluster (this is the name you assigned to the cluster during the installation on the first node). The description of the cluster can also be modified using the General tab (see Figure 9.3).

Using the Quorum tab of the Cluster Properties dialog box, you can change the location of the Quorum resource. The path and the size of the Quorum log (the default log size is 64K) can also be set (see Figure 9.4).

The Network Priority tab allows you to specify which network will be used for node-to-node communication. If the nodes are configured on a private subnet, this is the network connection that should be listed first. Selecting the Properties option from this dialog box, as shown in Figure 9.5, also allows you to reconfigure the type of communication the network is used for (private, public, or mixed).

The Security tab allows you to grant or deny administrative privileges to the cluster to users and groups (see Figure 9.6).

Renaming

From within the Cluster Administrator utility, it is possible to change the name that has been assigned to the cluster. This NetBIOS name was assigned to the cluster during the installation of the Cluster Service on the first node. Keep in mind when you are renaming the cluster that the name must follow the

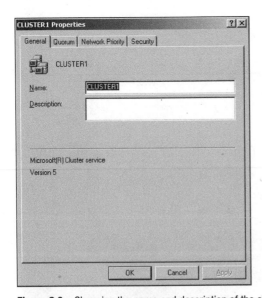

Figure 9.3 Changing the name and description of the cluster.

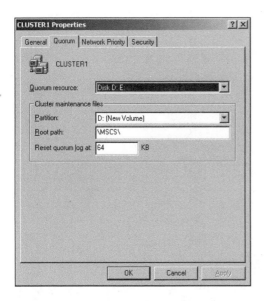

Figure 9.4   The Quorum tab of the Cluster Properties dialog box.

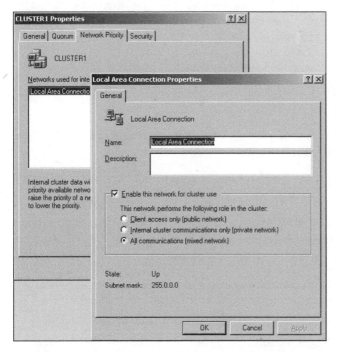

Figure 9.5   The Network Priority tab of the Cluster Properties dialog box.

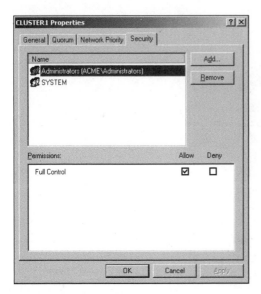

Figure 9.6   The Security tab of the Cluster Properties dialog box.

15-character NetBIOS naming convention and must not already be in use on the network. If you change the name of the cluster, it may also have to be updated in the DNS database if WINS is not in use.

To rename a cluster using the Cluster Administrator utility, follow these steps:

1. Open Start|Programs|Administrative Tools and select the Cluster Administrator utility.

2. From with the console, select the cluster name in the left pane. Then, from the File menu, select Properties.

3. From the Cluster Properties dialog box, select the General tab if it is not already active.

4. Type in the new NetBIOS name that you want to assign to the cluster. The new name will not be assigned to the cluster until the Cluster Name resource is taken offline and brought back online.

5. To take the Cluster Name resource offline, select the cluster name in the left pane if it is not already selected. Then, from the File menu, select the Take Offline option.

6. The Cluster Name resource can be brought back online by selecting the cluster name and then, from the File menu, choosing Bring Online. The new NetBIOS name will now take effect.

Pausing/Resuming

If you need to take a cluster offline to perform maintenance, the node can be paused and then resumed once maintenance has been completed. Pausing a node allows the Cluster Service to continue to run and communicate within the cluster.

To pause and resume a node using Cluster Administrator, follow these steps:

1. Open Start|Programs|Administrative Tools and select the Cluster Administrator utility.

2. From within the console, select the node to be paused in the left pane and from the File menu choose the Pause Node option.

3. Move any groups to the second cluster node by selecting the group and choosing the Move Group option from the File menu.

4. Perform any maintenance tasks on the node.

5. From within the console window, select the paused node and from the File menu select the Resume Node option.

Replacing

If you need to replace one of the nodes in the cluster, you will first have to evict one of the existing nodes (evicting a node is covered in the following section). Once one of the nodes has been evicted, it can be replaced with another system. Replacing a node means installing Windows 2000 Advanced Server and Cluster Service and configuring the new system to join the existing cluster.

Evicting

If a cluster node needs to be removed from the cluster, you can use the Evict Node option from within the Cluster Administrator utility. For example, if you want to replace an existing node with another system, you will first have to evict the node before the new one can join the cluster. The Evict Node option will logically remove the selected node from the cluster and update the cluster database. Once the node has been logically removed from the cluster, Cluster Service can be uninstalled and the node can then be physically removed. Keep in mind that before you evict a node from the cluster, it is a good idea to back up all nodes (refer to Chapter 13 for information on backing up and restoring your cluster).

To evict a node from a cluster, follow these steps:

1. Open Start|Programs|Administrative Tools and select the Cluster Administrator utility.

2. Before the node is evicted from the cluster, move all the groups to the second node. To move a group, select the group and choose the Move Group option from the File menu.

3. You will need to stop the Cluster Service on the node you want to evict. To stop the Cluster Service, select the node in the left pane and from the File menu select the Stop Cluster Service option. Once the service has been stopped, the node can be evicted from the cluster.

4. In the left pane of the console, select the node you want to remove from the cluster. From the File menu, select the Evict Node option. Once the node has been evicted, it can be physically removed from the cluster.

Once a node has been evicted from a cluster, the only way to have the system rejoin the cluster is to reinstall Cluster Services. If you want to perform maintenance on a node but not remove it from the cluster, use the Pause Node option instead. Evicting the node removes it from the cluster, whereas pausing a node allows it to remain a member of the cluster.

Adding a Node

If you are running Windows 2000 Advanced Server, only two nodes are supported. If you currently have two nodes in the cluster and want to add a new node, one of the existing ones will first need to be evicted from the cluster. Once a node has been logically and physically removed from the cluster, the new node can be added. This entails installing Windows 2000 Advanced Server and Cluster Service on the new system and configuring it to join the existing cluster.

Command-Line Administration

Another way to administer a cluster is to use the command-line utility. The tasks that can be performed from within the Cluster Administrator utility can also be performed from the command prompt using Cluster.exe. This command-line utility is installed by default into the %systemroot%/system32 directory when Cluster Service is installed. It is also installed when the Cluster Administrator is installed and can be used on any system running any of the following operating systems:

➤ Windows 2000 (any platform)

➤ Windows NT Workstation (with Service Pack 3 or later)

➤ Windows NT Server (with Service Pack 3 or later)

One of the advantages to using the command-line utility as opposed to the GUI utility is that the Cluster.exe command-line utility can be used in scripts and executed within a batch file (a short discussion of scripting as well as a sample script will be provided later in the chapter). This allows you to make global administrative changes to the cluster more efficiently and schedule the command to execute at specific or repeated times. Also, if you need to administer your cluster across a WAN link, it may be more efficient to use the command-line tool instead of Cluster Administrator.

You can use the following commands with the Cluster.exe utility:

➤ **Cluster**

➤ **Cluster Node**

➤ **Cluster Network**

➤ **Cluster Group**

➤ **Cluster Resource**

Also, several options can be used with these commands. The commands and their options are covered in the following sections.

Be sure you are familiar with the different **Cluster** commands, what they are used for, and the options available with each one. It is essential for exam success.

The **Cluster** Command

The **Cluster** command can be used to administer the cluster as a whole. The basic syntax for using the command is as follows:

```
Cluster [cluster name] /option
```

When you're using the **Cluster** command, specifying the cluster name is optional. The cluster name only needs to be included when you are remotely administering a cluster.

Specifying the cluster name within the command is optional. If you do not specify a cluster name, Cluster.exe will try to connect to the node that you are running the command on. Table 9.1 lists the options that can be used to administer the cluster using the **Cluster** command.

Table 9.1	The options that can be used to administer a cluster using the Cluster command.
Option	**Use**
Version	Displays the version number of the cluster.
List:*domain_name*	Displays a list of all clusters within the specified domain.
Rename:*cluster name*	Renames the cluster.
Quorum_Resource	Use this option to change the name and location of the Quorum resource and the size of the Quorum log.

A cluster can be renamed using the Cluster Administrator, but it can also be renamed using the command-line utility. The syntax for renaming a cluster using the **Cluster** command is as follows:

```
Cluster [cluster name] /rename:
```

For example, to rename a cluster named Cluster1 as Cluster2, use the following syntax:

```
Cluster Cluster1 /rename: Cluster2
```

The Cluster Node Command

The Cluster.exe utility can also be used to change the properties of a specific node. To make a change to a specific node, use the following syntax:

```
Cluster [cluster name] Node [node name] /option
```

Table 9.2 lists the options that can be used to administer a specific node within the cluster.

Table 9.2	A list of options that can be used to administer a specific node within a cluster.
Option	**Use**
Status	Displays the status of the node.
Properties	Displays the properties of the node.
Pause	Pauses the node.
Resume	Resumes the node.
Evict	Evicts the specified node from the cluster.

Pausing/Resuming

Using the command-line utility, you can pause a cluster node to perform maintenance on the system and then resume the node once maintenance is complete.

For example, to pause Server10, which is a member of Cluster1, you can enter the
following command at the command prompt (see Figure 9.7):

```
Cluster Cluster1 Node Server10 /pause
```

The following command can be used to resume the node once maintenance
is complete:

```
Cluster Cluster1 Node Server10 /resume
```

Evicting

If a node needs to be removed from a cluster, the **Evict** option can be used in
conjunction with the **Cluster** command to permanently remove the node. Remember that once the node has been evicted, the only way for it to rejoin the
cluster is for Cluster Service to be reinstalled.

For example, to evict Server10 from Cluster1, you can enter the following command at the command prompt:

```
Cluster Cluster1 Node Server10 /evict
```

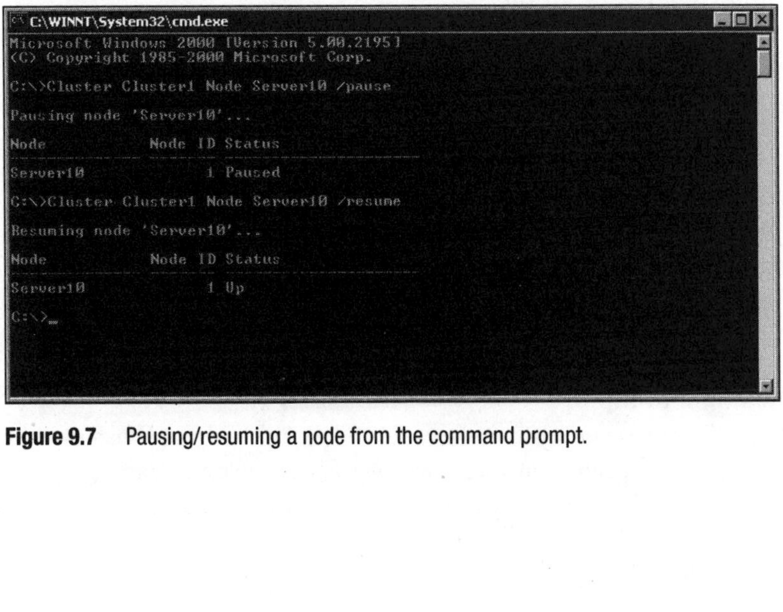

Figure 9.7   Pausing/resuming a node from the command prompt.

The **Cluster Network** Command

The **Cluster Network** command is used to view the status of the cluster network and configure network properties. The syntax for the command is as follows:

```
Cluster [cluster name] Network [network name] /option
```

Table 9.3 lists the options that can be used with the **Cluster Network** command. Using the **Cluster Network** command with the **Properties** option, you can display the properties of the network (see Figure 9.8). You can also alter certain properties of the network from the command prompt by using the **Properties** option. Table 9.4 lists the different properties that can be modified.

The **Cluster Group** Command

The **Cluster Group** command can be used to perform administrative tasks on groups, such as renaming them, moving them, and taking them offline. With some of the options, a timeout value can be set. The timeout value specifies how long to wait before canceling the issued command if it does not execute successfully. The basic syntax for the **Cluster Group** command is as follows:

```
Cluster [cluster name] Group [group name] /option
```

Table 9.5 lists the options that can be used with the **Cluster Group** command.

Creating/Deleting a Group

Groups can be created from the command prompt using the **Cluster** command with the **Create** option. For example, to create a new group called NewGroup on Cluster1, use the following syntax from the command prompt:

```
Cluster Cluster1 Group NewGroup /create
```

To delete the group NewGroup using the command-line utility, use the following syntax:

```
Cluster Cluster1 Group NewGroup /delete
```

Renaming a Group

Using the Cluster.exe utility from the command prompt with the **Cluster Group** command, you can easily change a group name. For example, to rename the group NewGroup on Cluster1 to OldGroup, use the following syntax:

```
Cluster Cluster1 Group NewGroup /rename:OldGroup
```

Table 9.3   The options available with the Cluster Network command.

Option	Use
Status	Displays the status of the cluster network. Specifying a network name is optional; the status of all cluster networks will be displayed if no network name is specified.
List Interfaces	Lists all the network interfaces connected to the network.
Rename: *network name*	Renames the network.
Properties	Displays the common network properties. This option can also be used to configure certain network properties.

Table 9.4   The commom properties that can be modified using the Cluster Network command.

Property	Description
Name	The name assigned to the network.
Address	The address assigned to the network.
AddressMask	The subnet mask assigned to the network.
Description	The description of the network.
Role	The role assigned to the network. The value supplied is a numeric one: 1—Use for internal cluster communication only 2—Use only for client access 3—Use for both cluster and client communication

Figure 9.8   Viewing the properties of a network.

Table 9.5	A list of the different options that can be used with the Cluster Group command.
Option	**Use**
Status	Provides information on the status of the specified group, such as whether it is online or offline.
Listowners	Provides a list of the preferred owners for the group.
Setowners	Allows you to specify a preferred owners list for a group.
Create	Creates a new group.
Delete	Deletes the specified group.
Rename: *group name*	Renames the specified group.
Moveto: *node name*	Moves a group to the node specified. Use this command with the **Wait** option to specify a timeout interval.
Offline: *node name*	Takes the group offline; can be used with the **Wait** option.
Online: *node name*	Brings the specified group online; can be used with the **Wait** option.
Properties	Displays and configures the common properties for the group. There are several group properties that can be configured using the **Properties** option (see Table 9.6 for the property list).

Moving a Group

Groups and their resources can be moved between cluster nodes using the command-line utility with the **Move** option. You can also use the **Wait** option to specify the timeout interval by specifying the time in seconds to wait before canceling the command if it does not execute. For example, to move the group OldGroup from Node1 to Node2 with a timeout internal of 120 seconds, use the following syntax:

```
Cluster Cluster1 Group OldGroup /moveto:Node2 /wait:120
```

Using the **Listowners** and **Setowners** Options

Groups can be assigned a preferred owner. This is the node that you prefer the group to run on. When a node in a cluster fails, the second node in the cluster will automatically take over the groups. Setting a preferred owner for a group means that the group will fail back to its preferred owner once it comes back online. If a preferred owner is not set for a group, it will not fail back once the failed node comes back online. Keep in mind that specifying a preferred owner does not mean automatic failback is configured. This option specifies which node the group should failback to. Automatic failback must be configured under the Failback tab of the group's Properties dialog box. The **Listowners** option displays a list of preferred owners for a group, and the **Setowners** option specifies the preferred owner list for a group.

For example, to view the preferred owner list for OldGroup, use the following syntax:

```
Cluster Cluster1 Group OldGroup /Listowner
```

To specify Node1 as the preferred owner for OldGroup, use the following command:

```
Cluster Cluster1 Group OldGroup /Setowners:Node1
```

Cluster Group Properties

Cluster groups all have a set of common properties. Using the **Properties** option with the **Cluster Group** command, you can display and configure the common properties. Table 9.6 lists the common group properties that are available for cluster groups. The syntax when using the **Properties** option is as follows:

```
Cluster [cluster name] Group [group name] /Properties
[propname:value]
```

The Cluster Resource Command

The **Cluster Resource** command allows you to display and configure settings for resources from the command prompt. You can use several options with this command to configure the different settings for cluster resources. The options are summarized in Table 9.7. The syntax for the command is as follows:

```
Cluster [cluster name] Resource [resource name] /option
```

Table 9.6 The common properties for cluster groups.	
Property	Use
Name	The name of the cluster group.
Description	The general description of the group.
FailoverThreshold	Specifies the number of times the Cluster Service will attempt to fail over a group.
FailoverPeriod	The interval (in hours) that the Cluster Service attempts to fail over a group.
AutofailbackType	To prevent fail back, set this property to ClusterGroupPrevent Failback (0). To allow fail back, set it to ClusterGroupAllow Failback (1) (see Figure 9.9).
FailbackWindowStart	Specifies the fail back start time (24 hour clock) of the specified group to its preferred node.
FailbackWindowEnd	Specifies the fail back end time (24 hour clock) of a group to its preferred node.

Table 9.7	Some of the options that can be used with the Cluster Resource command.
Option	**Use**
Create	Creates a new resource. Use this option with the **/Group** option to specify which group the resource should be a member of. Use it with the **/Type** option to specify the resource type.
Delete	Deletes a resource.
Rename:*resource name*	Renames a resource.
Fail	Initiates failure of the resource.
Properties	Displays and modifies the properties of a resource.
Moveto:Group	Moves the resource to the specified group.
Online	Brings a resource online.
Offline	Takes a resource offline.
Listowners	Lists the possible owners for the resource.
Addowner:*node name*	Adds the specified node to the list of possible owners.
Removeowner:*node name*	Removes the specified node from the list of possible owners.
List Dependencies	Displays the dependencies for the resource.
Adddependency:*resource*	Adds a dependency for the resource.
Removedependency:*resource*	Removes a dependency for a resource.

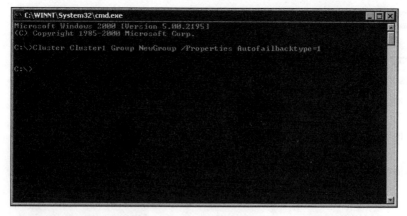

Figure 9.9 Setting the failback type for a cluster group.

Some properties are common to all cluster resources. These common properties can be modified using the **Properties** option along with the **Cluster Resource** command. Table 9.8 lists some of the different properties that can be modified using the **Properties** option. Use the following syntax to modify one of the common resource properties using the **Properties** option:

```
Cluster [cluster name] Resource [resource name] /Properties
[propname=value]
```

Scripting

All the commands available with the Cluster.exe utility can be used with scripts. The major benefit to this is that the execution of the commands can be made universally; they can be automated and scheduled by using batch files. Figure 9.10 provides an example of a batch file that creates a new group, creates a resource within the group, sets the owners for the group, and initiates failure of the resource.

Table 9.8 Some common resource properties.	
Property	**Use**
Description	Modifies the general description of the resource.
SeparateMonitor	Uses true and false values to determine whether a resource should run in a separate resource monitor.
LooksAlivePollInterval	Specifies the time (in milliseconds) that Cluster Service should poll the resource to see whether it appears to be functioning.
IsAlivePollInterval	Specifies the time (in milliseconds) that Cluster Service should poll the resource to determine whether it is online.
RestartAction	Specifies the action to take if a resource fails. The three possible actions are (see Figure 9.11): 0—ClusterResourceDon'tRestart 1—ClusterResourceRestartNoNotify 2—ClusterResourceRestartNotify
RestartThreshold	Specifies the number of times during the restart period that Cluster Service will attempt to restart a failed resource before the group is failed over.
RestartPeriod	Specifies the amount of time for restart attempts of the failed resource before the group is failed over.

Figure 9.10 Sample batch file.

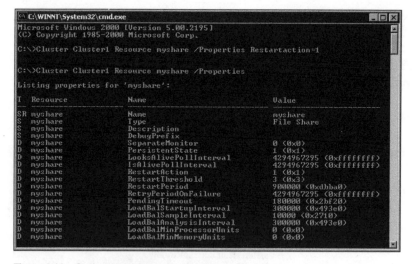

Figure 9.11 Setting the restart action for a cluster resource.

Practice Questions

Question 1

> You want to be able to administer your cluster from across the network using the GUI-based administration tool. Which of the following operating systems can the Cluadmin.exe utility be installed on? [Check all correct answers]
>
> ❑ a. Windows 2000 (any platform)
>
> ❑ b. Windows 2000 Server only
>
> ❑ c. Windows NT (with Service Pack 3 or later)
>
> ❑ d. Any Windows platform

The correct answers are a and c. The Cluadmin.exe utility can be installed on any Windows 2000 platform and on any system running Windows NT with Service Pack 3 or later. Answer b is incorrect because the administration tool can be installed on any of the Windows 2000 platforms. Answer d is incorrect because the administration tool can only be installed on Windows 2000 and Windows NT (Service Pack 3 or later).

Question 2

> You want to change the name that was assigned to the cluster during the installation from Cluster1 to Cluster2. What methods can be used to perform this action? [Check all correct answers]
>
> ❑ a. Open the Cluster Administrator, select the cluster name, and choose the Properties option from the File menu. Use the General tab to change the name assigned to the cluster.
>
> ❑ b. Open the Cluster Administrator, select the node hosting the resource, and choose the Properties option from the File menu. Use the General tab to change the name assigned to the cluster.
>
> ❑ c. **Cluster Cluster1 /rename:Cluster2**.
>
> ❑ d. **Cluster /rename:Cluster2**.

The correct answers are a, c, and d. The name of the cluster can be changed by using the General tab from the Cluster Properties dialog box. It cannot be changed from the node's Properties dialog box, thus making answer b incorrect. Answers c and d are correct because both commands can be used to rename a cluster. Note that specifying the cluster name is optional; it's only needed if you're connecting to a remote cluster.

Question 3

You change the name of the cluster from Cluster1 to Cluster2 using the GUI administration tool. However, the name change does not immediately take effect. What needs to be done after the cluster name is changed in order for this change to take effect?

- ○ a. Both cluster nodes need to be shut down and restarted.
- ○ b. The WINS database needs to be manually updated.
- ○ c. Cluster Service needs to be stopped and restarted on both nodes.
- ○ d. The Cluster Name resource needs to taken offline and brought back online.

The correct answer is d. In order for the name change to take effect, the Cluster Name resource needs to be taken offline and brought back online. Neither the nodes nor Cluster Service need to be physically restarted, thus making answers a and c incorrect. Answer b is incorrect because the WINS database does not have to be manually updated; the WINS database is dynamic.

Question 4

You currently have two nodes running Windows 2000 Advanced Server that are members of Cluster1. One of the nodes is going to be replaced by a new system. What must you do before the new system can join the cluster?

- ○ a. Install Cluster Service on the new node and configure it to join Cluster1.
- ○ b. Pause the node that will be replaced. Bring the new node online.
- ○ c. Physically disconnect the node that will be replaced.
- ○ d. Evict the node that will be replaced.

The correct answer is d. The node that will be replaced by the new system needs to be evicted from the cluster first in order for you to logically remove it from the cluster database. Answer a is incorrect because Windows 2000 Advanced Server only supports two nodes in a cluster, so one node has to be removed before the new one can be added. Answer b is incorrect because pausing the node does not remove it from the cluster database. A node that is paused is still a member of the cluster. Answer c is incorrect because the node needs to be logically removed from the cluster before it is physically disconnected.

Question 5

You create a group on Cluster1 using the following command:

```
Cluster Cluster1 Group NewGroup /create
```

Once the group is created, you want it to always fail back to Node1 when it becomes available. Which of the following commands will allow you to set the fail back for the new group?

○ a. **Cluster Cluster1 Group NewGroup**

○ b. **Cluster Cluster1 Group NewGroup /Listowners**

○ c. **Cluster Cluster1 Group NewGroup /Setowners:Node1**

○ d. **Cluster Cluster1 Group NewGroup /Properties:Node1**

The correct answer is c. This command will set Node1 as the preferred owner for NewGroup. Answer a is incorrect because this command will display the status of the group. Answer b is incorrect because this command will show the current list of preferred owners for the group. Answer d is incorrect because the Properties option is used to view and configure properties for a specific group. You cannot use the Properties option to set the owners for a group.

Question 6

You currently have two nodes in a cluster running Windows 2000 Advanced Server. You are planning to replace one of the nodes in the cluster with a new system. Put the following steps in order as they would occur when replacing one of the existing nodes with a new one. [Use only the required steps]

Pause the node to be replaced.

Physically disconnect the node to be replaced.

Move all groups to the remaining node.

Install Cluster Service on the new system.

Evict the node to be replaced.

Delete all groups from the node to be replaced.

Evict the node to be replaced.

The correct answer is:

Move all groups to the remaining node.

Evict the node to be replaced.

Physically disconnect the node to be replaced.

Install Cluster Service on the new system.

Question 7

You configure the **RestartThreshold** and **RestartPeriod** properties for a resource called NewShare on Cluster1. Once the restart threshold is exceeded within the restart period, you want Cluster Service to attempt to fail the group over to another node. Which of the following options used with the **Cluster** command will allow you to configure this? .

- ○ a. **Cluster Cluster1 Group NewShare /Properties / RestartAction=2**
- ○ b. **Cluster Cluster1 Resource NewShare /Properties / RestartAction=2**
- ○ c. **Cluster Cluster1 Resource NewShare /Properties / RestartAction=0**
- ○ d. **Cluster Cluster1 Resource NewShare /RestartAction=1**

The correct answer is b. This command will configure Cluster Service to attempt to fail the group over to another node. Answer a is incorrect because to configure the properties of a resource, the **Cluster Resource** command is used, not the **Cluster Group** command. Answer c is incorrect because setting the **RestartAction** value to 0 means no attempt will be made to restart the resource after failure. Answer d is incorrect because setting the **RestartAction** value to 1 means the Cluster Service does not attempt to fail the group over once the restart threshold is exceeded within the restart period.

Question 8

> You currently have a two-node cluster. Each node is configured with two network cards. There is a private network used for cluster communication only named LAN1. The public network (LAN2) is configured for client access only. To provide fault tolerance for cluster communication, you want to reconfigure the public network for both cluster and client communication. What methods can be used to reconfigure the public network? [Check all correct answers]
>
> ❑ a. From within the Cluster Administrator, use the Network tab of the Cluster Properties dialog box to change the network usage to All Communications.
>
> ❑ b. From within Cluster Administrator, use the General tab of the Cluster Properties dialog box to change the network usage to All Communications.
>
> ❑ c. **Cluster Network LAN2 /Role=3**
>
> ❑ d. **Cluster Network LAN2 /Interface=3**

The correct answers are a and c. To change the role of the network, you can use the Network tab of the Cluster Properties dialog box or the **Cluster Network** command with the **Role** option. Answer b is incorrect because the General tab only allows you to change the name and description of the cluster. Answer d in incorrect because **Interface** is not a valid option available with the **Cluster Network** command.

Question 9

You create a group called NewGroup on Node1. You decide to move the group to Node2. Which of the following commands will move the group to Node2 and specify that Cluster Service should cancel the execution of the command in 120 seconds if it does not execute?

○ a. **Cluster Node Node1 /Moveto: Node2 /Wait:120**

○ b. **Cluster Group NewGroup /MoveGroup:Node2 /Wait:120**

○ c. **Cluster Group NewGroup /Moveto:Node2 /Cancel:120**

○ d. **Cluster Group NewGroup /Moveto:Node2 /Wait:120**

The correct answer is d. This command specifies that the group will be moved from Node1 to Node2 and Cluster Service will cancel the command in 120 seconds if it does execute. Answer a is incorrect because to move a group, you use the **Cluster Group** command, not the **Cluster Node** command. Answer b is incorrect because you use the **Moveto** option to move a group. There is no **MoveGroup** option available with the **Cluster Group** command. Answer c is incorrect because you use the **Wait** option, not **Cancel**, to specify how long Cluster Service should wait before canceling the command.

Question 10

You create a resource called NewShare. Which of the following commands will allow you to initiate failure of the resource?

○ a. **Cluster Resource NewShare /InitiateFailure**

○ b. **Cluster Resource NewShare /Fail**

○ c. **Cluster Group NewShare /InitiateFailure**

○ d. **Cluster Group NewShare /Fail**

The correct answer is b. The **Cluster Resource** command along with the **Fail** option will initiate failure of the resource NewShare. Answer a is incorrect because **InitiateFailure** is not an option available with the **Cluster Resource** command. The Initiate Failure command is used within the Cluster Administrator. Answers c and d are incorrect because in order to initiate the failure of a resource, you use the **Cluster Resource** command, not the **Cluster Group** command.

Need to Know More?

 Libertone, David. *Windows 2000 Cluster Service Guidebook: A Guide to Creating and Managing a Cluster, Second Edition.* Prentice Hall, Upper Saddler River, NJ, 2000. ISBN 0130284696. This book provides detailed information on cluster administration using the command-line utility.

 Search TechNet on the Internet at **www.microsoft.com/technet/default.asp** or the TechNet CD for more information on cluster administration.

For more information on cluster administration, use the Windows 2000 Help. Click Start and then choose Help. Under the list of contents, choose Windows Clustering.

10

Installing Microsoft Applications on a Cluster

. . . .

Terms you'll need to understand:

✓ Exchange Virtual Server (EVS)

✓ Excluadmin.dll

✓ Exres.dll

✓ Generic resource DLL

✓ Exchange 2000

✓ SQL 2000

✓ Cluster-aware applications

✓ Non-cluster-aware applications

✓ Default instance

✓ Named instance

Techniques you'll need to master:

✓ Configuring Exchange 2000 in a cluster environment

✓ Configuring an Exchange Virtual Server

✓ Understanding the elements of an Exchange Virtual Server

✓ Configuring SQL in a cluster environment

✓ Installing a default instance of SQL Server

✓ Installing a named instance of SQL Server

✓ Understanding the elements of a SQL Virtual Server

✓ Understanding the difference between cluster-aware and non-cluster-aware applications

Many applications and services are capable of taking advantage of clustering technologies to increase their availability. Two of the most common cluster-aware applications in use today are Exchange 2000 and SQL 2000. This chapter discusses the configuration of these two applications in a cluster environment.

Exchange 2000

Exchange is one of the most powerful enterprise messaging systems. It provides businesses with an easy, quick way of creating, sharing, and storing information. Many businesses rely heavily on their messaging systems for their day-to-day operations and therefore require high availability. Exchange 5.5 was the earliest version of the messaging system to provide support for clustering technologies. The latest version, Exchange 2000, integrates seamlessly into the Windows 2000 environment. Exchange 2000 Enterprise Server provides support for the Cluster Service, which means businesses can increase the availability of their messaging systems by installing it in a cluster environment. Deploying Exchange 2000 in a cluster environment can eliminate some of the single points of failure, such as failed hardware or software components, associated with running a standalone messaging system. Planned outages for routine maintenance, upgrades, and configuration changes will result in little downtime if Exchange 2000 is installed in a clustered environment.

Note: Exchange 2000 comes in different versions: Enterprise Server and Standard Server. To take advantage of the cluster technologies offered with Windows 2000 Advanced Server and Windows 2000 Datacenter Server, you must install Exchange 2000 Enterprise Server. Exchange 2000 Standard Server does not support clustering.

Exchange 2000 supports an Active/Passive configuration and an Active/Active configuration. In an Active/Passive configuration, Exchange runs on a single cluster node, while the other node remains idle. All the resources reside on the active node while the other one remains available should the active member fail. Exchange 2000 in an Active/Active cluster configuration means that each node in the cluster is running Exchange 2000, with at least one virtual server for each node. Because the service is running on all nodes, in the event of failure, only the resources need to fail over to the second node, not the service itself. Each cluster node has the capability to support multiple virtual servers. For example, suppose Node A and Node B are both running Exchange 2000, and each is configured with an Exchange Virtual Server (EVS). If Node A were to fail, its EVS would fail over to Node B. Once the virtual server has failed over to the second node, clients can reconnect to it using its network name. The fact that the virtual server is now running on Node B is transparent to the user.

Exchange is comprised of several different components. Some of these components are supported in a cluster environment and some are not. Of the components that take advantage of clustering technologies, some support an Active/Active configuration, where an instance of the component runs on each node, whereas others support only an Active/Passive configuration, where there is only one instance per cluster. Table 10.1 lists some of Exchange's components and the type of cluster configuration each supports.

Note: NNTP is not supported in a cluster configuration but is still required to be installed on each node that owns or could own an Exchange Virtual Server. If it is not already present, it can be installed through the Add/Remove Programs icon in the Control Panel prior to installing Exchange on a cluster node.

Exchange 2000 Cluster Components

Once Exchange 2000 is installed, it is fully cluster aware and can take advantage of clustering technologies to provide high availability. The main components of Cluster Service that provide Exchange 2000 with this functionality are resource DLLs, resources, and cluster groups. Each of these components, in regards to Exchange 2000 clustering, are discussed in the following sections.

Resource DLLs

Resource DLLs are used by Cluster Service to communicate with the resources. Once Exchange is installed, it adds its own resource DLL called exres.dll, which is used by Cluster Service to monitor the status of Exchange resources. Cluster Service communicates with the Exchange DLL through a resource monitor. The DLL performs functions on Exchange resources, such as checking their status through IsAlive calls, reporting any resource failures, and bringing resources online.

Table 10.1 Components of Exchange 2000.	
Exchange Components	**Cluster Configuration**
Exchange System Attendant	Active/Active
POP3	Active/Active
SMTP	Active/Active
IMAP	Active/Active
NNTP	Not supported
Message Transfer Agent (MTA)	Active/Passive
Information Store	Active/Active
Key Management Services (KMS)	Not supported
HTTP	Active/Active

Here is the difference between cluster-aware applications and non-cluster-aware applications: Cluster-aware applications have custom DLLs written specifically for use in cluster environments, thus providing more functionality. Applications that are not cluster aware use a generic resource DLL.

The setup of Exchange 2000 also adds a second DLL: excluadmin.dll. This DLL is used by the Cluster Administrator utility to configure and manage Exchange resources.

Resources

If you recall from Chapter 3, *resources* are the logical entities controlled by the cluster. Once Exchange 2000 is installed on a cluster node, it adds its own application-specific resources to the Exchange Virtual Server. It also uses some of the Cluster Service resources, such as the IP Address resource, the Network Name resource, and the Disk resource.

Cluster Groups

Exchange 2000 uses virtual servers in a cluster environment. Virtual servers are equivalent to cluster resource groups. If you recall from Chapter 3, resource groups basically define units of fail over. If a resource within a group fails and needs to be moved to the second node in the cluster, all resources within the group are moved as well. Clustering Exchange 2000 means that the virtual servers are no longer linked with a single computer. If a resource within the virtual server fails, the virtual server can fail over to the second node in the cluster, thus providing minimal downtime for users. Each node in the cluster requires at least one virtual server. Each Exchange Virtual Server has the following requirements:

➤ A static IP address

➤ A unique NetBIOS name

➤ Shared storage space

➤ An Exchange System Attendant

Each virtual server is assigned it own IP address and unique network name (NetBIOS name). This is the name users will specify when connecting to their mailboxes, regardless of which node the virtual server is running on. This means if the virtual server fails over to the second node in the cluster, users can still access it by specifying the same network name. By setting up Exchange in an Active/Active configuration, you specify that each virtual server also requires its own disk volume on the shared storage space.

Exchange Virtual Servers also require an Exchange System Attendant resource. The Exchange System Attendant is one of the main components of Exchange and is responsible for tasks such as monitoring server services and messaging connectors. Once the Exchange System Attendant is added as a resource to the virtual server, it adds the remaining required resources.

Installing Exchange 2000 in a Clustered Environment

Installing Exchange 2000 in a cluster environment is basically a four-step process. The first two steps are preliminary steps, and the last two steps involve installing and configuring Exchange 2000 to run on the cluster nodes:

1. Install Windows 2000 Advanced Server and Service Pack 1 on both systems (refer to Chapter 2 for installation details).

2. Install Cluster Service on each node, one node at a time (refer to Chapter 5 for Cluster Service installation procedures).

3. Install Exchange 2000 on both cluster nodes, performing the installation one node at a time.

4. Configure at least one virtual server on each node.

 Cluster Service must be running on both nodes before you install Exchange 2000. It cannot be installed onto a non-clustered server and integrated into a cluster afterward. Cluster Service must be on the system before Exchange 2000 to take advantage of the clustering technologies.

Once Windows 2000 Advanced Server (or Windows 2000 Datacenter Server) is installed and Cluster Service is running on both of the nodes, you are ready to begin the installation of Exchange 2000 on the cluster nodes. As with the installation of most software, you need to complete some preliminary steps before you jump into the installation process. The preliminary steps that need to be completed before beginning the actual installation of Exchange 2000 are listed here:

1. Assign the Cluster Service account the appropriate permissions. The Cluster Service account needs to be made a member of the Schema Admins group and the Enterprise Admins group. The installation of Exchange 2000 will be done under the account created for Cluster Service, and because the installation of Exchange 2000 will make modifications to the schema, the account needs to be given permission to do so. The Cluster Service account can be added to the Schema Admins group and the Enterprise Admins group through the Active Directory Users And Computers snap-in.

2. Run the Forestprep utility to prepare Active Directory for the installation of Exchange. The Forestprep utility must be run under a user account that is a member of the Schema Admins group and the Enterprise Admins group (this is why the Cluster Service account is added to these two groups in the previous step). When the Forestprep utility is run without any previous versions of Exchange running, it adds Exchange-specific information into the schema, establishes the Exchange organization name and object within Active Directory, and grants Exchange Full Administrator permissions to the user account specified.

3. Run the Domainprep utility in the domain where Exchange 2000 will be installed. The Domainprep utility will set the appropriate permissions in the domain and identify the address list server responsible for the domain.

Once the preliminary steps have been completed, the installation of Exchange can be completed on each cluster node. The installation process for Exchange is the same regardless of whether you are installing the application in a clustered environment or on a standalone server. If you install Exchange 2000 on a cluster node, a message box will appear during the installation informing you that the cluster-aware version of Exchange is being installed (see Figure 10.1).

Configuring Exchange Virtual Servers

Once Exchange has been successfully installed on both cluster nodes, you can begin configuring the Exchange Virtual Servers (cluster resource groups) on each of the cluster nodes. Once the groups are created, you will be able to create the required resources. The following steps outline how to create the first Exchange Virtual Server through the Cluster Administrator utility and how to create the necessary resources.

To configure an Exchange Virtual Server, follow these steps:

1. Open Start|Programs|Administrative Tools and select the Cluster Administrator.

2. In the left pane of the Cluster Administrator console, right-click Groups, point to New, and choose the Group option. This will launch the New Group Wizard.

3. In the New Group dialog box, enter a name and description for the group. Click Next.

4. From the Preferred Owners dialog box, you can optionally select a preferred owner for the group. Click Finish and then click OK. You should now have a new group created, and you are ready to create the resources.

Figure 10.1   Message box stating the cluster-aware version of Exchange will be installed.

To create an IP Address resource, follow these steps:

1. In the left pane of the Cluster Administrator console, right-click the group you just created, point to New, and select the Resource option to launch the New Resource Wizard.

2. Enter a name and description for the new resource. Select IP Address to create a new IP Address resource for the EVS (see Figure 10.2). Click Next.

3. From the Possible Owners dialog box, verify that both nodes are listed as possible owners. Click Next.

4. From the Dependencies dialog box, verify that no dependencies for the resource are listed. Click Next.

5. From the TCP/IP Parameters dialog box, specify the IP address and subnet mask. This will be the IP address and subnet mask assigned to the EVS. Make sure the public network connection is selected. Click Finish and then click OK.

To create a Network Name resource, follow these steps:

1. In the left pane of the Cluster Administrator console, right-click the group created for the EVS, point to New, and select the Resource option.

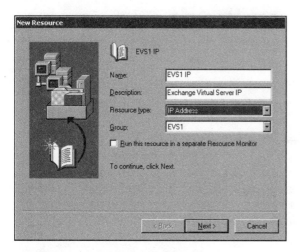

Figure 10.2   Creating an IP Address resource.

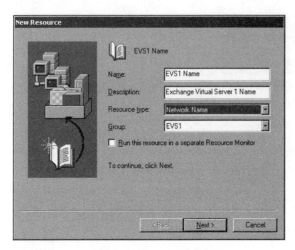

Figure 10.3 Creating a Network Name resource.

2. From the New Resource Wizard dialog box, type in a name and description for the resource. Select Network Name for the resource type (see Figure 10.3).

3. Click Next at the Possible Owners dialog box, making sure that both nodes are listed.

4. In the Dependencies dialog box, select the EVS IP Address resource from the list of available resources and click Add. Click Next.

5. Type in a network name (NetBIOS name) for the resource and click Finish. Click OK.

To create a Disk resource, follow these steps:

1. In the left pane of the Cluster Administrator utility, select Groups.

2. From within the Groups container, select the drive that will be assigned to the EVS.

3. Drag the drive onto the group created for the virtual server.

To create the Exchange System Attendant resource, follow these steps:

1. In the left pane of the Cluster Administrator console, right-click the group, point to New, and select the Resource option. Click Next.

The IP Address resource, the Network Name resource, and the Disk resource must first be online before you create the Exchange System Attendant resource.

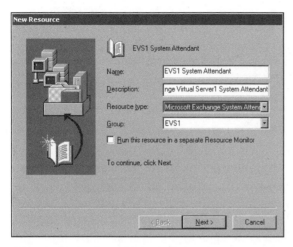

Figure 10.4 Creating an Exchange System Attendant resource.

2. Type a name and description for the resource. For the Resource Type option, select Exchange System Attendant. For the Group option, select the group you created for the EVS (see Figure 10.4). Click Next.

3. In the Possible Owners dialog box, verify that both cluster nodes are listed. Click Next.

4. In the Dependencies dialog box, add the Exchange Network Name and Disk resources to the list of dependencies by selecting each one and clicking Add. Click Next.

5. Verify the location of the data directory. Click Next.

Once the Exchange System Attendant resource has been added to the EVS, it adds the remaining required resources to the virtual server, as shown in Figure 10.5.

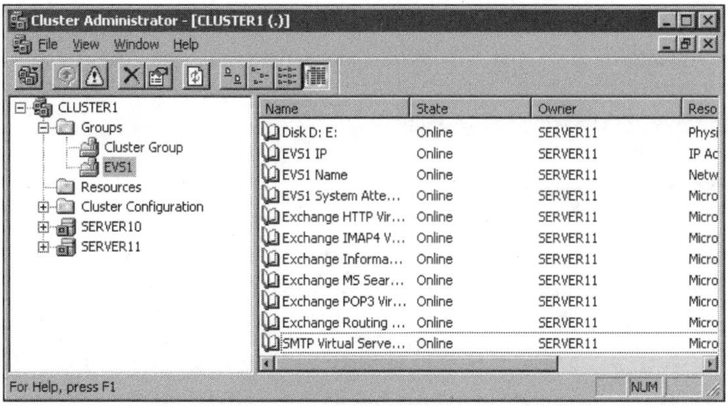

Figure 10.5 Resources added by the Exchange System Attendant.

Once the virtual server has been configured and brought online, right-clicking a resource and choosing the Initiate Failure option can test the virtual server's ability to failover. A resource failure can also be initiated using the **Cluster** command.

Exchange 5.5

Exchange 5.5 Enterprise Edition is also capable of functioning in a cluster environment. Keep in mind, though, that not all the services and components are cluster aware. Unlike Exchange 2000, Exchange 5.5 does not have an application-specific resource DLL and therefore uses the generic resource DLL. This means that Exchange 5.5 supports only an Active/Passive cluster model, and the application runs only on one node at a time.

There is no significant difference between Exchange 5.5 and Exchange 2000 in a cluster environment. Before Exchange 5.5 can be installed, Cluster Service must first be running. Exchange 5.5 also requires a resource group be created with an IP Address resource, a Network Name resource, and a Disk resource. Because Exchange 5.5 supports an Active/Passive cluster configuration, a full installation of the application is done only on one node (unlike clustering Exchange 2000, where a full installation of the application is done one each cluster node). In order for the application to fail over to the second node, the Exchange system libraries and extensions are installed on the second node and the Windows 2000 services are registered to make it Exchange aware. The second node is then able to act as a backup for the first node in the event of failure.

If you are currently running Exchange 5.5 in a cluster, you cannot upgrade directly to Exchange 2000. You have two options if you want to upgrade Exchange 5.5 to Exchange 2000 in a cluster environment. The first option is to do a fresh install of Exchange 2000, adding it to the existing site and moving the mailboxes into the new Exchange 2000 cluster. The second option is to back up the information store database and remove Exchange 5.5. You can then install Exchange 2000 on all the cluster nodes. This option only works if the cluster nodes are running Windows 2000 with Service Pack 1.

SQL 2000

To increase its availability, SQL 2000 supports failover clustering, which means that processing can automatically switch between cluster nodes if one fails. For a corporation, this means that in the event of failure, database services can quickly be restored. As with Exchange, certain components of SQL Server are supported in failover clustering. The supported components are listed here:

➤ Microsoft Search Service

➤ Multiple Instances

➤ SQL Server Enterprise Manager

➤ Service Control Manager

➤ Replication

➤ SQL Profiler

➤ SQL Analyzer

When configuring failover clustering for SQL Server, you have two options. The first option is to install SQL Server on all cluster nodes. For each installation of SQL, a virtual server is created (a *virtual server* is equivalent to a cluster resource group).

 As with Exchange, Cluster Service must first be installed and configured before you install SQL Server.

The second option is to configure multiple instances of SQL Server (with SQL 2000, you can install up to a maximum of 16 instances, each operating independently of one another). When an instance of SQL is installed, it operates as though it were on a separate server. Each instance that is installed has its own path for executable program files and its own location for storing data files. Every instance will have its own database and database files that are not shared between instances. When an instance of SQL is installed, the setup program automatically installs the needed executable files on both the cluster nodes (the executable files are installed in the same location on all cluster nodes) and places the database files in a cluster group (virtual server). The cluster node where the instance is installed then becomes the owner of the cluster group. In the event of failure, only the database will fail over, not the executable files, because they are already located on each cluster node.

Two types of instances can be configured on cluster nodes, as explained in the following list:

➤ *Default instance*—When SQL is installed for the first time on a cluster node, it is automatically installed as a default instance (this can be changed by deselecting the appropriate option during setup, as shown in Figure 10.6). You can enable client applications to connect to the default instance by specifying the network name of the computer (this obviously means that there can only be one default instance running on a computer).

> *Named instance*—Multiple instances of SQL Server can exist on a single node when you create named instances. You can enable client applications to connect to a named instance by specifying the computer name as well as the instance name (this is the main difference between a default instance and a named instance).

 Keep in mind that each instance of SQL Server must have a unique name between cluster nodes to avoid conflict.

SQL Virtual Server

A SQL virtual server is the equivalent of a cluster resource group. If a resource within a virtual server fails, the entire group and all its resources fail over to the second cluster node. Each SQL virtual server must contain the following:

➤ A Disk resource (each virtual server requires its own disk volume)

➤ A Network Name resource

➤ An IP Address resource

➤ One instance of SQL Server 2000 (per virtual server)

 Once an instance of SQL is added, resources are added to the virtual server. These resources include a SQL Server resource, a SQL Server Agent resource, and a Fulltext resource (as shown in Figure 10.7).

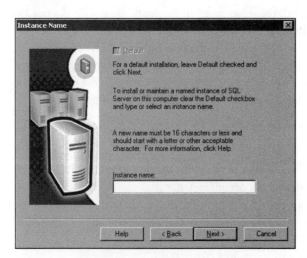

Figure 10.6   Changing the type of instance from default to named.

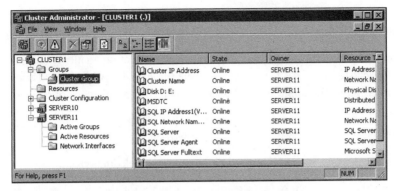

Figure 10.7 Resources added after an instance of SQL is installed.

Creating a SQL Failover Cluster

Before beginning the installation of SQL in a cluster environment, you need to complete a few preliminary steps. Obviously, Windows 2000 Advanced Server and Cluster Service need to be installed and configured. Once they are, you will need to verify that there is a Microsoft Data Transaction Coordinator (MS-DTC) resource created through Cluster Administrator.

SQL requires the MS-DTC for distributed queries. The MS-DTC is installed by default when Windows 2000 is installed, but when in a cluster configuration, the MS-DTC needs to be run in cluster mode. The MS-DTC can be put in cluster mode using the Component Cluster Wizard (Comclust.exe). Once the wizard is executed, it makes the following changes:

➤ It creates an MS-DTC resource.

➤ It creates an MS-DTC log file on one of the shared disks. Doing so ensures that the log file can be accessed from any node in the cluster.

➤ It places the necessary MS-DTC registry entries into the cluster registry.

Once configured in cluster mode, the MS-DTC Transaction Manager runs on a single node, which means that only one MS-DTC Transaction Manager is in control of the cluster at one time. Any calls made by the other cluster nodes are forwarded to the MS-DTC Transaction Manager that is in control of the cluster. If the MS-DTC Transaction Manager fails, it is restarted on another node in the cluster.

To configure MS-DTC to run in cluster mode:

1. Point to Start|Run and type "cmd". Click OK.

2. From within the command prompt window type "Comclust.exe".

3. Repeat the previous two steps on all remaining nodes in the cluster.

Once the MS-DTC is configured to run in cluster mode, you can begin the installation of SQL.

The following list outlines the basic steps involved in creating a failover cluster. Unlike the clustering of Exchange Server, where the virtual server is created after the installation of the application, the virtual server for an instance of SQL is created during setup.

To create a new SQL failover cluster, follow these steps:

1. Insert the SQL Server CD and click Next at the Welcome screen.

2. From the Computer Name screen, enter a name for the virtual server. If setup detects Cluster Service is running, the Virtual Server option is the default. Click Next.

3. Enter in the username and company name and click next. Click Yes to accept the Software License Agreement.

4. From the Failover Clustering screen, select the network from which clients will be accessing the virtual server and enter in an IP address for the virtual server. You can enter in multiple IP addresses if the virtual server needs to be accessible to clients on different subnets. Click Next.

5. From the Cluster Disk Selection screen, select a disk group. This is where the data files for this instance of SQL will be located. Click Next.

6. From the Cluster Management screen, remove any nodes that will not be part of the failover cluster by selecting the node and choosing Remove. Click Next.

7. The Remote Installation screen appears. Enter in a username and password for the remote cluster node. The user account specified must have administrative privileges on the node. Click Next.

8. From the Instance Name screen, choose the type of instance—default or named. You can specify a named instance by simply clearing the Default checkbox (refer back to Figure 10.6). Click Next.

9. Select the type of installation from the Setup Type screen. Click Next.

10. From the Services Account screen, select the account that the failover cluster will run under. Click Next.

11. From the Authentication Mode screen, select the authentication type—Windows authentication mode or mixed mode. Click Next.

12. Click Next at the Setup Copying Files screen. Click Finish.

To create another instance of SQL, repeat this entire procedure.

SQL 7.0

Support for Cluster Service is available with SQL 7.0 Enterprise Edition. Through SQL Server failover support, the availability of the application can be increased and downtime can be minimized. When SQL is installed in a cluster environment, it appears to the user as though it is running on a single server. Clients connect to a SQL virtual server using a network name, and the actual cluster node servicing their requests is transparent to them. In the event of failure, the resources are moved to the second node, and all users have to do is reconnect to the virtual server using its network name.

SQL 7.0 supports two types of failover cluster configurations: Active/Passive failover configuration and Active/Active failover configuration. In an Active/Passive configuration, one server is designated as being the active (or primary) server. This cluster node is running SQL Server. The second cluster node merely acts as a backup should the active node fail. To set up an Active/Passive configuration, install SQL Server on one node and the SQL Server utilities on the second node. Keep in mind that in order for the SQL virtual server to successfully fail over to the second node, the installation of SQL must be placed on the shared disk. In an Active/Active failover configuration, there are multiple instances of SQL Server running on the cluster, as opposed to a single instance. Each cluster node runs an independent copy of SQL Server, and there are two virtual servers, one for each instance of SQL. This configuration requires two separate shared volumes for each installation of SQL Server.

The installation process for clustering SQL Server 7.0 varies from that of SQL 2000. Before installing SQL 7.0 in a cluster environment, the MS-DTC must be configured to run in cluster mode using the **Comclust** command. Again, this command must be run on each node in the cluster.

*Note: The **Comclust** command only needs to be run once on a node, even if the node will be configured with multiple instances.*

Several services that may be running also need to be stopped to prevent them from interfering with the installation of SQL 7.0. Some of the services are:

➤ All Internet Information services

➤ All Microsoft Exchange services

➤ Any anti-virus software

➤ Any backup software or services

➤ MS-DTC

➤ Remote Access Autodial

➤ SMTP service

➤ SNMP service

➤ NNTP service

After the necessary services have been stopped, you can install SQL 7.0 on the cluster node. Doing so places both the program files and the data files on one of the shared cluster disks. Once SQL Server 7.0 has been installed on a cluster node, the Cluster Failover Wizard must be run to create the virtual server. The information you provide is used to create an IP Address resource and a Network Name resource for the virtual server. Running the wizard creates a virtual server with the required resources and puts the files needed to run SQL on to any other nodes in the cluster.

Practice Questions

Question 1

You install Exchange 2000 on Node A of Cluster 1. You create a new group for the Exchange Virtual Server called EVS1. What resources need to be added to the group before the Exchange System Attendant resource can be added? [Check all correct answers]

- ❑ a. IP Address resource
- ❑ b. File Share resource
- ❑ c. Network Name resource
- ❑ d. Disk resource
- ❑ e. Print share

The correct answers are a, c, and d. Before the Exchange System Attendant resource can be added to the group EVS1, an IP Address resource, a Network Name resource, and a Disk resource must be added to the virtual server. A File Share resource and Print share are not required for an EVS, thus making answers b and e incorrect.

Question 2

Exchange 2000 is a fully cluster-aware application. What custom DLLs does Exchange come with to enhance its functionality within a cluster environment? [Check all correct answers]

- ❑ a. A generic resource DLL
- ❑ b. Exres.dll
- ❑ c. Excluadmin.dll
- ❑ d. Exclures.dll
- ❑ e. Exresadmin.dll

The correct answers are b and c. Exchange 2000 adds Exres.dll and Excluadmin.dll when it is installed in a cluster environment. These are custom DLLs that make Exchange 2000 a cluster-aware application. Answer a is incorrect because a generic resource DLL is used for those applications that do not have custom DLLs defined for use within a cluster. A generic resource DLL provides limited functionality in a cluster environment. Answers d and e are incorrect because there are no such DLLs added via the installation of Exchange in a cluster environment.

Question 3

> You are setting up SQL Server 2000 in a failover cluster configuration. What
> is the maximum number of instances of SQL can be installed?
>
> ○ a. 8
>
> ○ b. 12
>
> ○ c. 16
>
> ○ d. 20

The correct answer is c. You can install up to a maximum of 16 instances of SQL
per failover cluster. Therefore, answers a, b, and d are incorrect.

Question 4

> Your corporation plans to implement Exchange 2000 and has expressed the
> need for minimal downtime. You decide to implement Exchange 2000 in a
> cluster environment to increase its availability. Put the following steps in the
> order they would occur when you're configuring the systems to run Cluster
> Service and Exchange 2000.
>
> Install Cluster Service on each system.
>
> Install Exchange 2000 on each node.
>
> Install Windows 2000 Advanced Server on each system.
>
> Configure an Exchange Virtual Server on each node.
>
> Apply Service Pack 1.

The correct answer is:

>   Install Windows 2000 Advanced Server on each system.
>
>   Install Cluster Service on each system.
>
>   Apply Service Pack 1.
>
>   Install Exchange 2000 on each node.
>
>   Configure an Exchange Virtual Server on each node.

Remember that Service Pack 1 needs to be installed before Exchange 2000. Also
keep in mind that Cluster Service must be installed and configured before you
install Exchange 2000 in a cluster environment.

Question 5

SQL Server 2000 supports multiple instances. What are the types of SQL instances that can be created? [Check all correct answers]

- ❏ a. Default
- ❏ b. SQL Server
- ❏ c. Network
- ❏ d. Named

The correct answers are a and d. The two types of instances that can be created are default instances and named instances. Answers b and d are incorrect because there are no such instances that can be created with failover clustering.

Question 6

You are setting up Exchange 2000 in an Active/Active cluster configuration. The cluster contains two nodes running Windows 2000 Advanced Server, and you install Exchange 2000 on each of the nodes. How many disk volumes will be required on the shared storage space?

- ○ a. One
- ○ b. Two
- ○ c. Three
- ○ d. Four

The correct answer is c. You will need at least three disk volumes. One volume will be dedicated to the Quorum resource, and the Exchange Virtual Server on each cluster node will each be assigned a separate volume because they cannot share the same physical disk. Therefore, answers a, b, and d are incorrect.

Question 7

You currently have two systems in a cluster configuration: Node A and Node B. You install a default instance of SQL Server 2000 on Node A. You would now like to add a second instance of SQL to Node A. How can a second instance of SQL be installed?

○ a. This cannot be done because a cluster can maintain only a single instance of SQL.

○ b. From within Cluster Administrator, create a new virtual server.

○ c. Run setup for SQL Server on Node A. During setup, create a named instance of SQL.

○ d. Run setup for SQL Server on Node A. During setup, create another default instance of SQL.

The correct answer is c. By running setup for SQL and choosing to create a named instance, a second instance of SQL can be created on the cluster. Answer a is incorrect because you can create up to 16 instances of SQL on a failover cluster. Answer b is incorrect because creating a new virtual server doesn't create a second instance of SQL. Answer d is incorrect because there can only be one default instance of SQL per computer.

Question 8

You successfully install Exchange 2000 on two cluster nodes and configure two Exchange Virtual Servers. You would like to test the failover of one virtual server from one node to another. How can you generate a failover for a virtual server to another cluster node? [Check all correct answers]

☐ a. From within Cluster Administrator, right-click one of the Exchange resources and choose the Initiate Failure option.

☐ b. Use the **Cluster Node** command with the **/InitiateFailure** option.

☐ c. From within Cluster Administrator, right-click one of the Exchange resources and choose the Test Failure option.

☐ d. Use the **Cluster Resource** command with the **/Fail** option.

The correct answers are a and d. You can generate a resource failure by right-clicking one of the Exchange 2000 resources and choosing the Initiate Failure option from within Cluster Administrator. Alternatively, you can use the **Cluster Resource** command with the **/Fail** option. You cannot initiate failure of a resource using the **Cluster Node** command; therefore answer b is incorrect. There is no **Test Failure** option in Cluster Administrator; therefore answer c incorrect.

Question 9

How many shared volumes do you need to set up three instances of SQL Server on a cluster?

○ a. One

○ b. Three

○ c. Four

○ d. Six

The correct answer is c. One volume will be required for each instance of SQL Server installed, and one volume will be required for the Quorum resource. Therefore, answers a, b, and d are incorrect.

Question 10

> Of the following items, which are elements of an SQL virtual server? [Check all correct answers]
>
> ❑ a. Network Name resource
>
> ❑ b. IP Address resource
>
> ❑ c. Disk resource
>
> ❑ d. One instance of SQL

The correct answers are a, b, c, and d. These are all elements of an SQL virtual server.

Question 11

> You are configuring multiple instances of SQL 2000 in an Active/Active configuration on your two-node cluster. The cluster is configured with three external drives. One drive is dedicated to the Quorum resource. The remaining two drives are each configured with three partitions. How many instances of SQL can be installed?
>
> ○ a. 1
>
> ○ b. 2
>
> ○ c. 4
>
> ○ d. 6

Answer b is correct. One drive has been dedicated to the Quorum Resource, which leaves two remaining drives. Each instances of SQL must be placed on a separate SCSI device. Because there are two remaining drives, two instances of SQL can be configured. Multiple instances of SQL cannot be placed on the same physical disk because a physical disk and its partitions can only be owned by one node in the cluster.

Need to Know More?

 Libertone, David. *Windows 2000 Cluster Service Guidebook: A Guide to Creating and Managing a Cluster, Second Edition.* Prentice Hall, Upper Saddler River, NJ, 2000. ISBN 0130284696. This book contains information on clustering SQL Server 7.0 and Exchange 5.5.

 Microsoft Corporation. *Microsoft Exchange 2000 Implementation and Administration.* Microsoft Press, Redmond, WA, 2001. ISBN 0735610282. Chapter 7 provides some information on Exchange 2000 in a cluster environment.

 Installing Exchange 2000 on a Windows 2000 Cluster: Step-by-Step Guide. Microsoft Corporation. Microsoft Corporation, Redmond, WA, 2000. This online document, found at **www.microsoft.com/Exchange/ techinfo/clusterinstall.htm**, provides step-by-step instructions on installing Exchange 2000 in a cluster environment.

 Search TechNet on the Internet at **www.microsoft.com/technet/ default.asp** or the TechNet CD for more information on clustering Exchange Server and SQL Server.

For more information on clustering Exchange 2000 and SQL 2000, use the Books Online documentation that comes with each application.

Optimization

Terms you'll need to understand:

✓ Disk subsystem
✓ Virtual memory
✓ Bottlenecks
✓ System Monitor
✓ Network Monitor
✓ Virtual disk

Techniques you'll need to master:

✓ Upgrading the disk subsystem
✓ Determining hardware that is causing a bottleneck
✓ Removing a bottleneck
✓ Using System Monitor to find cluster bottlenecks
✓ Using Network Monitor

This chapter presents you with information on optimizing your cluster server for better performance and reliability—two areas that are essential to all organizations. You will learn how to make your cluster nodes perform better for your network clients accessing them as well as how to make your cluster nodes more reliable in order to keep resources available to your network clients. You will also learn the process of testing performance on cluster nodes to determine areas causing a performance loss.

Resource Optimization

Most resources are not too server hardware-intensive, meaning they do not put a large load on all the server hardware. Most resources use only the disk and network resources of the node on which they are running.

The resources that require the physical disk as a dependency or that read/write database files will be disk intensive, which covers almost all the resources that can operate on a node in a cluster environment. To achieve better performance for the resources that use physical disk resources, the disk subsystem should be upgraded to a faster one.

Disk Subsystem Optimization

To optimize your disk subsystem, you must first be aware of what hardware is part of the subsystem. The disk subsystem is made up of all hardware used to read or write to the physical disk drives. This includes the disks themselves, the controller cards, and the bus to send to and receive data from the disk controller. The physical disks can be replaced with other disks that are larger and faster to provide more usable disk space and better access time.

If many network users are reading and writing to the physical disk, the disk buffer can become overrun, causing delays in disk access. Newer physical disks can provide better access time for reading and writing, thus improving performance for network clients. Newer physical disks can also improve the performance of resources that use their own database on a shared disk resource, such as the DHCP Cluster resource. If DHCP can read and write to its database faster, the DHCP service can issue IP addresses faster to network clients, so that clients obtain an IP address faster.

Controller cards can be upgraded to provide better throughput to and from the physical disk as well as the data bus on the motherboard. If the controller is creating a bottleneck, consider using a new controller with a larger data bus. For example, you could upgrade a SCSI controller card from an ISA card (8 or 16 bits) to a PCI card (32 or 64 bits) to allow for much higher throughput. Finding bottlenecks will be discussed later in this chapter.

Another way to upgrade the disk subsystem for better performance is to implement a hardware Redundant Array of Inexpensive Disks (RAID) solution, which provides faster performance when reading and/or writing to the physical disk. See Table 11.1 for a list of RAID implementations and their performance improvements.

Implementing a RAID option not only provides fault tolerance of the data on the RAID disks, but also improves some performance for the disk subsystem.

Note: RAID 0 is not fault tolerant. Also, any other implementation of RAID will not be fault tolerant and will result in slower performance if one hard disk in the implementation fails. Once the disk is replaced, the implementation will be fault tolerant again and also provide performance improvements.

Another way to improve disk performance is to minimize the number of file shares that are managed by a cluster node. Any node can become overburdened if there are too many requests for file share access by network clients.

Network Optimization

Almost all cluster resources use the network for sending and receiving data, and thus the network can become a bottleneck for the cluster as well as the disk subsystem. The network interface card (NIC) installed in the cluster node and the network cabling and hardware are two components of the network that can create problems.

Network Interface Card (NIC) Optimization

Because most of the information used by a cluster is coming in or going out through the network connection, the NIC is very susceptible to creating a bottleneck.

The NIC can handle only the throughput it was designed to handle. If there are many users on the network accessing a cluster resource on a node, the NIC might not be able to manage all the I/O required to produce acceptable results for the network clients.

Table 11.1   RAID implementations and performance improvements.

RAID Type	Performance Improvement
0—Disk striping without parity	Best read, best write, no fault tolerance
1—Disk mirroring, normal	Moderately better read, slow write
1—Disk mirroring, duplex	Moderately better read, better write
2—Disk striping with Error Correction Code (ECC)	Better read, better write
3—Disk striping with ECC as parity	Better read, better write
4—Disk striping with large blocks	Better read, better write
5—Disk striping with parity	Better read, better write

If the NIC's response time is unacceptable, it may need to be replaced with a faster card that can handle a faster throughput on the data bus. This is accomplished in the same manner as upgrading the disk controller in the disk subsystem. If the network card is using too much of its buffer to pass and receive data to and from the data bus, it can be upgraded to a newer card that has a larger data bus so that it can pass and receive more data to and from the motherboard at one time. If an IDE NIC (8- or 16- bit) is being used, it can be upgraded to a PCI NIC (32- or 64- bit) bus type to allow for more data to pass between the NIC and the motherboard.

If in a switched network, an additional network card could be placed in the cluster nodes to allow for more throughput of data. A bottleneck can occur if the throughput is too small for the number of clients accessing the cluster.

Network and Network Hardware Optimization

If the bottleneck is not occurring between the motherboard and the NIC but rather between the cluster and the network clients, the problem can be resolved in several ways.

When the bottleneck is caused by too much data being transmitted on the network or too many users, the network must be divided or upgraded. You can use bridges, switches, or routers to segment the network into smaller networks that have fewer clients accessing the segment to which they are connected. Take a look at Figure 11.1. If there were 100 users on this network and all were competing for network access at the same time, the network access time could be improved by splitting the network into segments so that fewer users compete for access to their segment of the network.

If the number of users is so great that dividing the network does not remove the bottleneck, the network throughput can be increased by upgrading the network as a whole. This can be achieved by upgrading from a network that supports a small amount of throughput to one that supports a larger amount of throughput, such as replacing a 10Mbps network with a 100Mbps network or even a 1Gbps network. This allows for throughput rates over 10 times greater than before.

To upgrade a network in this manner may require you to replace of all NICs, bridges, switches, routers, hubs, and cabling. All devices that transmit or receive data across the network cable (including the network cable) must support the data transmission speed you want to achieve. The network as a whole is only as fast as the slowest component operating on it. This means that if all the switches, bridges, routers, and hubs were replaced with 100Mbps components, and all NICs but one were replaced, the client using the slower NIC would not benefit from the other improvements.

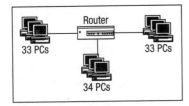

Figure 11.1   A divided network.

Note: When you're upgrading a network to a higher bandwidth, all network components should be replaced with components that support the higher bandwidth. This can be done in stages, but the end result should be that all components support the higher bandwidth.

Server Application Optimization

Server-based applications use more server hardware, so each node that is a possible owner of the Application resource will require more hardware to perform well if and when it becomes the owner of the resource.

Server applications can be very memory and CPU-intensive. Network clients access these applications, but the server performs the main processing, as well as all calculations and data retrievals. Exchange Server and SQL Server are examples of server applications. Some of these applications are accessed by a "client" application, in much the same way that Outlook can be used to access Exchange. Most of the processing occurs on the Exchange Server due to the fact that the user's mailbox is located there. Outlook will access the server and request a list of messages, which the Exchange Server will then process.

In a cluster, memory and CPU optimization are important to keep the resources available at all times. When one node fails, the node that assumes ownership of the resources must have enough memory and CPU resources available to handle not only its own resources, but also the resources it takes over for the failed node.

Memory Optimization

If a server running memory-intensive applications seems to be running slowly, it can be optimized in several ways when you're dealing memory.

More memory can be added, which will usually solve the problem of a slow server. You may see some improvement by upgrading the memory modules to a faster speed, but this same improvement can be achieved by just adding more memory.

Virtual memory also affects memory bottlenecks. *Virtual memory* is the memory area that is actually stored as a physical file on a hard disk. When the majority of the physical memory is being used and almost gone and more memory is required, Windows will take memory from RAM and give it to the swap file on the hard disk. The information that is removed from physical memory into the swap file includes portions or all of an application that has not been accessed for a while. When the memory area is cleared, the other application or service that originally requested memory for its use will be given that memory area to use. When you access a program that has portions of its executed code in memory (physical RAM) and that was swapped to the swap file (hard disk), the program will be recalled back into physical memory to a place that is available or cleared by the previous process.

To improve memory responsiveness, the disk to which the swap file is written should not be the same disk that holds the operating system. Because the operating system must access its own files, the disk will usually have some overhead associated with the OS. If the swap file is not on the same disk as the OS, the process of swapping memory to the file won't compete with the OS disk for access time. The swap file should be on a physical drive separate from the OS (not a different partition on the same physical disk), and preferably on a different controller. If the swap file is on a different controller, the disk will not have to share a data bus with the hard disk containing the OS.

Another option is to improve the disk subsystem architecture, as discussed earlier in this chapter in the section titled "Disk Subsystem Optimization."

Network performance can be degraded when the cluster is installed on domain controllers. The domain controllers' responsibility to the network clients is to validate logon usernames and passwords. Managing user validation is an overhead that could affect the overall ability of the cluster. By not putting the cluster services on domain controllers, you can alleviate the overhead, but the cluster relies on domain controllers and must therefore rely on another server that might not be fault tolerant. This could be a single point of failure if the cluster is unable to contact a domain controller when the cluster is only made up of non-domain controller servers. To correct a possible point of failure, connect the cluster nodes to a domain controller on a separate network by adding an additional network card to all servers involved. This solution will provide a second connection for the cluster nodes to contact the domain controllers for logon validation.

CPU Optimization

The server's CPU can become overburdened by the processing requirements needed to answer requests from network clients. In these situations, the server CPU will need to be upgraded to a faster processor that can handle a higher load.

Another solution to the problem of an overburdened CPU is to add other processors to the server (if its motherboard is capable of using multiple processors). Adding a second processor can effectively double the load the server can handle, so that it can easily manage processor requests and calculations without being overburdened.

A third solution is to spread the cluster resources across multiple nodes or even multiple clusters within the organization. This will decrease the number of instructions being sent to a processor on a given server.

Application Optimization

Any applications that reside on the cluster are either cluster-aware or non-cluster-aware applications. Cluster-aware applications are those applications written specifically to operate on a cluster, and they take full advantage of the Cluster Services. Cluster-aware applications also take full advantage of all the capabilities of Cluster Server and allow for better failover performance.

Non-cluster-aware applications, on the other hand, are not aware of the Cluster Services and don't take full advantage of the cluster's capabilities. These types of applications may not fail over in case of a node failure. Non-cluster-aware applications are not optimized for cluster use and may cause some performance degradation on the cluster itself. Cluster applications will be labeled as cluster-aware applications.

 Try to use applications that are cluster aware for best cluster performance.

Determining Bottlenecks

The hardware in a server can be checked to determine whether it is creating a bottleneck that hinders server performance or network client response time. Once the hardware is determined to be a bottleneck, the bottleneck can be resolved by using the aforementioned options for increasing server performance.

Bottlenecks can be determined by using either System Monitor (previously known as *Performance Monitor* in Windows NT 4) or Network Monitor, which comes as a built-in utility with Windows 2000.

System Monitor

The System Monitor allows you to monitor the hardware to test for bottlenecks.

Note: The System Monitor monitors hardware, including the network interface card, but you must use the Network Monitor utility to monitor the network.

To open System Monitor, got to Start|Programs|Administrative Tools and select Performance. Another option is to go to Start|Run and type in "PERFMON". Either method will open the System Monitor, as shown in Figure 11.2.

When opened, the System Monitor will not be monitoring any hardware. Hardware options must be selected to start monitoring hardware. Options added are called *counters*. System Monitor can manage multiple counters at once.

Note: Running System Monitor causes a slight load on the server. The extra load will be included in the results of the counters and must be taken into account.

To add a counter, click the button with the plus sign (+) icon in the shortcut bar above the right pane. Once this button is selected, you are given another dialog box from which to choose the counters, as shown in Figure 11.3.

The first option allows you to select whether counters will be used to check the local system or a remote system.

The second option allows you to select the hardware that will be monitored from the Performance Object drop-down list. Then you can select all counters or a specific counter. Each hardware component can have multiple counters to monitor various values of the hardware capability. The counter you use will vary depending on the function of the hardware being monitored. To determine which counter to use, select a counter and then click the Explanation button to see a

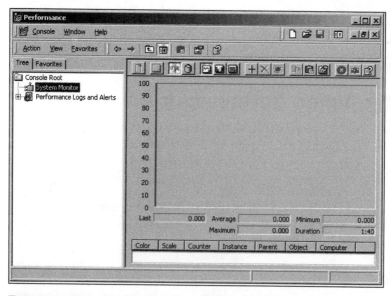

Figure 11.2 System Monitor.

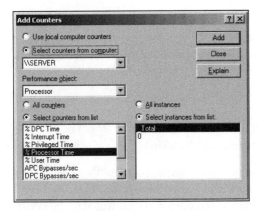

Figure 11.3 System Monitor's Add Counters dialogue box.

description of what value the counter is monitoring. Once you have selected the appropriate counter, click the Add button and then click Close to view the monitor. You can select other counters before you click the Close button.

When you're using multiple counters, each counter will be displayed in a different color on the monitor. Each counter will have an acceptable range, and if any counter falls outside of its acceptable range, the hardware must be upgraded. For examples, see Table 11.2.

After running Performance Monitor and monitoring specific counters, you will be able to pinpoint bottlenecks during peak hours or after new users are added. Performance Monitor should be used at different times of the day so that you can

Table 11.2 System Monitor counter values.		
Counter	Acceptable Values	Resource Fix
Memory:Pages/Sec.	0 to 20, the lower the better	If this counter is higher han 20 consistently, upgrade RAM.
Memory:Available Bytes	Greater than 4MB	If this counter is less than 4MB, upgrade RAM.
Memory:Committed Bytes	Less than physical RAM	If this counter is greater than the physical amount of RAM, upgrade RAM.
Processor:% Processor Time	Between 0 and 80	If this counter is consistently greater than 80%, upgrade or add a CPU.
System:Processor Queue Length	Less than 2	If this counter is consistently over 2, upgrade or add a CPU.

determine a baseline and have a comparison of counter values to other counter values taken at different times. You should check the values after adding more users to the network to see whether the server is still capable of handling the load produced by the new network users.

Network Monitor

The Network Monitor is a utility for monitoring network traffic. The Network Monitor is not installed by default and must be added.

To install the Network Monitor, select Start|Settings|Control Panel. When the Control Panel is opened, double-click Add/Remove Programs. Then, in the left panel, select Add/Remove Windows Components, which will start the Windows Components Wizard, as shown in Figure 11.4. When all files are copied, select Finish to close the wizard.

Once Network Monitor is installed, start it by opening Start|Programs| Administrative Tools and selecting Network Monitor.

Scroll down and select Management And Monitoring Tools; then select the Details button. The next screen shows a list of management and monitoring tools. Check the box next to Network Monitor Tools, click OK, and then click Next. The files will be copied from the source directory, if available, or you will be prompted to insert the Windows 2000 CD-ROM.

Once started, as shown in Figure 11.5, Network Monitor needs to be enabled to capture network traffic. Select Capture from the Menu options and then select Start. Starting the capture will allow Network Monitor to start logging all packets coming into and out of the server being monitored.

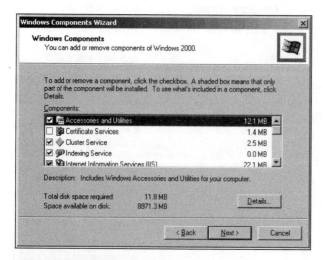

Figure 11.4 The Windows Components Wizard.

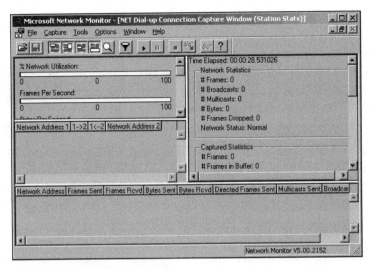

Figure 11.5   Network Monitor display screen.

When you're done logging all packets, select Capture from the menu and then select Stop and View to quit the capture and look at the results. You will be shown a list of the packets that were captured. For more information on Network Monitor, see Chapter 7.

Availability

For optimization in an Active/Active cluster, keep both nodes available at all times. If any node should fail, the other node will run the groups and resources for both nodes. This will cause a decrease in available hardware resources.

There are many ways to keep the cluster nodes available and performance at an acceptable level for all the groups and their resources; for example, by making the cluster and the network fault tolerant, clients can always access the nodes in the cluster.

Cluster Fault Tolerance

A cluster, by definition, is fault tolerant, but there are other ways to improve the fault tolerance of a cluster to keep availability higher than normal.

As with the cluster model types discussed in Chapter 3, you can implement a standby node, as in the hot spare cluster model, by having a physical computer that is not being used but standing by in case one of the active nodes on the cluster has a hardware failure. A standby node will supply spare parts to replace the failed hardware on the faulty node. Another option is to just have the main hardware parts available as replacements.

The parts to have on hand include all internal parts of the PC—even all expansion cards, especially the SCSI adapter. The external parts include all the SCSI or Fibre Channel cabling and connectors. External SCSI hard disks should definitely be kept on hand to replace any failed SCSI disks that are used as shared disks for the cluster. The external SCSI disks should be implemented as a hardware RAID to allow for fault tolerance. This will allow your cluster to function even after a shared hard disk failure.

The internal hard disk that contains the operating system files should be implemented as RAID 1 with two hard disk controllers. This will allow the server to still function even if the internal hard disk fails or if the controller that manages the hard drive on which the operating system is installed fails. These changes will make the operating system and the Cluster Service more fault tolerant.

Network Fault Tolerance

Even if a node doesn't fail, the network is yet another point of failure. The network clients must be able to access the cluster at all times. In case of a network failure, the cluster cannot be accessed and the clients cannot access the network.

To keep the network available, you must make the network fault tolerant. Again, this requires that you keep spare hardware on hand, such as routers, switches, hubs, and network cards. If any hardware fails, it can be replaced as soon as the fault is detected.

Another option is to set up the network with multiple routers to form a "loop." In Figure 11.6, you can see how this works. For performance issues, the network is divided into three separate networks and connected by routers to provide the fault tolerance (that is, it can still function in case one router fails).

For example, as shown in Figure 11.6, if Router A fails, users on Network 1 would not be able to communicate with users on Network 3 if Routers B and C did not exist. However, because Routers B and C are present, all users on any network segment can still communicate with any other user on the network as a whole, because data packets can be routed through the routers that are still available.

Configuring the network in a loop using multiple routers allows for network fault tolerance in the case of a router failure. This setup also improves network performance by splitting the network into smaller segments, with fewer users per network segment.

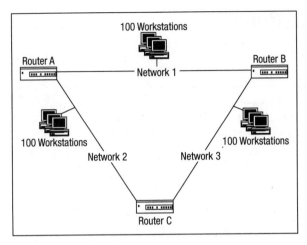

Figure 11.6   A routed network.

Practice Questions

Question 1

If you are managing a two-node cluster that has groups and resources running on both nodes at the same time, what type of cluster are you managing?

O a. Active-Active

O b. Active-Passive

O c. Passive-Active

O d. Passive-Passive

The correct answer is a. This is an Active-Active type of cluster. Each node owns and is running groups and resources.

If either node is not running any groups or resources, the type would be Active-Passive. Therefore, answer b is incorrect. Any node running groups or resources is Active, and any node that is not is Passive. Passive-Active is the same as Active-Passive. Therefore, answer c is incorrect. There is no Passive-Passive cluster type. This would defeat the purpose of having a cluster. Therefore, answer d is incorrect.

Question 2

If a resource requires the use of a database to store information for itself, which hardware resource will most likely be a bottleneck for this resource?

O a. CPU

O b. Memory

O c. Physical disk

O d. Network card

The correct answer is c. If a resource must keep data on a shared physical disk, the disk will be the most likely bottleneck.

Any resource that requires a lot of computations will most likely have a CPU bottleneck. Therefore, answer a is incorrect. Any resource that requires a lot of memory to execute and manage network clients will most likely have a bottleneck with memory. Therefore, answer c is incorrect. Any resource that communicates a lot with network clients will possibly have a network card bottleneck. Therefore, answer d is incorrect.

Question 3

> Which of the following can remove a physical disk bottleneck? [Check all correct answers]
>
> ❏ a. More RAM
>
> ❏ b. RAID
>
> ❏ c. A hard disk with a faster access time
>
> ❏ d. An extra CPU

The correct answers are b and c. Implementing RAID can increase the read and/or write performance of a hard disk. This can be enough to improve performance and remove a bottleneck. A hard disk with a faster access time can result in an increase in read/write performance and thus remove the bottleneck. More RAM and an additional CPU will not improve the disk subsystem, but it will improve the performance of applications running on the server and the processing of client requests. Therefore, answers a and d are incorrect.

Question 4

> Which of the following utilities can be used to determine bottlenecks on server hardware on a Windows 2000 Cluster?
>
> ○ a. Performance Monitor
>
> ○ b. System Monitor
>
> ○ c. Bottleneck Tester
>
> ○ d. Network Monitor

The correct answer is b. In Windows 2000, System Monitor is used to check for hardware bottlenecks.

Network Monitor is used to monitor network throughput and individual packets on the network. Therefore, answer d is incorrect. Performance Monitor is the same as System Monitor, except it's used on Windows NT systems, but the Performance Monitor utility is not on a Windows 2000 Server. Therefore, answer b is incorrect. Bottleneck Tester does not exist. Therefore, answer c is incorrect.

Question 5

> What is a virtual disk?
>
> ○ a. A mapped drive to a hard disk on another node in the cluster
>
> ○ b. A partition that is mapped to a directory on another partition on the same server
>
> ○ c. A partition that has two drive letters
>
> ○ d. A part of a disk that is used as RAM

The correct answer is d. A *virtual disk* is a file that is used to copy RAM contents to for freeing parts of RAM for other programs to use. This allows a system to use a little less RAM than would be required to run all the applications that are normally executed.

A mapped drive to a disk on another node is simply a network mapped drive. Therefore, answer a is incorrect. A partition that is mapped as a directory, instead of as a drive letter on a hard disk, is basically extending the capacity of a hard disk by joining two disks together. For example, a partition could be set up as the directory C:\DATA and any files or folders put in the DATA directory will actually go to the mapped partition. Therefore, answer b is incorrect. A partition that has two drive letters is one that is mapped twice over the network or is local and mapped as a network drive. Therefore, answer c is incorrect.

Question 6

> Which of the following are included in the disk subsystem? [Check all correct answers]
>
> ❑ a. Disk controller
>
> ❑ b. Disk drive
>
> ❑ c. Molex plug
>
> ❑ d. Data bus

The correct answers are a and b. Disk subsystem hardware joins the hard disk to a server's data bus. This hardware includes the hard disk, disk controller, and ribbon cable.

The Molex plug is used to deliver power to the hard disk, which is not part of the disk subsystem, but rather the power subsystem. Therefore, answer c is incorrect. The data bus is part of the motherboard and transfers information between components. Therefore, answer d is incorrect.

Question 7

> Which of the following applications are best suited for cluster performance?
> [Check all correct answers]
>
> ❏ a. Cluster-aware applications
>
> ❏ b. Non-cluster-aware applications
>
> ❏ c. DOS-based accounting software
>
> ❏ d. Exchange 2000

The correct answers are a and d. Cluster-aware applications provide better performance on a cluster due to the fact that they can fail over much more easily than non-cluster-aware applications. This will keep the application available in case of a node failure. Exchange 2000 is a cluster-aware server application.

Non-cluster-aware applications are not suited for running on clusters because they cannot fail over in case of a node failure. This means that the applications are not available and their performance is zero. DOS-based applications are not usually cluster aware and are not recommended anyway on Windows 2000 operating systems. Therefore, answers b and c are incorrect.

Question 8

> Which of the following actions will optimize the performance of a shared physical disk for a two-cluster node?
>
> ○ a. Using software RAID
>
> ○ b. Using hardware RAID
>
> ○ c. Making the shared disk the virtual disk
>
> ○ d. Installing the operating system of both nodes on the shared disk

The correct answer is b. Windows 2000 clusters cannot use software RAID on the shared physical disk; they can only use hardware RAID implementations. Therefore, answer a is incorrect. The shared physical disk cannot be the virtual disk, nor can it have the operating system installed on it. Therefore, answers c and d are incorrect.

Question 9

> Which of the following actions should be taken to improve the fault toler-
> ance of a single node in a cluster? [Check all correct answers]
>
> ❑ a. Have the disk with the operating system installed in a RAID 5 software
>   implementation
>
> ❑ b. Have the disk with the operating system installed in a RAID 1 software
>   implementation
>
> ❑ c. Have the shared physical disk installed in a RAID 5 hardware
>   implementation
>
> ❑ d. Have the shared physical disk installed in a RAID 1 hardware
>   implementation

The correct answers are b, c, and d. The operating system can only be installed in
a RAID 1 implementation (mirroring) if it is a software implementation. Therefore, answer a is incorrect.

The shared disk can be any RAID implementation as long as it is a hardware
implementation. The trick is to remember is that a cluster cannot use software
RAID implementations for the shared disks, and the operating system itself cannot be implemented as anything but RAID 1.

Question 10

Your company has three buildings that are serviced on the corporate network. Each building has its own network, and all three are connected by routers. The headquarters is located on Network A and has the majority of the 200 users. The other two networks each have roughly an equal number of network users. The company CEO wants you to determine the layout of the network and suggest how to improve it. This includes the layout of the users and where the cluster server should be placed. Using the following diagram, where should the users and cluster be placed? (Note that not all options will be used, and some may be used more than once.)

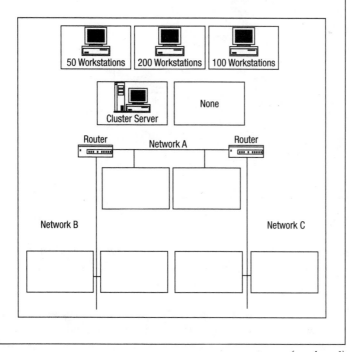

(continued)

Question 10 *(continued)*

The correct answer is:

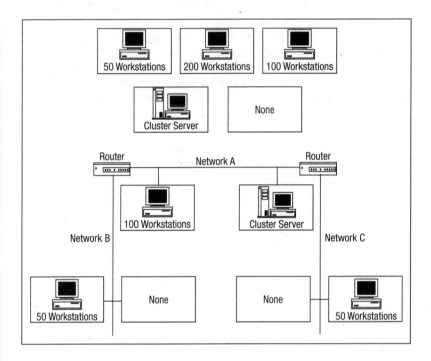

Because the majority of the users are located on Network A, the cluster server should be placed on Network A. This will also provide better communication without packets needing to be passed to a router.

Not all 200 users should be placed on one of the subnets, so the 100 users should be placed on Network A because this is the corporate office and it houses the majority of the network users. The other two networks should be somewhat equal, so they contain 50 users each and no cluster server.

The trick here is to remember is that for better performance, the cluster should be placed on the segment with the most users. The segments should be spread out in such a way that no segment will bear the brunt of network traffic if the clients all need access to the cluster. This would happen if the cluster were to be placed on the "end" of the network, which would cause the network traffic to be routed through the "center" segment to reach the cluster and then out again to send the response to the client from the cluster.

Need to Know More?

 Lee, Richard R. *Windows NT Microsoft Cluster Server*. Osborne/ McGraw-Hill, Berkley, CA, 1999. ISBN 0078825008. This book includes information on RAID solutions for clusters.

 Microsoft Corporation. *Windows 2000 Server Resource Kit Deployment Planning Guide*. Microsoft Press, Redmond, WA, 2000. ISBN 1572318058. The *Deployment Planning Guide* covers the design of a cluster and network configuration for better fault tolerance.

 Search TechNet on the Internet at **www.microsoft.com/technet/ default.asp** or the TechNet CD for more information on cluster optimization on a Windows 2000 Advanced Server PC.

 Search Exam Notes on the Internet at **www.examnotes.net/mcse2000/ 70223/index.shtml** for more information on cluster optimization.

Troubleshooting

Terms you'll need to understand:

✓ -fixquorum

✓ -noquorumlogging

✓ -resetquorumlog

✓ Clusrest.exe

✓ Cluster log

✓ Dumpcgf.exe

✓ Event Viewer

✓ **Net View** command

✓ Performance Monitor

✓ Ping

✓ Task Manager

Techniques you'll need to master:

✓ Identifying the tools available to troubleshoot a cluster

✓ Identifying and troubleshooting common SCSI bus and device problems

✓ Performing the steps necessary to repair a failed cluster

✓ Identifying and troubleshooting common cluster group and resource problems

✓ Troubleshooting network connectivity problems between cluster nodes

✓ Troubleshooting client-to-cluster communication problems

✓ Identifying and troubleshooting Quorum resource problems

This chapter provides an overview of some of the tools available for trouble-shooting clusters. It also covers some of the common Cluster Service problems you may encounter, as well as possible solutions.

Troubleshooting Utilities

Several utilities that come with Windows 2000 can aid you in troubleshooting a cluster. Being aware of the different utilities available, their functions, and how they can be used to troubleshoot a cluster will assist you in detecting, diagnosing, and troubleshooting problems. Table 12.1 lists some of the troubleshooting utilities that come with Windows 2000.

Installation of Cluster Service

The installation of Cluster Service is a relatively straightforward process. To eliminate some of the problems that can occur during the installation of Cluster Service, make sure the requirements for running Cluster Service are met and then complete all the preliminary steps prior to installation. Use the following checklist prior to installing Cluster Service:

➤ System components are on the Hardware Compatibility List (HCL) for Windows 2000 Advanced Server and Cluster Service.

➤ Windows 2000 Advanced Server (or Datacenter, if more than two nodes will be used in a cluster configuration) is present.

➤ Both systems are configured as either member servers or domain controllers (both systems must be in the same domain).

➤ Name resolution is enabled.

➤ There are two disk controllers per system (one for the private disk and one for the shared disk).

➤ Each system is connected to at least one shared disk (using a SCSI bus or Fibre Channel hub).

➤ The shared disk is a basic disk formatted with NTFS.

➤ Drive letter assignment for the shared disk is the same from each system.

➤ There are two network adapters per system (recommended).

➤ A domain user account for Cluster Service to run under is set up (must be a member of the Administrators group).

Table 12.1   Windows 2000 troubleshooting utilities.

Utility	Function
Cluster Log	Use the Cluster Log to view detailed information about the cluster. Cluster logging is enabled by default.
Device Manager	Device Manager can be used to ensure that the SCSI controllers don't have any conflicts and that the drivers are loaded properly.
Disk Administrator	Disk Administrator is used to verify drive recognition, drive letter assignment, and drive status.
Event Viewer	Use the System Log in the Event Viewer to view any messages generated by the Cluster Service.
Net View command	Use this command to verify that you can connect to a cluster, cluster nodes, and Network Name resources using NetBIOS names.
Network Monitor	Network Monitor is used to capture and analyze network traffic to monitor RPC connectivity between nodes and heartbeat messages.
Performance Monitor	Performance Monitor can be used to monitor the realtime performance of system components, applications, and services.
Ping	The ping utility can be used to test TCP/IP connectivity between clients and cluster nodes and between the cluster nodes themselves. You can also use the Pathping utility to trace a path to a remote host. It will report any packet losses that occur at each router to assist in determining network problems.
Services icon	The Services icon in the Control Panel is used to verify that the Cluster Service is running.
Task Manager	Task Manager can be used to view which processes are running on a system. The main processes pertaining to Cluster Service are Clussvc.exe and Resrcmon.exe.

Failed Installation on the First Cluster Node

Consider the following points when attempting to troubleshoot a failed installation of Cluster Service on the first node:

➤ Is the system hardware listed on the HCL for Cluster Service?

➤ Is the first node properly connected to the shared disk/disks? (Cluster Service requires that the system be connected to at least one shared disk prior to installation.)

➤ Is the shared disk a basic disk, and has it been formatted with NTFS?

➤ Is the cluster name unique on the network?

➤ Has the Cluster Service user account been added to the Administrators group?

 Discovering at what point during the installation Cluster Service fails will help you to identify and correct the problem.

Failed Installation on the Second Cluster Node

Consider the following points when troubleshooting a failed installation of Cluster Service on the second node:

➤ Is the first node online?

➤ Is Cluster Service running on the first node?

➤ Is the RPC service running? (Use the Services option to verify whether the service has been started.)

➤ When the second node is joining the cluster, is the correct network name being specified?

➤ If the correct cluster name is being used, try pinging the cluster network name resource (by IP address and network name) to make sure it is accessible.

SCSI Troubleshooting

Due to the way the Cluster Service uses the SCSI bus and devices, most problems will occur in this area.

Because the use of the SCSI bus requires complex functions, ensure that the SCSI controllers are of the same brand and model to avoid possible command differences. Also, the controllers you use must be listed on the Microsoft Hardware Compatibility List (HCL). Unpredictable results can arise if noncompliant hardware is used.

When problems with the SCSI bus or devices arise, check the following:

➤ Is the bus properly terminated?

➤ Is the cabling within length limitations? Each controller has a specific bus cable length set forth by the manufacturer. This length should not be exceeded.

➤ Are the cables damaged or are pins bent/missing?

➤ Are all SCSI IDs unique throughout the bus? Each controller and device connected to the bus must have a unique ID. (Microsoft recommends that the controllers be assigned IDs 6 and 7.)

➤ Are the controller cards recognized by Windows and are the correct drivers loaded? Check Device Manager to confirm that the controllers are enabled and have no hardware conflicts.

SCSI Termination

To ensure the stability of the SCSI bus, proper termination is a must. Termination prevents stray signals from entering the bus and corrupting communication between the nodes and the shared resource.

To properly set up SCSI devices, you must use termination at each end of the chain. If proper termination is not applied, devices will misbehave or fail completely. This will prevent the Cluster Service from starting, and shared resources will fail to come online.

Termination can be applied in several ways. If external SCSI devices are used, the controllers can be used to terminate the bus. Termination on controllers is usually enabled by default. If you suspect a termination fault, check the SCSI setup.

Using the termination built into the controller is not recommended, because some controllers don't provide termination when the power to them is removed. Consider using SCSI Y-cables, because termination can be achieved at all times, regardless of adapter termination. If you use SCSI Y-cables, make sure the bus is terminated properly and no termination appears in the middle of the SCSI bus.

SCSI Device IDs

All SCSI devices on the SCSI bus must have unique IDs assigned. If two devices have the same ID, neither will work properly because both devices will try to act on commands destined for that ID. This also applies to the SCSI controllers participating on the bus. It is recommended that the controller cards be assigned IDs 6 and 7 in a two-node cluster.

The ID numbers for controller cards can be set using the controller's setup program. See the controller documentation for instructions on how to enter the setup utility.

Setting ID numbers on SCSI disks is usually accomplished using DIP switches. Again, because each device is unique in configuration, see the documentation that comes with the device for instructions on how to change the ID.

Bus Length

Each controller has a limit as to the length of the SCSI bus. If this length is exceeded, signals could be lost, and as a result, the cluster will fail over repeatedly or not work at all.

The maximum length for most SCSI controllers is 12 meters for Ultra2 buses. To find out the maximum cable length of the bus the cluster uses, refer to the documentation that comes with the controller.

Fibre Channel

Three general areas could cause a Fibre Channel bus to fail: the adapter, the cabling, and any connectivity devices between them (such as hubs and switches).

Host Bus Adapter (HBA) Failure

If the failure of a host bus adapter occurs, only the computer that the adapter resides in will be affected. Due to the nature of fiber communications, there is no interruption in service on other nodes. If the node owned the cluster group with the failed adapter, it will fail over to a working node.

To resolve this issue, simply replace the adapter with an identical controller. Once the controller is installed and verified to be functioning, it will resume activity within the cluster.

Fiber Cable Failure

Depending on the topology being used, cable failures can affect a single node, a group of nodes, or the whole fiber trunk. If a star topology is being used, a cable failure will affect only the devices on each end of the failed cable. For example, if a cable fails between the hub and controller, only that controller is affected. Other nodes on the bus will continue to function. However, if the cable between a shared resource and hub fails, all nodes will lose communication to that shared disk.

Remedying this situation simply involves replacing the faulty cable. If fiber-optic cable is in use, care must be observed so that no fractures occur during cable replacement.

Fiber Hub/Switch Failures

The failure of a fiber hub or switch will result in all devices connected to it losing connection with each other—that is, the hub/switch is a single point of failure (SPOF)—unless some form of fiber mirroring is in place. In the case of a cluster, all nodes connected to the failed hub will lose contact with the shared disk, and the shared resource will go offline. The hub must be replaced or an alternate solution implemented before the shared resource can be brought back online.

Troubleshooting the Quorum Resource/Shared Disk

The Quorum resource is an integral part of the Cluster Service. Because the Quorum resource is used to determine the cluster configuration at any given moment, failure of the Quorum resource will prevent the Cluster Service from starting. If a shared disk fails, it will affect only the resources that depend on that shared disk (that is, cluster items that are dependent on the failed disk).

Complete Quorum Resource Failure

If the Quorum resource fails, Cluster Service will not start. To remedy this, you can start the cluster service by bypassing the Quorum resource. To do so, follow these steps:

1. Shut down all cluster nodes but one.

2. Stop the Cluster Service on the remaining node.

3. Open the Services applet in Control Panel and enter the **-fixquorum** parameter in the Cluster Service Startup Parameters field. Instead of using the Services icon, you can enter **net start clussvc -fixquorum** at the command prompt.

4. Start the Cluster Service. Open Cluster Administrator and modify the cluster's properties to designate a new Quorum resource.

5. Stop and restart the Cluster Service. This clears the parameter previously passed to the service.

6. Start all nodes.

Be sure you know how to pass startup parameters to the Cluster Service by using the Services applet in Control Panel. Also, remember that once parameters are entered, they are removed once the service is stopped and restarted. There is no need to remove them manually.

Corrupt Quorum Disk or Quorum Log

When the cluster service detects a corrupt Quorum Log, it will attempt to repair it automatically. This is indicated by an entry in the Event Log. If Cluster Service cannot repair the log automatically, the service will not start and the log will have to be reset or repaired manually. Also, if Cluster Service fails to detect a corrupt quorum, an ERROR_CLUSTERLOG_CORRUPT message will appear in the Cluster Log file.

You can attempt to repair a corrupt Quorum Log by following these steps:

1. From the command prompt, switch to the Cluster directory and type "clussvc -debug -resetquorumlog".

Note: Using the –resetquorumlog startup parameter, Cluster Service will attempt to create a new log file based on the configuration information stored in the cluster's Registry hive.

2. Stop and restart Cluster Service using the **net start** command. If the log file cannot be reset, start Cluster Service using the **-noquorumlogging** parameter.

3. Start the Cluster Service on one node with the **-noquorumlogging** parameter entered in the Cluster Service startup parameters (see Figure 12.1).

4. Run **chkdsk** on the Quorum disk. If **chkdsk** finds errors, elect to repair them. If no errors are found, delete the quolog.log file and any temporary files located in the MSCS directory on the Quorum disk.

5. Stop and restart the Cluster Service on the one node.

Once you delete the quolog.log file, any configuration changes that were in the log and not communicated to all nodes will be lost. However, because the log is corrupt, that information is irretrievable from the log, and this is the only course of action to take.

Shared Disk Does Not Come Online

Once a disk is part of a cluster, any physical configuration changes applied to the disk can have an adverse effect on the Cluster Service.

For example, suppose an administrator determines that the partitions as defined on a shared application disk are not sufficient. Therefore, he backs up the disk, repartitions it, and restores the data. As a result of merging two partitions into one, a drive letter assignment has changed. Once the administrator restarts one node to apply the change, Cluster Service will not start because a dependent disk (the deleted partition) cannot be found. The preventive measure to take would be to remove the resource from the cluster group, make the configuration changes, and add the resource back to the group once the changes have been successfully made. After the changes have been successfully applied, all nodes must be restarted to obtain the latest disk configuration.

This also applies to drive letters on shared disks. All nodes must have the same drive letter assignments for a shared disk (that is, Node 1 must assign the E: drive to the same disk that Node 2 assigns the E: drive). If you need to change a drive

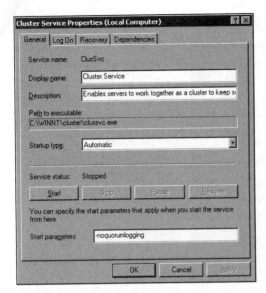

Figure 12.1 The **-noquorumlogging** startup parameter.

letter assignment, remove the resource from the cluster, make the drive letter change, add the resource back to the cluster, and restart all nodes to reflect the change.

If changes to shared disk configurations must be done, remove the resource from the cluster before making any changes. Once the changes have been made, add the disk back to the cluster and restart all nodes to reflect the changes.

Groups and Resources

This section describes some of the common problems that arise involving cluster resources and groups, and the various steps to troubleshoot these problems.

Resources

When a resource fails, Cluster Service should attempt to bring it back online. If a resource fails but is not brought back online, check the following:

➤ Does the resource have any dependencies, and are they properly configured?

➤ Is a dependent resource offline?

➤ Has the resource reached its maximum threshold? (Recall that the threshold defines how many times Cluster Service will attempt to fail the resource over.)

➤ From the Properties dialog box for the failed resource, make sure the Do Not Restart checkbox is cleared (see Figure 12.2).

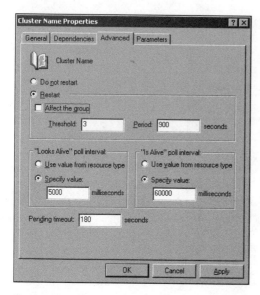

Figure 12.2 A cluster resource's Properties dialog box.

Groups

If you are unable to manually move a cluster group to the second node or if the group does not automatically fail over, check the following:

➤ Is the second node in the cluster designated as a possible owner for the group? If the second node is not designated as a possible owner, it cannot own the group, and therefore failover will not occur.

➤ Is automatic failback configured for the group? Is the current owner set as the preferred owner for the group? If the preferred owner is online, failback will occur as soon as the resource fails over.

➤ Are the resources in the group properly configured? Make sure the Restart and Affect The Group options are selected in the Properties dialog box for the resource (see Figure 12.3).

If a cluster group fails over to the second node in the cluster but does not fail back to the original node, check the following:

➤ Is the Prevent Failback option selected? If so, clear it from the group's Properties dialog box (see Figure 12.4).

➤ Is the original node configured as the preferred owner? If the node is not configured as the preferred owner for the group, failback will not occur.

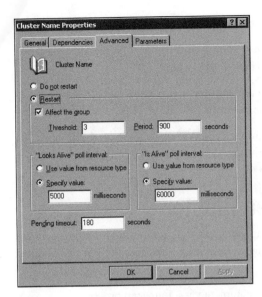

Figure 12.3 The Restart and Affect The Group options in the cluster resource Properties dialog box.

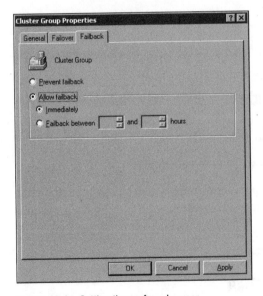

Figure 12.4 Setting the preferred owner.

If a cluster group fails and does not come back online, check the following:

➤ Is the node the group has been running on offline? If so, make sure the second node is listed as a possible owner for the group.

➤ Has the maximum threshold and failover period been met? If so, the group will have to be brought online manually.

➤ Has a static entry been configured in the WINS database for the group? If so, when the group fails over to the second node, it will be unable to register the network name and the group will fail to come online.

Repairing a Failed Cluster

It is possible to experience a complete cluster failure, meaning that both cluster nodes as well as the cluster disk fail. This section describes the steps to perform when repairing a failed cluster.

Repairing a cluster that has failed completely is a four-step process:

1. Restore the first node.

2. Restore the cluster disk.

3. Restore the second cluster node.

4. Test the repaired cluster.

Restoring the First Node

The first step in restoring a cluster that has failed completely is to perform a restore of the first node. To do so, follow these steps:

1. Install a new copy of Windows 2000 Advanced Server on the first node.

2. Once the installation is complete, restore the system and boot partition, the system state data, and any other information.

3. Once the information has been restored from backup, restart the cluster node and proceed to restore the cluster disk.

Restoring the Cluster Disk

Once the first node has been repaired, you can restore the cluster disk. Restoring the cluster disk entails restoring the disk signature file. This file contains information necessary to identify and mount volumes. Obviously, if a disk is replaced, the disk with the original disk signature file will have to be restored. Here are the steps to restore the cluster disk:

1. To restore the disk signature file, use the Dumpcfg.exe utility. This resource kit utility can be used to extract the signature file from the Registry and restore it to a new disk.

2. Stop the Cluster Service.

3. Restore the cluster system state data from backup. The contents of the Quorum disk are placed into a temporary directory.

4. Use the Clusrest.exe utility to restore the contents of the temporary directory to the node's registry.

5. Restart the Cluster Service.

Restoring the Second Node

Once the cluster disk has been restored and Cluster Service has successfully started on the first node, the second node can then be restored. The steps to restore the second node are identical to the steps used to restore the first node—the only difference is that the cluster disk does not have to be restored a second time.

Testing

The final step in repairing a failed cluster is to test it to ensure that the repair was successful. Here are the steps to follow:

➤ Verify that the cluster resources are online.

➤ Verify that the different cluster groups and resources can successfully fail over to the second cluster node.

➤ If preferred owners are configured, verify that the groups and resources are failing back.

Client Communication

Clients communicate with the cluster and access the cluster resources using TCP/IP. To ensure that clients can access the cluster, it is therefore important that TCP/IP be configured correctly. Most issues that arise with client-to-cluster communication are related to TCP/IP. This section covers some of the common communication problems that can occur and the steps to take to troubleshoot these problems.

Recall from Chapter 10 that a *virtual server* is the equivalent of a cluster resource group and contains a Network Name resource and an IP Address resource. If a client cannot connect to a virtual server, follow these steps to troubleshoot the problem:

1. Ping the IP address assigned to the virtual server to test for network connectivity between the client and the cluster.

2. Ping the network name assigned to the virtual server to test for network connectivity as well as name resolution.

3. If the virtual server contains a File Share resource, try to connect to it using the **Net Use** command.

4. Use the **Ipconfig /all** command to verify that TCP/IP is properly configured for all network adapters.

In the event of a failover, clients are temporarily disconnected from the cluster. If a group fails over to the second node, clients should be able to reconnect to the group once it has been restarted. If clients cannot connect to a group that has failed over, check the following to help determine the problem:

➤ If the client is attempting to reconnect to a resource, is the resource online?

➤ Is the physical connection between the client and the cluster available?

➤ Is the physical connection between the cluster nodes available?

 How Cluster Service deals with a network failure depends on how the networks have been configured for cluster use. If the public network is configured for mixed use, cluster nodes will be able to maintain communication in the event that the private network becomes unavailable.

Once a cluster resource is brought online, it should be accessible to clients. Check the following if clients cannot access a cluster resource:

➤ Are both the IP Address resource and the Network Name resource for the group to which the resource belongs online?

➤ Are the dependencies configured correctly for the resource? The resource should be dependent on either the IP Address resource or the Network Name resource.

➤ Is the client configured with some form of name resolution (DNS or WINS)? The client needs to be configured with name resolution to map the network name of the group to an IP address.

 A lack of communication between clients and a cluster can usually be attributed to a misconfiguration in TCP/IP parameters or a failed network connection.

Node-to-Node Communication

Node-to-node communication is necessary for the cluster to monitor the status of each node and the cluster resources. Network Monitor is one of the best tools that can be used to troubleshoot communication problems between cluster nodes. Using Network Monitor to capture network traffic, you can verify that regular heartbeat messages are being sent between cluster nodes. Once a capture of network traffic has been done, verify that Cluster Service is using UDP port 3343 to send and receive heartbeat messages.

When troubleshooting node-to-node communication, use Network Monitor to verify that RPC communication is occurring between nodes. Cluster Service uses RPCs to make calls on other nodes and monitor the status of cluster resources (refer to Chapter 7 for more information on using Network Monitor to monitoring node communication).

Practice Questions

Question 1

Place the following steps in the order they would occur when a cluster is being repaired:

Restore the second node.

Use the Dumpcfg.exe utility to restore the signature file.

Restore the first node.

Test the restore.

Use the Clusres.exe utility to restore the Quorum disk.

The correct answer is:

Restore the first node.

Use the Dumpcfg.exe utility to restore the signature file.

Use the Clusrest.exe utility to restore the Quorum disk.

Restore the second node.

Test the restore.

Question 2

You want to verify that regular heartbeat messages are being sent and received among members of the cluster. What tool allows you to capture and analyze node-to-node traffic?

- ○ a. Performance Monitor
- ○ b. System Information
- ○ c. Ping
- ○ d. Network Monitor

The correct answer is d. Network Monitor, which comes with Windows 2000, allows you to capture and analyze network traffic. Answer a is incorrect because Performance Monitor allows you to monitor different system components and services. Answer b is incorrect because System Information can be used to determine device conflicts. Answer c is incorrect because the ping utility allows you to test network connectivity, but it doesn't allow you to capture network traffic.

Question 3

The Quorum resource disk fails and Cluster Service will not start. You need to redesignate the Quorum resource. How can you gain access to the cluster and redesignate the Quorum disk if Cluster Service fails to start?

- ○ a. Restart one of the cluster nodes to restart Cluster Service.
- ○ b. Open the Services icon in the Control Panel and restart Cluster Service.
- ○ c. Use the **-fixquorum** startup option to bypass the Quorum resource and start Cluster Service.
- ○ d. Use the **-noquorum** startup option to bypass the Quorum resource and start Cluster Service.

The correct answer is c. Open the Services icon in the Control Panel and enter the -fixquorum parameter in the Cluster Service startup parameters. This allows you to bypass the Quorum resource to start Cluster Service. Answer a is incorrect because if the Quorum disk has failed, restarting a cluster node will not remedy the problem. Answer b is incorrect because if the Quorum disk has failed, Cluster Service will not be able to start unless the startup parameters are changed. Answer d is incorrect because there is no such startup parameter for Cluster Service.

Question 4

> You create a file share resource called FileShare1, which is a member of the cluster group MyGroup1. FileShare1 is dependent on the Network Name resource and the Physical Disk resource. The file share fails but MyGroup1 does not fail over to the second node. What could be a possible cause of this problem?
>
> ○ a. The dependencies are configured incorrectly.
>
> ○ b. Under the properties of FileShare1, the Affect The Group checkbox is selected.
>
> ○ c. Under the properties of MyGroup1, the Affect The Group checkbox is selected.
>
> ○ d. Under the properties of FileShare1, the Affect The Group checkbox is not selected.

The correct answer is d. If the Affect The Group option is not selected under the properties for the resource, the group will not fail over if the resource fails. Answer a is incorrect because a file share must be dependent on the Network Name resource and the Physical Disk resource. Answer b is incorrect because if the Affect The Group option is checked, the group should fail over when the resource fails. Answer c is incorrect because the Affect The Group option is configured for resources, not groups.

Question 5

Cluster Service fails to start because the Quorum Log is corrupt. You do not have a backup of the Quorum Log file. You start the Cluster Service with the **-noquorumlogging** option and run **chkdsk** on the Quorum disk. Chkdsk finds no errors. What is the next step?

○ a. Delete the quorum.log file and re-create the log using the **-fixquorum** option.

○ b. Delete the quolog.log file and re-create the log using the **-fixquorum** option.

○ c. Delete the quorum.log file and re-create the log using the **-resetquorumlog** option.

○ d. Delete the quolog.log file and re-create the log using the **-resetquorumlog** option.

The correct answer is d. Deleting the quolog.log file still prevents the cluster from starting. Starting the service with the **-resetquorumlog** option rebuilds the quolog.log file from entries in the cluster hive. Answers a and c are incorrect because there is no such file as the quorum.log. Answer b is incorrect because the **-fixquorum** parameter is used to start the Cluster Service when the Quorum disk has failed.

Question 6

You suspect a fault in the shared SCSI bus. Which of the following items can contribute to a SCSI bus failure? [Check all correct answers]

❑ a. Active termination is used.

❑ b. SCSI controllers are set to SCSI ID 7.

❑ c. Two different brands of controllers are used.

❑ d. Cluster Service failed to start on one node.

The correct answers are b and c. All SCSI devices need unique IDs if they are on the same bus. This includes SCSI controller cards. If two different brands of controller cards are used, the commands used by each can vary, thus causing unpredictable results. Answer a is incorrect because active termination is the method recommended by Microsoft to be used in a cluster. Answer d is incorrect because Cluster Service failing to start has no bearing on the SCSI bus.

Question 7

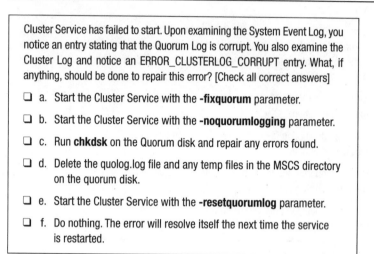

Cluster Service has failed to start. Upon examining the System Event Log, you notice an entry stating that the Quorum Log is corrupt. You also examine the Cluster Log and notice an ERROR_CLUSTERLOG_CORRUPT entry. What, if anything, should be done to repair this error? [Check all correct answers]

- ❑ a. Start the Cluster Service with the **-fixquorum** parameter.
- ❑ b. Start the Cluster Service with the **-noquorumlogging** parameter.
- ❑ c. Run **chkdsk** on the Quorum disk and repair any errors found.
- ❑ d. Delete the quolog.log file and any temp files in the MSCS directory on the quorum disk.
- ❑ e. Start the Cluster Service with the **-resetquorumlog** parameter.
- ❑ f. Do nothing. The error will resolve itself the next time the service is restarted.

The correct answers are b, c, d, and e. To repair a corrupt Cluster Log, start the service with the **-noquorumlogging** parameter, run **chkdsk** against the Quorum disk, and repair any errors found. Then restart the Cluster Service. If the service still fails to start, start the service with the **-noquorumlogging** parameter again and then delete the quolog.log file and any temp files in the MSCS directory on the Quorum disk. Finally, stop the service and start it with the **-resetquorumlog** parameter to re-create the quolog.log file from entries in the cluster hive. Answer a is incorrect because the **-fixquorum** parameter is used to start the Cluster Service with no Quorum resource to allow a new one to be configured. Answer f is incorrect because, by doing nothing, the corrupt quolog.log file will prevent the cluster service from starting.

Question 8

A node in the cluster has failed. This node was the current owner of the group MyGroup1, and the group and its resources have not failed over to the other node. When you open Cluster Administrator, it states that the cluster group is offline. You attempt to start the resource manually with no success. What is a possible cause for this?

○ a. The Prevent Failover checkbox has been enabled for this group.

○ b. The second node isn't specified as a possible owner.

○ c. A dependent resource in another group has failed to come online.

○ d. The Prevent Failback checkbox has been enabled for this group.

The correct answer is b. If the second node is not specified as a possible owner, the group will not fail over. Answer a is incorrect because there is no Prevent Failover option for a group. Answer c is incorrect because a resource within another group would have no bearing on MyGroup1 not failing over. Answer d is incorrect because the Prevent Failback option still allows a group to fail over; the group will not fail back when the original node comes back online.

Question 9

A node in the cluster has failed. This node was the current owner of MyGroup1. The group and its resources fail over to the second cluster node. The first node comes back online. You open Cluster Administrator and see that MyGroup1 is still owned by the second node. What could be preventing the group from failing back to the original node? [Check all correct answers]

❑ a. The first node is not specified as a possible owner.

❑ b. The first node is not specified as the preferred owner for the group.

❑ c. The Prevent Failback option is checked under the properties for MyGroup1.

❑ d. A dependent resource in another group has failed to come online.

The correct answers are b and c. If the first node is not specified as a preferred owner for the group, it will not fail back to the original node when it comes back online. If the Prevent Failback option is selected for the group, the group will not fail back. Answer a is incorrect because the first node was the original owner and therefore would be a possible owner for the group. Answer d is incorrect because a resource within another group would have no bearing on the group's ability to fail back.

Question 10

The quolog.log file is corrupt. Place the following steps needed to fix this problem in order of execution:

Delete the quolog.log file on the Quorum disk and any temp files present in the MSCS directory.

Stop the Cluster Service on all nodes.

Run **chkdsk** against the Quorum disk and repair any errors found.

Restart the Cluster Service on all nodes.

Start the Cluster Service with the **-noquorumlogging** parameter.

Start the Cluster Service with the **-resetquorumlog** parameter.

The correct answer is:

Stop the Cluster Service on all nodes.

Start the Cluster Service with the -**noquorumlogging** parameter.

Run **chkdsk** against the Quorum disk and repair any errors found.

Delete the quolog.log file on the Quorum disk and any temp files present in the MSCS directory.

Start the Cluster Service with the -**resetquorumlog** parameter.

Restart the Cluster Service on all nodes.

Stop the Cluster Service on both nodes and start the Cluster Service on one node with the -**noquorumlogging** parameter to allow access to the Quorum disk. Run chkdsk on the Quorum disk to repair errors in the quolog.log file. If no errors are detected by **chkdsk**, you should delete the quolog.log file and any temp files and then use the -**resetquorumlog** parameter to re-create the log based on entries in the cluster's Registry hive. Restart Cluster Service on both nodes.

Need to Know More?

Libertone, David. *Windows 2000 Cluster Server Guidebook: A Guide to Creating and Managing a Cluster, Second Edition.* Prentice Hall, Upper Saddle River, NJ, 2000. ISBN 0130284696. This book provides detailed information on problems that can occur within a cluster environment and some possible solutions to those problems.

Search TechNet on the Internet at **www.microsoft.com/technet/ default.asp** or the TechNet CD for more information on cluster troubleshooting.

For more information on cluster troubleshooting, use the Microsoft Windows 2000 Help. Click Start, and then choose Help. Under the list of contents, choose Windows Clustering.

Disaster Recovery

Terms you'll need to understand:

✓ Full backup

✓ Incremental backup

✓ Differential backup

✓ Copy backup

✓ Restore

✓ Emergency Repair Disk

Techniques you'll need to master:

✓ Planning for disaster and recovery

✓ Using the Windows 2000 Backup program to back up files

✓ Using the Windows 2000 Backup program to restore files

✓ Creating an Emergency Repair Disk

✓ Backing up and restoring the Quorum

This chapter presents you with information on providing a final resolution for data loss or corruption. Disaster recovery is important on all computer systems, even those that employ fault-tolerant devices and configurations.

When it comes to lost or corrupted data, no company is exempt. Any company can lose valuable files, and the company may have to close if the lost data is so important that it causes loss of business.

Disaster Planning

Because data can be lost or corrupted by various means, it is very important for most companies to devise a strategy for recovering from data loss.

Most companies manage their disaster recovery by performing a backup of all data or any data that has changed since the last backup. This allows company administrators to recover from data loss at any time and can prevent any downtime due to data loss.

Performing a daily backup of data can help prevent data loss because you can restore the files that are lost or corrupted. However, this plan does not allow you to recover from natural disaster. In the case of a natural disaster, such as a fire, earthquake, or flood, the backup store of data is worthless if the physical hardware from which the backup was made is no longer usable. Therefore, some companies have a spare server that is identical to the one in use but is stored a distant facility, such as a branch office.

If a natural disaster occurs, business can resume from the branch office when all the data is restored to the duplicate server hardware. This can prevent a company from having to close, which is extremely important, especially if there is an Internet presence that the company hosts internally.

To plan for a disaster, the administrator needs to determine how many days of data can be lost without the company feeling severe repercussions. This timeframe can determine how often data backups must be performed. The administrator must also determine how long the server can be offline for data to be restored when data loss occurs as well as how long the server can be offline while data files are being backed up. Once these decisions are made, the administrator can then determine which backup strategy is the best for the company.

Backup Strategies

When backing up data, a company has a few different ways to back the data up, depending on time requirements during the backup or restore process. When a company is planning its backup and restore strategies, it must decide whether it wants a quick backup and slower restore or a slower backup and faster restore. This decision then determines which backup type is most beneficial to the company.

Full Backup

A full backup is performed by smaller organizations that have less data to back up or larger corporations that can afford faster backup equipment. A full backup consists of copying all files to a backup device. When the full backup is done, each file backed up will have its Archive attribute turned off.

Note: The Archive attribute is a setting on each file that shows whether the file has been modified. When a file is created or modified, the Archive attribute is turned on. When some backup types are performed, files with the Archive attribute are backed up and then the attribute is turned back off. This allows only changed and new files to be backed up.

Incremental Backup

An incremental backup backs up files that have changed since they were last backed up or those with the Archive attribute turned on. Once a file is backed up, its Archive attribute is turned off, so it will not be backed up again unless it is changed or a full backup is performed.

Differential Backup

A differential backup is almost the same as an incremental backup, except when a file is backed up, the Archive attribute is not turned off. Leaving the Archive attribute on means that the file will be backed up again, regardless of whether the file has changed after the last differential backup. This basically means that all files that have changed since the last full backup will be backed up during the differential backup.

Copy Backup

A copy backup is where all files are backed up, but the Archive attribute is not changed. A copy backup is the same as a full backup, but it does not change the Archive attribute. This lets the administrator back up all files without causing a change in the regular backup schedule.

Backup Schedule

A company's backup schedule depends on whether the backup time or restore time is more important. For most companies, if time permits, a full backup should be performed every night. This means that the backup could take quite awhile and is dependent on the amount of data to be backed up.

If there are five files, for example, the backup will take the time required to read all five files and then write them to the backup media every day. Of course, a company will have more than five files, but for the interests of this chapter, we will keep the examples simple.

If a company needs to have backups performed in a short period of time each night, it should implement an incremental backup schedule. The first day of the week, usually Sunday, a full backup is performed. Because the company data is not usually in use, the backup can be performed during the day and not cause any downtime by requiring files to be closed for backup. Also, with large amounts of data, a longer period of time is required to perform a full backup of all files. This usually means that a full backup can only be done on the weekend.

Once the full backup is performed, all Archive attributes are turned off. Any files changed on Monday will have the Archive attributes turned back on, as shown in Figure 13.1. File 2 and file 5 have been modified in some manner. This means that because their Archive attributes have been turned on, these files will be backed up during the Monday night backup and their Archive attributes will be turned back off when they are backed up. Files 1, 3, and 4 will not be backed up because their Archive attributes are still turned off. There is no reason to back them up because they were backed up during the full backup on Sunday night and have not changed at all. The Archive attributes on files 1, 3, and 4 will not be changed after the backup.

On Tuesday, files 3 and 5 are modified, which turns on their Archive attributes. During the Tuesday night backup, only files 3 and 5 are backed up and then their Archive attributes are turned off again. This continues throughout the week, as shown in Figure 13.1. You can see that the backup time will vary depending on the number of files that have been modified and the sizes of the changed files.

Because the amount of time for the backup will vary each night, the number of backup media will also vary each night. Although the amount of time varies, it is still less than the time required for a differential backup during the span of a week.

When a differential backup is performed, the files that have the Archive attribute turned on are backed up, but the attribute is not turned off when the files are backed up. This is shown in Figure 13.2.

With the same files and the days on which they are changed as before, the backup schedule is performed each night starting on Sunday with a full backup, which turns the Archive attributes off on all files.

On Monday, files 2 and 5 are changed, which means they will be backed up on Monday night. However, because their Archive attributes are not turned off, these files will continue to be backed up every night for the rest of the week. This shows that the time required to back up the files and the number of media required to write the files will increase.

Incremental Backup
Day of the Week

	Sunday			Monday			Tuesday		
	Before	Copied	After	Before	Copied	After	Before	Copied	After
File 1		X							
File 2		X		√	X				
File 3		X					√	X	
File 4		X							
File 5		X		√	X		√	X	

	Wednesday			Thursday			Friday		
	Before	Copied	After	Before	Copied	After	Before	Copied	After
File 1				√	X				
File 2	√	X		√	X		√	X	
File 3				√	X		√	X	
File 4	√	X					√	X	
File 5	√	X		√	X				

√ — denotes that the archive attribute is turned on
Before — is the status of the archive attribute before the backup occurs
Copied — will have an "X" if the file was included in the backup
After — is the staus of the archive attribute before the backup occurs

Figure 13.1 Incremental backup schedule.

Differential Backup
Day of the Week

	Sunday			Monday			Tuesday		
	Before	Copied	After	Before	Copied	After	Before	Copied	After
File 1		X							
File 2		X		√	X	√	√	X	√
File 3		X					√	X	√
File 4		X							
File 5		X		√	X	√	√	X	√

	Wednesday			Thursday			Friday		
	Before	Copied	After	Before	Copied	After	Before	Copied	After
File 1				√	X	√	√	X	√
File 2	√	X	√	√	X	√	√	X	√
File 3	√	X	√	√	X	√	√	X	√
File 4	√	X	√	√	X	√	√	X	√
File 5	√	X	√	√	X	√	√	X	√

√ — denotes that the archive attribute is turned on
Before — is the status of the archive attribute before the backup occurs
Copied — will have an "X" if the file was included in the backup
After — is the staus of the archive attribute before the backup occurs

Figure 13.2 Differential backup schedule.

On Tuesday, files 3 and 5 are modified, but because the Archive attribute on file 5 is already on, the file is again ready to be backed up. Therefore, on Tuesday night, files 2, 3, and 5 are backed up during the differential backup. For the rest of the week then, files 2, 3 and 5 are backed up.

Looking at Figure 13.2, you can see that each day more and more files are backed up. This requires more time to back up the files and also more backup media. By the end of the week, the backups are almost equal to the time and media required to perform a full backup. Figure 13.3 shows that as the week goes on, the differential backup requires more and more time and media, whereas the incremental backup uses a minimal amount of time and media, depending on the day.

Depending on your requirements for backing up your organization's data, you should choose incremental backups if you need to take a short amount of time to perform the backups.

If a full backup takes too long and the time to restore files is not an issue, then differential backups should be performed.

Backup Log

Backup logs contain logged information about backups. A log will contain information such as when a backup was performed, how long it took, what backup media were used, the number of files backed up, which files were backed up, and, for the important part of the log, which files were not backed up or resulted in some type of error.

It is very important to keep the backup logs. You should even print them out to keep a hard-copy record of all backups. Keeping a record of your backups can allow you to determine when a file was last backed up and possibly why it was not backed up since then, if there were problems.

Restoring Data

Once data files are lost or corrupted, they need to be copied from the backup media back to the source location so that the data can be accessed again. Just copying files from the backup media back to the source location is not the means by which to restore all files or even some files of a backup. Because some files are part of the operating system and also part of programs, special care must be given to the restore so that the operating system or program can function again. Depending on the type of backup performed and the files to be restored, the restore process can vary.

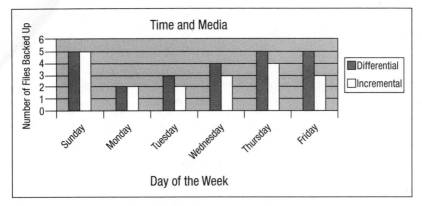

Figure 13.3 Time and media differences in backup types.

Full Restore

When a full backup is performed every night, a full restore can be done to recover from a complete loss of data. If a whole system needs to be replicated, then a full backup should be done on the source system and a full restore done on the target system. If the system crashes the day after a full backup, a full restore needs to be done to bring it back to its original state.

Doing a full restore involves taking all the files that were backed up during a full backup and copying them back to the original system or another system. In most cases, this will involve restoring the operating system as well.

Full restores are almost always done when a system crash has occurred and all files are lost. A system crash could result from failed hardware, such as a failed hard disk on which the files resided. A crash could also result from a computer virus that has corrupted the operating system and/or the allocation table of the hard disk. There are many other ways in which corruption or data loss can occur.

No matter how the data was lost or corrupted, doing a full restore is usually the quickest way to get the data back and the system online again. Doing a restore from a full backup almost guarantees that all files will be restored to the state they were in when the backup was done.

If a file has been changed between the time the full backup was done and the time of the data loss, all changes made to the file are lost.

Incremental Restore

Restoring from the full backup is a simple process because all files should be present on the full backup. However, if you are performing incremental backups, the process of restoring files changes.

Because an incremental backup backs up only some of the files, the process of restoring all the files is as follows:

1. The last full backup must be restored.

2. Every incremental backup must be restored that was done since the last full backup, in the order in which they were done.

This puts back all the files that were on the system when the full backup was done as well as every changed file since then. Any file that was changed more than once would be overwritten by a later restore of the file from later in the week.

If you look back at Figure 13.1, you'll see that after doing a full restore of Sunday's backup, there are still many changed files throughout the week. After restoring Monday's backup, you will have an updated version of files 2 and 5. But looking on, you would not have the updates that were included in the backup on Wednesday night for files 2 and 5. If any day is skipped by not restoring the incremental backup from that night, you may miss a file that is not backed up again. For example, by restoring all files from every night's backup, but skipping Thursday's backup, you will not have an updated file 1, and file 5 would not be the most up-to-date version.

Therefore, when restoring from an incremental backup, you must restore the full backup and every incremental backup since the full backup to the time of the system crash to recover completely or as close as possible without losing much data.

If a single file or multiple files must be restored, but not the whole system, you should consult the backup logs and determine when the required files were last backed up and restore those files.

For example, if files 2 and 5 from Figure 13.1 needed to be restored, then looking at the chart, you can determine that file 2 should be restored from Friday's backup and file 5 should be restored from Thursday's backup. This example shows how important the backup logs can be when restoring individual files instead of all files. Without the backup log, you would have to restore files 2 and 5 from each backup, starting with the full backup on Sunday and every backup thereafter, which would be time consuming.

Incremental restores require more time. Therefore, if your company wants the backups to take less time and the restores to take longer, an incremental backup is the backup strategy to use.

Differential Restore

Restoring files from a differential backup is a process somewhat similar to restoring from an incremental backup, except the number of tapes required differs.

When you're restoring all files from a differential backup, the process is as follows:

1. Restore the files from the last full backup.

2. Restore the files from the last differential backup.

As this process shows, the differential restore requires only two backup sets to be restored.

Note: A backup set is the collection of files that were backed up during one backup session. A backup set can span multiple backup media types.

For example, if backups are done at a company as shown in Figure 13.2, and the system fails on Friday morning, after the system is repaired, only two backup sets are required to put the system and all the data back in the state they were in before the crash. The two backup sets would be from Sunday night (to restore all the files) and from Thursday night (to update all the changed files since Sunday).

The differential restore requires less time, but the differential backup requires more time as the week progresses. Therefore, if your company does not care about the time it takes to back up a server but wants the server to be restored as quickly as possible, the differential backup type is the best solution.

Trial Restores

Every so often, data that is backed up should be temporarily restored to an alternate location to determine whether the backup is being performed without error.

Sometimes companies back up their file servers on a regular basis only to learn at a later date when a file needs to be restored that no backups have been occurring. The backup media tapes are all blank. There were no errors in any of the backup logs, and all seemed normal; however, the backup hardware had failed and no errors were generated.

Windows 2000 Backup Utility

The Windows 2000 Backup utility is included with Windows 2000 products. It is used for backing up and restoring system and data files on a local or remote system.

To start Windows 2000 Backup, select Start|Programs|Accessories|System Tools|Backup. This will bring up the initial welcome screen, as shown in Figure 13.4.

This screen contains four tabs and three buttons, of which we will be discussing two tabs and all three buttons. The buttons are Backup Wizard, Restore Wizard, and Emergency Repair Disk. The two tabs we will be covering are Backup and Restore.

Note: The Backup and Restore Wizard are available only on Advanced Server.

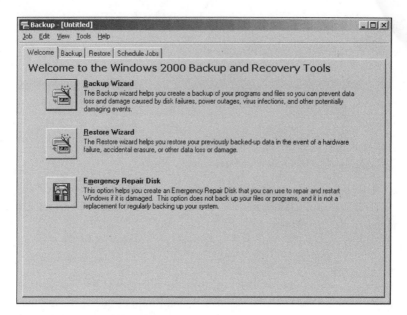

Figure 13.4   The Windows 2000 Backup Welcome screen.

Backup Wizard Button

Once you select the Backup Wizard button from the Welcome screen, you will be presented with another Welcome screen for the Backup Wizard, as shown in Figure 13.5.

After selecting Next, you are presented with the screen shown in Figure 13.6, which allows you to choose whether to back up all files, some files, or the System State data. Once you make a selection, you click Next to continue to the next step.

Figure 13.5   The Windows 2000 Backup Wizard Welcome screen.

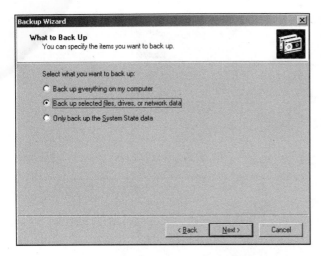

Figure 13.6   The Windows 2000 Backup Wizard options screen.

After selecting to back up all files or the System State data, you are presented with a screen to select the backup media. The System State data includes the Active Directory (if the PC is a domain controller), Windows boot files, Cluster Quorum, COM+ Class Registration database, and Registry and System Volume. The Cluster Quorum backup consists only of the Recovery Log and the checkpoints. The option to back up all files will back up the System State data and all other files located on the server.

If you select the option for backing up selected files or drives, you are presented with the screen shown in Figure 13.7, where you can select individual drives or files.

Just as when using Windows Explorer, you can use this screen to look through the list of folders and files. Check the box to the left of files and folders to select the file or folder to be included in the backup. Click Next when all files and folders have been selected and then select the backup media type to copy the selected files and folders to.

Restore Wizard Button

The Restore Wizard button takes you through the steps for restoring backed up files. After selecting the Restore Wizard button, you are shown the Restore Wizard's Welcome screen, which is similar to the Backup Wizard's Welcome screen, shown previously in Figure 13.5.

After clicking Next, you are shown a screen that lists the backup media types and the backup sets available for restoring. Select a backup set to restore and click Next to continue. The next screen shows a summary of what is to be performed. Click Finish to perform the selected restore.

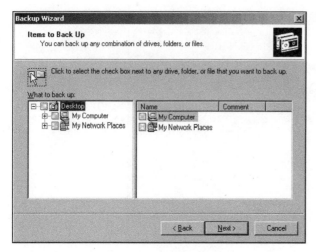

Figure 13.7   The Windows 2000 Backup Wizard file-selection screen.

Emergency Repair Disk Button

Selecting the Emergency Repair Disk button allows you create an Emergency Repair Disk, similar to the Emergency Repair Disk used by Windows NT. After selecting the button, you are presented with the screen shown in Figure 13.8, which prompts you to insert a floppy disk and gives you the option of copying the Registry to the Repair directory on the hard disk.

Insert your disk and select OK to continue the Emergency Repair Disk creation process. The repair diskette will give you the ability to restore a corrupted registry as well as the operating system boot files.

Backup Tab

The Backup tab's function is somewhat the same as the option to back up selected files in the Backup Wizard. This screen is similar to Windows Explorer, as shown in Figure 13.9. It allows you to select files and folders by checking the boxes next to the files and folders to be backed up. Once all files and folders are selected from the necessary drives, the backup media can be selected.

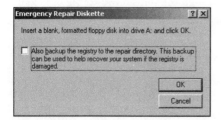

Figure 13.8   The Emergency Repair Disk prompt.

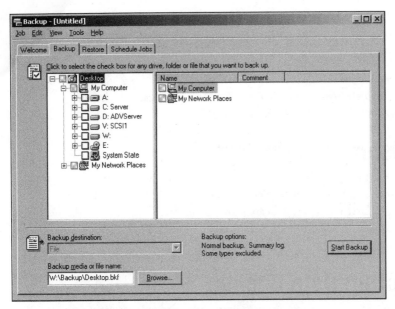

Figure 13.9   The Backup tab of the Windows 2000 Backup utility.

Select the backup media from the Backup Destination drop-down box and give a name to the backup set to be created. Click the Start Backup button when you're finished setting options to begin the backup to the selected media.

Restore Tab

The Restore tab gives the same options as the Restore Wizard button. When you select this tab, you can choose a media type and an available backup set. Then, in the right pane, you can choose the individual folders and files included in the backup set to restore. At the bottom of the window, you can use the drop-down box to specify whether to restore the files to the original location, to an alternate location, or to a single folder. When all choices are set, select the Start Restore button to start copying the files from the backup media to the specified location.

Cluster Data Backup

Once you are familiar with the workings of the Backup utility, backing up the cluster's data files is a simple task. Backing up cluster data is the same as backing up any other type of data, with one exception: The node that owns a resource is the only node that can back up the data for that resource.

For example, if Node A owns Group 1, which contains physical disk W: and a File Share resource, then only Node A can back up the files contained in the file share and the files located on physical disk W:. Node B can back up the data if it owns Group 1. In this example, the only other way for Node B to back up the files in Group 1 is for Node B to be connected to physical disk W: through the administrative share and to back it up as a network drive.

Note: An administrative share is indicated by the drive's letter and a dollar sign. For example, Server1 has drives C, D, and E, which can be connected to using \\Server1\C$, \\Server1\D$, and \\Server1\E$.

Cluster Data Restore

The option to restore cluster files and applications is the same as restoring any other files and applications. Select the files to be restored and leave the destination set to Original. Then you can begin the restore. To restore to a Physical Disk resource from a node, the node must own the Physical Disk resource or be mapped to the administrative share and restored over the network.

Quorum Data Backup

You can back up the Quorum data on a cluster node by selecting the Back Up Everything On My Computer option from the Backup Wizard button or by selecting the Only Back Up System State Data option. This will work from any node, regardless of which node owns the Quorum resource. To correctly back up the Quorum data, you must stop the Cluster Service.

 Do *not* use the option Back Up Selected Files, Drives Or Network Data to back up the Quorum data. The Quorum data will be backed up as it was when the backup was started. Any changes made in the Quorum data during the backup will not be included in the backup.

Backing up the Quorum data on other nodes is not required after backing up the Quorum data on a node, but the data files in the CLUSTER\CLUSDB folder should be backed up from all nodes. The Quorum data is the same for all nodes and only needs to be backed up once, whereas the files in the CLUSTER\CLUSDB folder can be unique to each node.

Quorum Data Restore

The Restore Wizard in the Windows 2000 Backup utility can be used to restore the Quorum data after it has been backed up.

The Restore option in the Backup utility performs the following actions:

1. The Cluster Service is stopped on all nodes.

2. The signature of the Quorum disk is restored to its original signature if the signature has changed (this is important if the Quorum disk has been replaced due to hardware failure). The signature is only modified on the Quorum disk.

3. The Quorum data is restored and the checkpoints are added.

4. The Cluster Service is restarted on the restored node.

The process is continued on the next node where the Cluster Service is already stopped so that the Cluster Service is not stopped on all nodes. The process continues until that node is restored and the Cluster Service is brought back online. This allows you to recover a failed node if the data or system as a whole is corrupted.

Practice Questions

Question 1

Which of the following is the quickest solution for recovering lost or corrupted data?

○ a. RAID 0

○ b. RAID 1

○ c. RAID 5

○ d. Backup

The correct answer is d. A backup is the best solution for recovering lost or corrupted data. If data is lost or corrupted on a RAID volume, it cannot be restored because the data itself is lost or corrupted (which is the trick to this question). RAID 0 has no fault tolerance for any data. Therefore, answer a is incorrect. In a RAID 1 implementation (mirroring), both disks will have the same duplicated corrupted errors or neither will contain the data required. Therefore, answer b is incorrect. RAID 5 cannot recover lost or corrupted data due to the fact that the parity bits are based on the data available, which is corrupted or missing. Therefore, answer a is incorrect.

Question 2

Which of the following are valid backup types? [Check all correct answers]

❏ a. Incremental

❏ b. Total

❏ c. Differential

❏ d. Full

The correct answers are a, c, and d. The valid backup types are full, incremental, differential, and copy. Total is an incorrect backup type. Therefore, answer b is incorrect.

Question 3

> Which attribute is used to show that a file has been changed or modified?
>
> ○ a. Hidden
>
> ○ b. Read-Only
>
> ○ c. Archive
>
> ○ d. System

The correct answer is c. The Archive attribute is used to signify that a file has been modified since the last full backup.

The Hidden attribute is used to hide a file from standard users. Therefore, answer a is incorrect. The Read-Only attribute is used to make a file read-only so that it cannot be changed or deleted. Therefore, answer b is incorrect. The System attribute is used to signify that a file is part of the operating system. Therefore, answer d is incorrect.

Question 4

> Which backup types change the Archive attribute when they finish copying a file? [Check all correct answers]
>
> ❏ a. Full
>
> ❏ b. Differential
>
> ❏ c. Incremental
>
> ❏ d. Copy

The correct answers are a and c. A full backup will copy all files, regardless of their Archive attribute setting. It then turns off the Archive attribute. An incremental backup backs up only the files with the Archive attribute on, but it turns off the attribute when done.

A differential backup backs up all files with the Archive attribute on but does not turn off the attribute when done. Therefore, answer b is incorrect. A copy backup backs up all files, regardless of the state of the archive attribute, and then leaves the attribute in the same state.

Question 5

> If a company performs a full backup on Sunday night and incremental back
> ups every night, with each backup using one tape cartridge, how many
> tapes would be required to restore the system and data if a crash occurs
> Friday before noon?
>
> ○ a. One
>
> ○ b. Two
>
> ○ c. Four
>
> ○ d. Five

The correct answer is d. The restore would require the last full backup and every incremental backup done since the last full backup. This requires the tapes from Sunday, Monday, Tuesday, Wednesday, and Thursday, which means five tapes if all nightly backups are on separate tapes. Therefore, answers a, b, and c are incorrect.

Question 6

> If a company performs a full backup on Sunday night and differential backups
> every night, with each backup using one tape cartridge, how many tapes would
> be required to restore the system and data if a crash occurs Friday before noon?
>
> ○ a. One
>
> ○ b. Two
>
> ○ c. Four
>
> ○ d. Five

The correct answer is b. The restore would require the last full backup and the last differential backup done before the crash. This requires the tapes from Sunday and Thursday, which means two tapes if all nightly backups are on separate tapes. Therefore, answers a, c, and d are incorrect.

Question 7

> Which of the following are included in the System State data? [Check all correct answers]
>
> ❑ a. Registry
>
> ❑ b. Active Directory
>
> ❑ c. Windows boot files
>
> ❑ d. Cluster Quorum

The correct answers are a, b, c, and d. All these items are included in the System State data. Other items included are the COM+ Class Registration database and the System volume.

Question 8

> If there are two nodes in a cluster, which of the following items can be backed up from one node? [Check all correct answers]
>
> ❑ a. The local operating system
>
> ❑ b. The local Registry
>
> ❑ c. All Physical Disk resources owned by the local node
>
> ❑ d. All Physical Disk resources owned by the other node

The correct answers are a, b, c, and d. All local resources can be backedup by the Backup utility and any remote resources that can be connected via a network drive mapping. This allows the local node to back up the resources on a Physical Disk resource on another node if there is a mapped drive, such as an administrative share, through which to access it.

Question 9

> Which two options can be selected to back up the Quorum data? [Check all correct answers]
>
> ❏ a. Back Up Everything On My Computer
>
> ❏ b. Back Up Quorum Data
>
> ❏ c. Back Up W:
>
> ❏ d. Back Up System State Data

The correct answers are a and d. Backing up all files and folders or the System State data will back up the Quorum data. There is no option to back up the Quorum data. Therefore, answer b is incorrect. Also, drive W: might not be the Quorum resource. Therefore, answer c is incorrect.

Question 10

Match the backup types shown in the following figure with their performance descriptions.

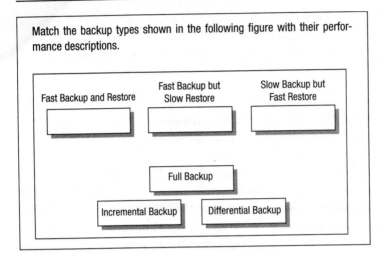

The correct answer is:

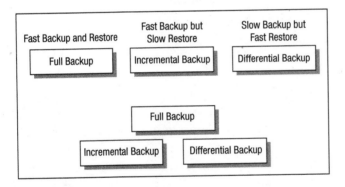

A full backup allows for a slow backup and a fast restore. An incremental backup allows for a fast backup but a slow restore. A differential backup allows for the slowest average backup but a restore faster than an incremental restore.

Need to Know More?

Lee, Richard R. *Windows NT Microsoft Cluster Server.* Osborne/McGraw-Hill, Berkley, CA, 1999. ISBN 0078825008. This book includes information on backing up and restoring cluster data.

Introducing Windows 2000 Advanced Server. Microsoft Corporation, Redmond, WA, 2000. Found at **www.microsoft.com/WINDOWS2000/guide/server/solutions/overview/advanced.asp,** this white paper includes information on the Windows 2000 Backup utility.

Server Cluster Backup and Restore. Microsoft Corporation, Redmond, WA, 2001. Found at **www.microsoft.com/windows2000/en/advanced/help/default.asp?url=/WINDOWS2000/en/advanced/help/sag_mscsusing_9.htm,** this white paper includes information on backing up and restoring data and Quorum resources on a cluster.

Search TechNet on the Internet at **www.microsoft.com/technet/default.asp** or the TechNet CD for more information on backing up and restoring Quorum data.

Sample Test

Question 1

You are installing and configuring the hardware for a two-node cluster. Your supervisor wants you to install four SCSI hard drives in the cluster, two in each node. In Node A, you set the SCSI IDs to 5 and 6. The SCSI adapter in Node A is set at the SCSI ID default of 7. Which of the following SCSI IDs should be used for the other two SCSI hard disks and the SCSI adapter? [Check all correct answers]

❑ a. SCSI hard disk IDs 4 and 5

❑ b. SCSI hard disk IDs 3 and 4

❑ c. SCSI adapter ID 2

❑ d. SCSI adapter ID 7

Question 2

In the following diagram of a SCSI bus, check which device(s) must be terminated.

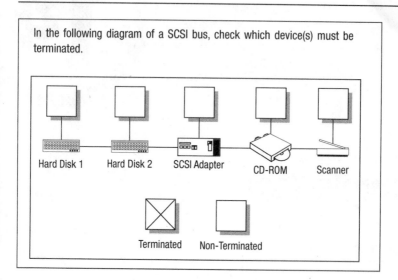

Hard Disk 1   Hard Disk 2   SCSI Adapter   CD-ROM   Scanner

Terminated   Non-Terminated

Question 3

Your supervisor wants you to add an internal CD-ROM drive in Node A of the cluster.

You must fulfill the following requirements that your supervisor specifies:

➤ The clients must be interrupted very little in their daily tasks.

➤ The CD-ROM needs to be installed as soon as possible before the end of the day.

➤ The cluster must function as it did before the CD-ROM was installed.

You perform the following tasks:

➤ You move all groups from Node A to Node B.

➤ You install the CD-ROM on the only SCSI adapter in Node A.

➤ You terminate the CD-ROM and disable the termination on the SCSI adapter.

➤ You power on Node A and move the groups back that were running on Node A originally.

Which of the required tasks have you succeeded in performing?

○ a. You performed one of the required tasks.

○ b. You performed two of the required tasks.

○ c. You performed all the required tasks.

○ d. You performed none of the required tasks.

Question 4

The accounting department is responsible for ordering PCs for all the departments in your company. Recently the accounting department ordered a new PC for a department that has called you for help to get the PC functioning on the network. When you arrive at the department, you look at the PC and realize that the Fibre Channel card installed in the PC has the wrong connector type to connect to the company network. What can you do to resolve this issue in a timely fashion?

○ a. Send the PC back.

○ b. Send the Fibre Channel card back.

○ c. Replace the GBIC on the Fibre Channel card.

○ d. Connect the Fibre Channel cable to the SCSI adapter in the PC.

Question 5

Your supervisor asks you to help propose a solution that will ensure your company's Web servers are almost always available for client access from the Internet. The Web designers who are proposing the design of the Web pages need access to a database for updating order information about the orders clients place on your Web site. Which of the following would you recommend to your supervisor as being an optimal choice to allow for high availability of the company Web site and database?

- ○ a. Two-node cluster
- ○ b. Four-node cluster
- ○ c. *N*-tier cluster
- ○ d. Network Load Balancing

Question 6

You are the administrator for your company's network and manage the company's two-node cluster. On Monday morning, you arrive at work and find that all the groups are running on Node B and that Node A has owner-ship of no groups. After consulting the log files in Event Viewer, you find that Node A failed late on Friday night and has been running fine ever since it rebooted itself. You are concerned that the groups that were running on Node A have not returned to run on Node A. What is the most likely reason for this problem?

- ○ a. The time specified for failback to occur has not been reached.
- ○ b. Failback is not enabled.
- ○ c. Failback Threshold is set too high.
- ○ d. Failback Period is set too low.

Question 7

You are given the task of installing a two-node cluster. Several clusters already exist on the company network. Each cluster supports its own subnet. You are told the cluster you will create will support a new subnet, 130.10.128.0/17, on the company network. The individual nodes must use the last two addresses in the subnet, and the cluster IP address will use the first address in the subnet. Place the appropriate IP addresses where they should go to follow the company standards.

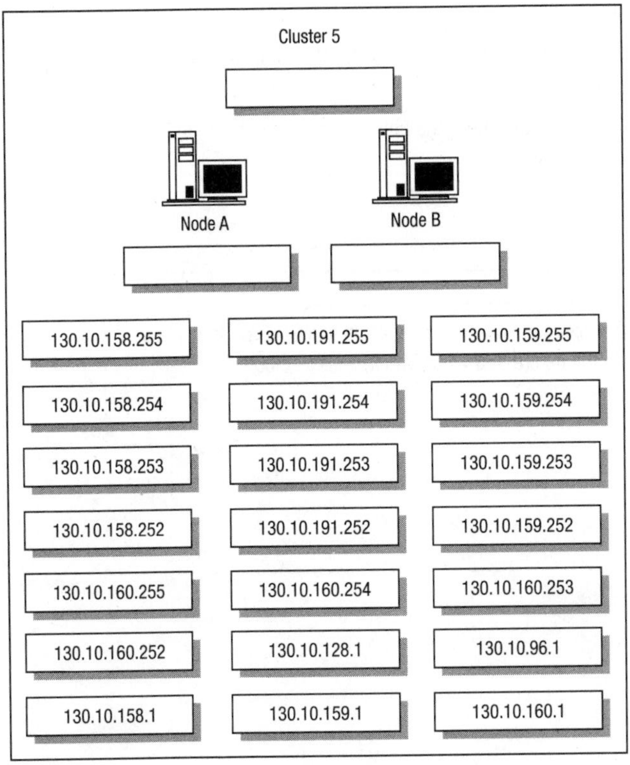

Question 8

You are the network administrator for a company and your primary responsibility is to maintain the cluster. You need to enable a share on the cluster that will be moved to the second node if a failure occurs on the first node. You need to set specific security on the share. Where would you set the share permissions?

○ a. Under the Security tab of the folder's Properties dialog box

○ b. In Cluster Administrator, under the Advanced tab of the share's Properties dialog box

○ c. In Cluster Administrator, under the General tab of the share's Properties dialog box

○ d. In Cluster Administrator, under the Parameters tab of the share's Properties dialog box

Question 9

On a new cluster that has four shared hard disks in a SCSI chain, how many default Disk groups will be created when you install the cluster?

○ a. One

○ b. Two

○ c. Three

○ d. Four

Question 10

Place the required dependencies in the appropriate place for the WINS Service resource.

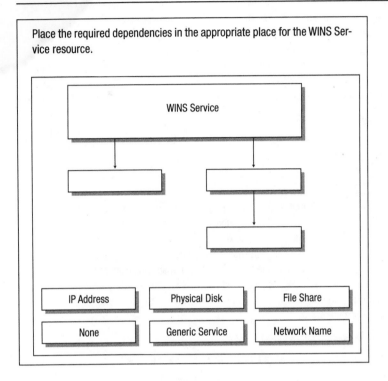

Question 11

Which resources are used to create a virtual server? [Check all correct answers]

❏ a. IP Address resource

❏ b. Physical Disk resource

❏ c. Generic Service resource

❏ d. Network Name resource

Question 12

Your supervisor wants to implement the users' personal drives on the cluster so they will be able to access their personal data even if the server goes offline. He wants a Users top-level shared directory, with access for the administrators to be able to manage the users' directories. Each user should have his own subdirectory under the Users directory that should be shared but not visible when Network Neighborhood is browsed. After creating all the directories, how should you implement the shares to meet your supervisor's requirements?

○ a. Use Explorer to share the directories.

○ b. Set up File Share resources for each directory and subdirectory.

○ c. Set up a File Share resource for the Users directory.

○ d. Set up a File Share resource for the Users directory and select Share And Hide Subdirectories.

Question 13

What action is required to delete a group that contains three resources?

○ a. Remove all resources from the group.

○ b. Take all resources offline.

○ c. Initiate a failure on all resources.

○ d. Nothing.

Question 14

What are possible solutions for optimizing an over-utilized CPU? [Check all correct answers]

❑ a. Adding more RAM

❑ b. Upgrading the existing processor

❑ c. Adding a second processor

❑ d. Adding a second hard disk

Question 15

What action can you take to get better throughput with a SCSI controller card?

○ a. Get a larger SCSI hard disk.

○ b. Upgrade to a higher bit card.

○ c. Get a thicker SCSI connector cable.

○ d. Make all SCSI IDs low numbers.

Question 16

If there is data on a cluster's shared disk in a shared directory, what must be done to back up the data?

○ a. The Cluster Service must be stopped on all nodes.

○ b. The shared resource must be taken offline.

○ c. The group the shared resource is in must be taken offline.

○ d. Nothing.

Question 17

Where should a virtual drive be located to improve operating system performance and memory swapping?

○ a. On the system disk

○ b. On the Quorum disk

○ c. On a separate hard drive and controller from the system disk

○ d. On an external hard drive connected by a parallel port

Question 18

On your cluster server, you have created a virtual server that is no longer needed. What one step can you perform to delete the virtual server?

○ a. Delete the Network Name resource.

○ b. Delete the IP Address resource.

○ c. Delete the Virtual Server resource.

○ d. This cannot be done in one step.

Question 19

Your supervisor has asked you to set up and configure the hardware on a server that will join an existing server to be used for the company's new cluster. Each server has the same hardware, but your supervisor wants you to set up the hardware on the new server to make sure the hardware all works. Each server has two SCSI adapters—SCSI Adapter A having only internal connectors and SCSI Adapter B having only external connectors. The external SCSI shared bus must have more hard drive space than the internal disks used for the operating system and other data. In the following diagram, place the hard disks in the appropriate place to meet the requirements.

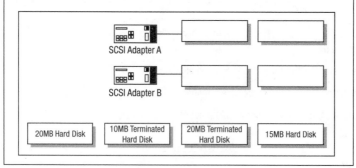

Question 20

Your company has a TCP/IP application that has a problem. When more than 10 people access it at one time, the application fails and causes the Generic Application resource to fail. Your supervisor wants you to change the settings that restart the resource so that a failover is not caused in the nine-hour period that the cluster is accessed during business hours. The most times the resource has failed in any given day is five, but your supervisor wants you to make the setting for six failures in a day, just to be safe. On the following screen, make the appropriate setting changes.

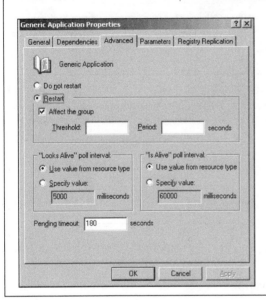

Question 21

You administer your company's cluster server. You have had many users call to complain that they cannot get access to the company's database program, which is on the cluster. You verify that the cluster is online by pinging both nodes and the cluster itself. What could be wrong?

○ a. The users are not logging on correctly.

○ b. The node containing the database program is offline.

○ c. The network is a bottleneck.

○ d. The Database group has failed.

Question 22

Which mechanism allows the nodes in a cluster communicate with one another on a private network?

○ a. LPC

○ b. RPC

○ c. Dfs

○ d. SMTP

Question 23

Your company currently has two Web servers in a cluster configuration. You are planning a rolling upgrade of the nodes to Windows 2000 Advanced Server. Each node is running Windows NT Server 4.0 Enterprise Edition, Service Pack 4, and Microsoft Cluster Service. Hardware-level RAID has been implemented on the shared disks. You want to implement software-level RAID on the local disks in each node. Which of the following methods can be used? [Check all correct answers]

❑ a. Upgrade both nodes to Windows 2000 Advanced Server. Leave the disks as basic disks and create a new stripe set with parity on each node.

❑ b. Before upgrading to Windows 2000 Advanced Server, create a new stripe set with parity and then perform the upgrade.

❑ c. Upgrade both nodes to Windows 2000 Advanced Server. Convert the disks from basic to dynamic. Create a new striped volume with parity on each node.

❑ d. Before upgrading to Windows 2000 Advanced Server, convert the disks from basic to dynamic, create a new striped volume with parity on each node, and then perform the upgrade.

Question 24

You are planning the installation of Cluster Service. Place the following steps in the order they would occur when installing Cluster Service on two systems.

➤ Power on the first node.

➤ Install Cluster Service on the second node.

➤ Power on the shared disk.

➤ Power off the second node.

➤ Install Cluster Service on the first node.

➤ Power on the second node.

Question 25

Your company is running a two-node cluster to increase the availability of a mission-critical application. Node1 of the cluster is better equipped to host the Application resource (AppGroup) and is therefore the preferred node. Node2 is capable of running the application in case Node1 fails, but you want the group to fail back to Node1 when it becomes available. To configure this property for the group using the cluster.exe command-line utility, which option should you use?

○ a. **FailbackType=1**

○ b. **AutoFailbackType=1**

○ c. **Setowners=Node1**

○ d. **Preferrednode=Node1**

Question 26

You add a new resource, App1, to a cluster group named S1. You attempt to initiate failure of the resource to test failover. When App1 fails, S1 does not fail over. You check the dependencies to determine whether they are configured correctly. What are some possible causes as to why S1 does not fail over when App1 fails? [Check all correct answers]

❏ a. Failback is not configured for the group.

❏ b. The second node is not configured as the preferred owner.

❏ c. The Affect The Group option is not enabled.

❏ d. The second node is not listed as a possible owner.

Question 27

You are setting up two systems in a cluster configuration and are trying to determine whether the private disks and the shared disk should be basic or dynamic. You are also trying to determine the file system to implement. The only requirements given to you are that software-level RAID will be implemented on the private disks, and file-level security will be required. Place the following options on each of the disks based on the requirements you have been given and the requirements of Cluster Service.

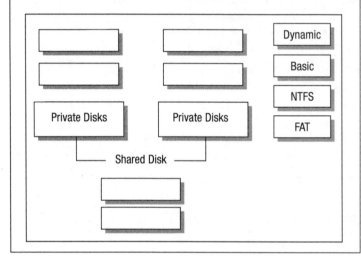

Question 28

> Your company recently migrated all its servers and desktop computers over to Windows 2000. Three domains are configured—a forest root and two child domains. You are in charge of adding two more servers to the structure, which will be configured in a two-node cluster to host the company's Exchange Server application. The two nodes will be added to one of the existing domains. The nodes will be placed on their own subnet, and each is configured with two network cards—one for the private subnet and one for the public network. Based on the recommended configuration and the requirements for Cluster Service, what components need to be in place before you proceed with the installation of Cluster Service on the systems? [Check all correct answers]
>
> ❑ a. A single-domain user account
>
> ❑ b. LMHOSTS
>
> ❑ c. WINS
>
> ❑ d. Service Pack 1
>
> ❑ e. A single static IP address
>
> ❑ f. Two static IP addresses
>
> ❑ g. DNS
>
> ❑ h. Internet Information Server 4.0
>
> ❑ i. Four static IP addresses
>
> ❑ j. Two domain user accounts (one for each node)

Question 29

> You are in the process of restoring your cluster disks. You run the backup program to restore the cluster database and the Quorum Log. The backup program runs successfully, and the System State data is restored. You do notice, however, that the cluster files were not restored to the Quorum disk. How should you proceed?
>
> ○ a. Use the Dumpcfg.exe utility to restore the signature file.
>
> ○ b. Use the Clusrest.exe utility to restore the database and configuration files.
>
> ○ c. Run Clussvc.exe with the **repair** switch to rebuild the Quorum disk.
>
> ○ d. Do nothing but restart Cluster Service.

Question 30

You've set up a two-node cluster. The nodes are configured on a private subnet. Each node is configured with two network cards, and you assign each one a static IP address as shown in the following figure. You soon discover that the IP addresses have been incorrectly assigned. What changes need to be made to correct the problem?

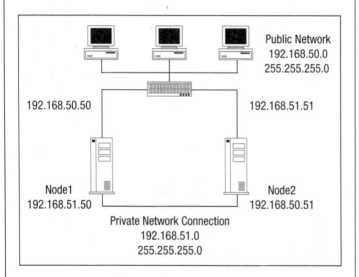

Public Network
192.168.50.0
255.255.255.0

192.168.50.50   192.168.51.51

Node1   Node2
192.168.51.50   192.168.50.51

Private Network Connection
192.168.51.0
255.255.255.0

○ a. Change the private adapter on Node1 to 192.168.50.50.

Change the public adapter on Node1 to 192.168.51.51.

○ b. Change the private adapter on Node2 to 192.168.51.51.

Change the public adapter on Node1 to 192.168.50.51.

○ c. Change the private adapter on Node2 to 192.168.51.51.

Change the public adapter on Node2 to 192.168.50.51.

○ d. Change the private adapter on Node1 to 192.168.50.50.

Change the public adapter on Node2 to 192.168.51.50.

Question 31

Your network administrator plans to implement a cluster and has asked you to install Windows 2000 Advanced Server on two systems. Both of the systems are currently running Windows NT Server 4.0, Service Pack 4, and IIS 4.0. How should you proceed with the installation?

○ a. Insert the Windows 2000 Advanced Server CD and choose the option to upgrade the operating system.

○ b. Connect to a network share containing the distribution files and run Winnt32.exe.

○ c. Install a new copy of Windows 2000 Advanced Server on both systems.

○ d. Upgrade to Windows 2000 Server and then upgrade to Windows 2000 Advanced Server.

Question 32

You successfully install Cluster Service on two nodes. You verify that the nodes are communicating and that clients can access the cluster. During the installation, you configured the private network for cluster communication and the public network for client access. After the installation, you test the capability of Cluster Service to see whether it can recover from a private network failure. You discover that after a private network failure, cluster communication does not fail over to the public network. What is causing the problem?

○ a. The private network should be configured for All Communications.

○ b. Cluster Service is not capable of recovering from a private network failure.

○ c. The public network should be configured for All Communications.

○ d. The public network should be configured for cluster communication only.

Question 33

You want to automate the installation of Windows 2000 Advanced Server and Cluster Service on two nodes that have identical hardware. What is the best method to use?

○ a. Configure a test computer. Use Sysprep to create a disk image of the installation. Place the cluscfg.exe utility into the GUIRUNONCE section of the sysprep.inf file.

○ b. Manually create an unattend.txt file. Set the cluster component within the file to "On". Place the cluscfg.exe utility into the GUIRUNONCE section of the text file.

○ c. Automate the installation of Windows 2000 Advanced Server by creating an unattend.txt file. Manually install Cluster Service on each system because it does not support an automated installation.

○ d. Configure a test computer. Use the cluscfg.exe utility to create an image of the system.

Question 34

You are in charge of creating and maintaining cluster resources. You create a cluster group called MyGroup on Cluster1 and add a Network Name resource, an IP Address resource, and a Physical Disk resource. The Network Name resource is dependent on the IP Address resource, which is dependent on the Physical Disk resource. You need to add a file share resource, MyFileShare1, to the group. Using the cluster.exe command-line utility, you type the following:

```
Cluster Cluster1 Resource MyFileShare1 /Create
/Group:MyGroup /Type:"File Share"

Cluster Cluster1 Resource MyFileShare1 /
Addowner:Node2

Cluster Cluster1 Resource MyFileShare1 /
Privprop ShareName="FileShare"

Cluster Cluster1 Resource MyFileShare1 /
Privprop Path="g\FileShare"
```

You create the resource and then set the share name and path. What command option must be used next in order for the resource to be accessible to users?

○ a. **Adddependency**

○ b. **Setowners**

○ c. **Listdependencies**

○ d. **Preferredowners**

Question 35

You have been given the task of upgrading two cluster nodes to Windows 2000 Advanced Server. Your network administrator is concerned about down-time during the upgrade process. You assure him that by performing a roll-ing upgrade, downtime will be minimal. Before you proceed with the rolling upgrade, what software requirements need to be met? [Check all correct answers]

❑ a. Windows 2000 Advanced Server

❑ b. Internet Information Server 4.0

❑ c. Windows NT Server 4.0, Enterprise Edition

❑ d. Service Pack 4

❑ e. Windows NT Server 4.0

❑ f. Microsoft Cluster Service

Question 36

Users have reported that they cannot access any resources on the cluster. You open the Event Viewer on one of the nodes and notice an ERROR_ CLUSTERLOG_CORRUPT message in the System Log. You attempt to restart Cluster Service, but it fails. You need to restore the Quorum Log. You per-formed a full system backup the previous night. How should you proceed?

○ a. Start Cluster Service with the **–noquorumlogging** parameter.

○ b. Start Cluster Service with the **–resetquorumlog** parameter.

○ c. Start Cluster Service with the **–fixquorum** parameter.

○ d. Start Cluster Service with the **–restorequorumlog** parameter.

Question 37

You install Exchange 2000 and are attempting to create an Exchange Virtual Server. You create a new group for the virtual server. What resources must be added to the group before the Exchange System Attendant resource can be added? [Check all correct answers]

○ a. IP Address resource

○ b. Generic Application resource

○ c. File Share resource

○ d. Physical Disk resource

○ e. Network Name resource

○ f. Print Share resource

Question 38

Which of the following is required to install Cluster Service?

○ a. Windows 2000 Server

○ b. Internet Information Server 4.0

○ c. Service Pack 1

○ d. Windows 2000 Advanced Server

○ e. DHCP

Question 39

Your supervisor has put you in charge of implementing a two-node cluster. The cluster will be used to increase the availability of your company's mail service. Your supervisor presents you with a list of requirements that must be met by your cluster configuration. The list of requirements is as follows:

➤ Use the existing corporate domain structure.

➤ Isolate node-to-node traffic.

➤ Eliminate the private cluster network as a single point of failure.

➤ Eliminate IP addressing as a single point of failure.

You perform the following tasks:

➤ Configure the cluster nodes as members of an existing domain.

➤ Configure each node with two network cards and place the nodes on their own subnet.

➤ Assign static IP addresses to each network adapter in each node.

➤ Configure the private network for Internal Cluster Communication only.

➤ Configure the public network for Client Access only.

Which of the requirements did you meet?

○ a. You met one of the requirements.

○ b. You met two of the requirements.

○ c. You met three of the requirements.

○ d. You met all the requirements.

○ e. You met none of the requirements.

Question 40

Users have reported that they cannot access any resources on the cluster. You open the Event Viewer on one of the nodes and notice an ERROR_CLUSTERLOG_CORRUPT message in the System Log. You attempt to restart Cluster Service, buy it fails. You need to restore the Quorum Log. You do not have a backup of the Quorum Log file. You navigate to the &systemroot%\Cluster directory. What is your next step in attempting to fix the problem?

- ○ a. Start Cluster Service by typing "clussvc –debug -noquorumlogging".

- ○ b. Start Cluster Service by typing "clussvc –debug -resetquorumlog".

- ○ c. Start Cluster Service by typing "clussvc –debug -fixquorum".

- ○ d. Start Cluster Service by typing "clussvc –debug -restartquorumlog".

Question 41

You configure an EVS in the cluster. To allow clients access to the virtual server, you add a static mapping to the WINS database for the virtual server. The virtual server is running on Node1. Node1 restarts because of a bug check, and the virtual server fails over to Node2. Now clients can no longer access the virtual server. Upon opening Cluster Administrator, you notice that the virtual server is offline. What is the cause of the problem?

- ○ a. The virtual server needs to be restarted manually.

- ○ b. Because there is already a static mapping in the WINS database for the virtual server, Node2 is unable to register the network name.

- ○ c. The IP address for the virtual server is changed when it fails over to Node2.

- ○ d. Node2 is not listed as a possible owner for the virtual server and therefore cannot bring it online.

Question 42

During the course of the day, a power failure occurs while you are offsite.
You return to discover that users can no longer access the cluster resources.
They report that the power outage lasted for two and a half hours. The UPS
is rated for 45 minutes. You open the Event Viewer on one of the nodes and
discover a ERROR_CLUSTERLOG_CORRUPT message in the System Log.
You want to run **chkdsk** to see whether the error to the log is repairable.
Which parameter would you enter to do this? Enter your answer on the
following screen:

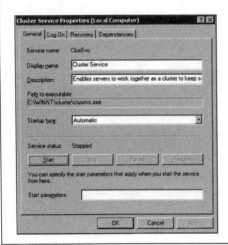

Question 43

You are an administrator for a medium-sized company. One of your primary
responsibilities is to maintain a two-node cluster. The cluster is configured
with three external shared disks that are not in a RAID configuration. The
disk holding the Quorum resource fails and Cluster Service will not start.
You need to designate a new disk for the Quorum resource. If Cluster Service fails to start, how can you gain access to the cluster to redesignate the
Quorum disk?

○ a. Restart Cluster Service using the **net start** command.

○ b. Shut down one of the nodes and restart Cluster Service once the
      node is back online.

○ c. Use the **–noquorum** startup parameter.

○ d. Use the **–fixquorum** startup parameter.

Question 44

Your company has a TCP/IP application that has a problem. When more than 10 people access the application at one time, the application fails and causes the Generic Application resource to fail. Your supervisor wants you to change the settings so that a failover is not caused in the nine-hour period that the cluster is accessed during business hours. The most times the resource has failed in any given day is five, but your supervisor wants you to make the setting for six failures in a day, just to be safe. Using the cluster.exe command-line utility, which options should you use to configure the settings for the resource?

- ○ a. **RestartAction=6**

   PendingTimeout=32400

- ○ b. **RestartThreshold=6**

   RestartPeriod=540

- ○ c. **LooksAlivePollInterval=6**

   IsAlivePollInterval=32400

- ○ d. **RestartThreshold=6**

   RestartPeriod=32400

Question 45

You are given the task of setting up a two-node cluster. The nodes are placed on a private subnet and are also connected to the public network. You are aware of the importance of node-to-node communication and want to configure the networks to isolate cluster traffic while ensuring cluster communication in case the private network becomes unavailable. How should the networks be configured during the installation of Cluster Service?

- ○ a. Configure the private network for All Communications and the public network for All Communications.

- ○ b. Configure the private network for All Communications and the public network for Client Access only.

- ○ c. Configure the private network for Internal Cluster Communication only and the public network for Client Access only.

- ○ d. Configure the private network for Internal Cluster Communication only and the public network for All Communications.

Answer Key

For asterisked items, see the answer text for the specific questions.

1. b, c
2. *
3. a
4. c
5. c
6. b
7. *
8. d
9. c
10. *
11. a, d
12. d
13. a
14. b, c

15. b
16. d
17. c
18. b
19. *
20. *
21. d
22. b
23. b, c
24. *
25. b
26. c, d
27. *
28. a, g, i
29. b
30. c

31. c
32. c
33. a
34. a
35. c, d, f
36. a
37. a, d, e
38. d
39. c
40. b
41. b
42. *
43. d
44. d
45. d

Question 1

The correct answers are b and c. The SCSI IDs must be unique on the SCSI chain. If the IDs are not unique, the devices might not work correctly, if at all. Because the IDs 5, 6, and 7 are already used on Node A, Node B only has the IDs 0 through 4 available. Therefore, answers a and d are incorrect.

Question 2

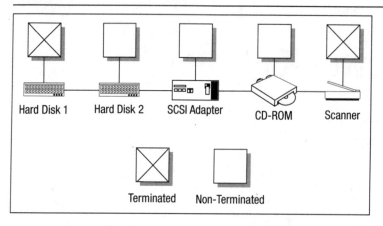

| Hard Disk 1 | Hard Disk 2 | SCSI Adapter | CD-ROM | Scanner |

Terminated   Non-Terminated

The two ends of a SCSI chain need to be terminated to prevent a signal from bouncing back from the ends of the cable. In this instance, the first internal hard disk and the scanner are the "end" devices and must be terminated.

Question 3

The correct answer is a. You have only succeeded in one of the tasks. By moving the groups on Node A to Node B, you have minimized the interruptions to the network clients. The rest of the procedure should not be performed. Any extra components that will not be shared by the nodes (hard disks) should not be on the shared SCSI bus. The CD-ROM should be installed on its own SCSI adapter—one that's different from the SCSI adapter that controls the shared SCSI bus. This will leave the cluster in a state that will interfere in the normal cluster functions. Therefore, answers b, c, and d are incorrect.

Question 4

The correct answer is c. Fibre Channel devices are very modular in fashion, and the connectors, or *Gigabit Interface Converters (GBICs)*, can be replaced to take advantage of different cabling types without your having to replace the whole Fibre Channel card.

Sending the whole PC or Fibre Channel card back to be replaced will not be a timely solution to the problem. Therefore, answers a and b are incorrect. Fibre Channel cables usually carry pulses of light, which is not compatible with SCSI cards due to the fact that they use electrical signals instead. Therefore, answer d is incorrect.

Question 5

The correct answer is c. The optimal choice is to use *n*-tier clustering. *N*-tier clustering allows network load-balanced servers to manage the Web site with a collection of nodes to maintain high availability as well as high performance. This also gives you a two-node cluster that runs the database to manage client orders for the NLB nodes to access. Two- or four-node clusters will not provide the stellar results for Web-site access that network load balancing gives. On the other hand, network load balancing will not provide for database fault tolerance, which cluster does provide. The only solution is to combine the two and have an *N*-Tier clustering solution.

Question 6

The correct answer is b. The failback option must be disabled. If the failback time was specified, the failback would have happened, because the failback time can only be scheduled within a 24-hour period, and more than 24 hours have passed. The only valid option would be that the failback settings were not enabled on the groups that were to be failed back to the node that had failed. Choices c and d are not valid because the Period and Threshold settings only exist only for failover and not for failback.

Question 7

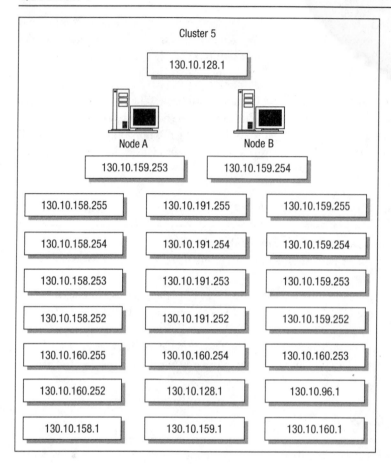

The subnet defined by 130.10.128.0/17 is split into the following subnets:

➤ 130.10.32.0–130.10.63.0

➤ 130.10.64.0–130.10.95.0

➤ 130.10.96.0–130.10.127.0

➤ 130.10.128.0–130.10.159.0 (this is the subnet you were assigned)

➤ 130.10.160.0–130.10.191.0

➤ 130.10.192.0–130.10.223.0

Because the range 130.10.128.0–130.10.159.0 was assigned for your use by your supervisor, this is the range from which you will select your IP address. Because Node A and Node B need to be the last two addresses in the range, they are

130.10.159.253 and 130.10.159.254. The cluster, itself, must be assigned the first address in the subnet, which is 130.10.128.1.

Question 8

The correct answer is d. File share permissions are set in Cluster Administrator on the Parameters tab of the file share's Properties dialog box. The Parameters tab has a Permissions button that allows you to set the security settings on the file share. Therefore, answers a, b, and c are incorrect.

Question 9

The correct answer is c. The number of Disk groups created is one for each hard disk, minus one for the Cluster group created, which has the Quorum resource as a resource. In this case, the number of Disk groups created is three. Therefore, answers a, b, and d are incorrect.

Question 10

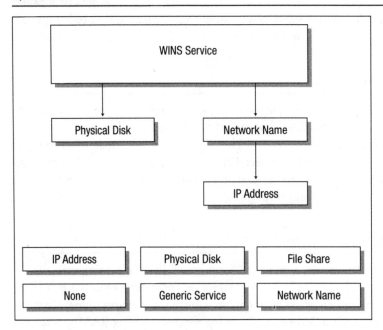

The WINS Service resource requires the Physical Disk, Network Name, and IP Address resources. The IP Address resource is a dependency of the Network Name resource, which is why the IP Address resource is placed under the Network Name resource.

Question 11

The correct answers are a and d. The virtual server is a resource that allows a node to appear as more than one PC, thus allowing certain resources to be accessed as if they were on a standalone server dedicated to the specific tasks of those resources. An example is the WINS Service resource, which can be given a specific network name and IP address to appear as a different server. A physical disk and Generic Service resource are not required to make a virtual server. They could be included but are not necessary, so choices b and c are incorrect.

Question 12

The correct answer is d. The file share should be created with Cluster Administrator making a Shared File resource. If you want to share all the subdirectories with their own share, select Share Subdirectories on the Parameters tab's Advanced button. Then, if you want the subdirectories to be hidden, select the Hide Subdirectories checkbox.

Explorer cannot be used to administer cluster-aware file shares, so choice a is incorrect. Choice b is a possibility but is not the best solution because it would take too long to implement. Choice c would only do part of the needed sharing. It would only make the initial administrative share on the top-level folder.

Question 13

The correct answer is a. Before you can delete a group, the group must be empty. All resources must be deleted or moved to other groups. The resources cannot just be offline when you remove the group—they must not be part of the group at all. Therefore, answer b is incorrect. Choice c is incorrect because a failure would only cause the group to move to another node. Choice d is incorrect because groups can be deleted only if the group is empty.

Question 14

The correct answers are b and c. To optimize a CPU that is being overutilized, you should add a second processor or upgrade the existing processor to a faster one. Another option would be to remove some of the resources from the system. This would result in less processing being required. Adding RAM or a second hard disk will not relieve the processing requirements for the server but will only add more memory resources and more disk space.

Question 15

The correct answer is b. The higher the bit bus a card supports, the greater the throughput between the card and the motherboard. For example, if the SCSI adapter is 16 bit, it could be upgraded to 32 or 64 bit to increase the throughput between the card and its devices. Another way to improve the devices' throughput somewhat is to assign them higher SCSI IDs that have higher priorities. Therefore, answer d is incorrect.

Thicker cables are used to support longer cable runs without experiencing interference and signal degradation. Therefore, answer c is incorrect. Larger SCSI hard disks have no bearing on the performance of the adapter card. Therefore, answer a is incorrect.

Question 16

The correct answer is d. Nothing special must be done to back up cluster data in a File Share resource. The data can be backed up just as any normal files would be backed up. Therefore, answers a, b, and c are incorrect.

Question 17

The correct answer is c. For best results, the virtual drive should be located on a disk separate from the operating system, and it should use a different controller card. Therefore, answers a, b, and d are incorrect.

Question 18

The correct answer is b. If the IP Address resource is deleted, the Network Name resource will also be deleted because it is a dependency; therefore answer a is incorrect. You cannot delete a Virtual Server resource because it does not exist as one entity but rather as two. Therefore, answer c is incorrect. Answer d is incorrect because this can be accomplished in one step.

Question 19

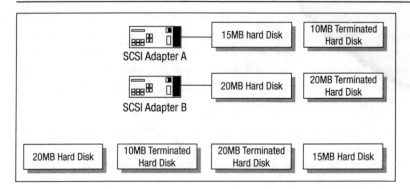

Because the most drive space will be used for the shared disks, the two 20MB hard disks will be placed on SCSI Adapter B, because this is the SCSI adapter that has the external connectors. The 20MB SCSI hard disk that is terminated must go on the end of the chain. With SCSI Adapter B, the two smaller hard disks will be used as specified with the terminated hard disk on the end of the SCSI chain. No other termination is required because there are no other connectors on the adapters that will be terminated at the card automatically.

Question 20

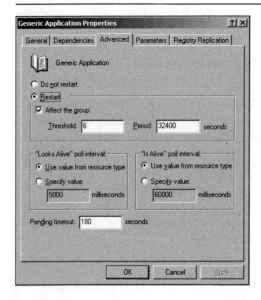

Threshold is set to 6, as specified by your supervisor, to make sure the most number of noncritical failures specified is met. Setting the threshold to 6 will allow you to make sure the General Application is not failed over unnecessarily. Period is the amount of time in which, if the Threshold setting is reached, the resource will be failed over. Period should be set to 32400 seconds (which is 9 hours).

Question 21

The correct answer is d. The only probable answer is that the group has failed completely and has exceeded its threshold in the specified period.

It is not probable, however, that so many users cannot log in correctly. Therefore, answer a is incorrect. The cluster and both nodes are online because you were able to ping them, which also proves the network is functioning. Therefore, answer b is incorrect. If there were a dramatic bottleneck issue, you might not be able to ping the servers at all. Therefore, answer c is incorrect.

Question 22

The correct answer is b. Node-to-node communication is accomplished via remote procedure calls (RPCs) on the private network.

LPC is used by communication internal to a system, not between systems. Therefore, answer a is incorrect. Dfs is a directory-sharing structure that allows for multiple shares on multiple systems to be accessed as if they were on one system. Therefore, answer c is incorrect. SMTP is used to transfer email messages. Therefore, answer d is incorrect.

Question 23

The correct answers are b and c. You have two options in this scenario. The first option is to create a striped set with parity under Windows NT 4.0, Enterprise Edition before upgrading the operating system. The second option is to perform the upgrade first, convert the disks to dynamic, and then create a striped volume with parity on each node. Software-level RAID must be in place before the upgrade is performed; otherwise, the disks will have to be converted to dynamic for any form of software-level RAID to be implemented, therefore answer a is incorrect. Answer d is incorrect because Windows NT 4.0 does not support dynamic disks, which are a new feature introduced in Windows 2000.

Question 24

Here is the correct order of installation:

➤ Power on the shared disk.

➤ Power off the second node.

➤ Power on the first node.

➤ Install Cluster Service on the first node.

➤ Power on the second node.

➤ Install Cluster Service on the second node.

Question 25

The correct answer is b. To have the group automatically fail back to its preferred owner once it becomes available, set the **AutoFailbackType=1** option using the Cluster.exe utility. This can also be done through the group's Properties dialog box in Cluster Administrator. Answers a and d are incorrect; there are no such options as FailbackType and Preferred Node. Using the Setowners option with the Cluster Group command allows you to specify a preferred owner but auto failback must be enabled first; therefore c is incorrect.

Question 26

The correct answers are c and d. There are two possible causes as to why the group is not failing over when the resource fails. If the Affect The Group option is disabled under the resource's Properties dialog box, the group will not fail over if the resource fails. Also, if the second node is not listed as a possible owner for the resource, it cannot fail over. Answer a is incorrect because configuring failback will have no impact on the group initially failing over to another node. Answer b is incorrect because configuring the second node as the preferred node means the group will always run on that node if it is available. The issue presented in the question is the group is not failing over.

Question 27

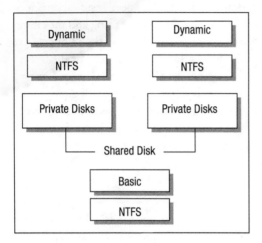

The private disks must be dynamic in order for software-level RAID to be implemented under Windows 2000. The private disks must also be formatted with NTFS to meet the requirement for file-level security. The shared disk must remain a basic disk; Cluster Service does not support dynamic disks. Cluster Service only supports NTFS, so it must be used on the shared disk.

Question 28

The correct answers are a, g, and i. Before beginning the installation of Cluster Service on the systems, you should create a single user account that is granted administrative privileges. This user account is used by both nodes, so only one account is needed. Active Directory uses DNS for name resolution, so the systems will need to be configured with the IP addresses of the DNS servers. The recommended configuration is to assign static IP addresses to the systems that will be used in a cluster. Each node is configured with two network adapters, so four static IP addresses will be required. Because the systems are configured for DNS, WINS and LMHOSTS are not needed for name resolution; therefore answers b and c are incorrect. Answer d is incorrect because service pack 1 in not required to install Cluster Service. Each node is configured with two network adapters and will need four static IP addresses; therefore e and f are incorrect. Answer h is incorrect because IIS 4.0 is required only to perform a rolling upgrade of a cluster that has an IIS resource. Answer j is incorrect because the nodes are configured as members of the same domain; a single domain user account can be used.

Question 29

The correct answer is b. Once the System State data has been restored on one of the nodes, use the Clusrest.exe utility to restore the Quorum Log and the cluster database to the node's Registry. Answer a is incorrect because the Dumpcfg.exe utility is used to restore the signature file to a disk if it is replaced or the bus re-enumerated. This utility would be used before the Clusrest.exe when restoring a cluster disk. There is no Repair option with Clussvc.exe that will allow you to restore the information to the node's registry; therefore answer c is incorrect. Answer d is incorrect because attempting to stop and restart Cluster Service will not restore the necessary information to the node's registry.

Question 30

The correct answer is c. To correct the problem, change the IP address assigned to the adapter connected to the public network on Node2 to 192.168.50.51 and change the IP address assigned to the adapter connected to the private cluster network on Node2 to 192.168.51.51. Therefore, answers a, b, and d are incorrect.

Question 31

The correct answer is c. Windows NT Server 4.0 cannot be upgraded to Windows 2000 Advanced Server. A clean installation will have to be performed and all applications reinstalled under the new operating system. The only operating system that can be upgraded directly to Windows 2000 Advanced Server is Windows NT Server 4.0, Enterprise Edition, therefore answers a,b,and d are incorrect.

Question 32

The correct answer is c. Cluster Service can recover from a private network failure if the public network has been configured for All Communications. Therefore, answers a, b, and d are incorrect.

Question 33

The correct answer is a. Because both systems have identical hardware, the best way to automate the installation is to configure a test computer and use the Sysprep utility to create a disk image. The installation of Cluster Service can be automated by placing the cluscfg.exe utility under the GUIRUNONCE section of the sysprep.inf file. Therefore, answers b, c, and d are incorrect.

Question 34

The correct answer is a. A file share resource should have a network name and disk dependency. Once the resource is added to the group, use the **Adddependency** option to configure the dependencies for the resource. Making the resource dependent on the Network Name resource would configure the required dependency. Therefore, answers b, c, and d are incorrect.

Question 35

The correct answers are c, d, and f. To perform a rolling upgrade of the nodes to Windows 2000 Advanced Server, you must ensure that each node is running Windows NT Server 4.0, Enterprise Edition; Service Pack 4 or later; and Microsoft Cluster Service; therefore answers a and e are incorrect. Internet Information Server 4.0 is only required if there is an IIS resource. Therefore, answer b is incorrect.

Question 36

The correct answer is a. Because there is a backup of the log file, you should start Cluster Service using the **–noquorumlogging** parameter. This will allow you to delete the corrupt log file and restore from backup.

The **–resetquorumlog** parameter would be used if there were no backup of the Quorum Log. With this parameter, a new log file is created based on the configuration information stored in the Registry of the local system. Therefore, answer b is incorrect. The **–fixquorum** parameter is used to start Cluster Service with no Quorum resource to allow another one to be configured. Therefore, answer c is incorrect. There is no **-restorequorumlog** startup parameter for Cluster Service. Therefore, answer d is incorrect.

Question 37

The correct answers are a, d, and e. Before adding the Exchange System Attendant resource to the group, you first need to add an IP Address resource, Network Name resource, and Physical Disk resource to the group. Therefore, answers b, c, and f are incorrect.

Question 38

The correct answer is d. Of the software listed, Windows 2000 Advanced Server is the only one required by Cluster Service. Therefore, answers a, b, c, and e are incorrect.

Question 39

The correct answer is c. You have succeeded in meeting three of the requirements. By placing the nodes in an existing domain but on their own subnet, you use the existing domain structure while isolating node-to-node traffic. Assigning static IP addresses to the nodes eliminates IP addressing as a point of failure. In order to eliminate the private network as a point of failure, the public network should be configured for All Communications instead of Client Access only. Therefore, answers a, b, d, and e are incorrect.

Question 40

The correct answer is b. Because there is no backup of the Quorum Log file, your first step in attempting to fix the problem is to navigate to the %systemroot%\Cluster directory and start Cluster Service using the –**resetquorumlog** parameter. Cluster Service will attempt to create a new log file based on the configuration information stored in the Registry of the local system.

The –**noquorumlogging** parameter would be used if there is no backup of the log file or if the log file cannot be reset. Therefore, answer a is incorrect. The –**fixquorum** parameter is used to start Cluster Service with no Quorum resource to allow another one to be configured. Therefore, answer c is incorrect. There is no –**restartquorumlog** startup parameter for Cluster Service. Therefore, answer d is incorrect.

Question 41

The correct answer is b. Static entries for WINS should not be used for cluster groups because they can fail over at any time. Because there is already a static mapping for the virtual server in the WINS database, the second node will be unable to register the network name when the group fails over.

Starting the virtual server manually will have no impact if the network name cannot be registered. Therefore, answer a is incorrect. The IP address assigned to a group does not change when it fails over. Therefore, answer c is incorrect. If the second node is not listed as a possible owner for the group, it will not fail over. In the scenario, the group has already failed over to the second node. Therefore, answer d is incorrect.

Question 42

The correct answer is:

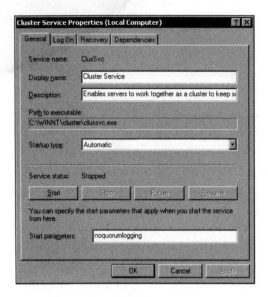

The **noquorumlogging** parameter would have to be used to start Cluster Service so that **chkdsk** can be run on the Quorum disk.

Question 43

The correct answer is d. Enter the **–fixquorum** parameter in the Cluster Service startup parameters. This allows you to bypass the Quorum resource to start Cluster Service. Once it is started, you can redesignate the Quorum disk through Disk Administrator.

If the Quorum disk has failed, Cluster Service will fail to start, even if you're using the **net start** command or you shut down and restart the node. Therefore, answers a and b are incorrect. There is no **–noquorum** parameter. Therefore, answer c is incorrect.

Question 44

The correct answer is d. Using the **RestartThreshold** option and setting the value to 6 ensures that failover of the group does not occur unnecessarily. Cluster Service will attempt to restart the resource six times before failing over the group. The **RestartPeriod** option is used to configure the amount of time (in seconds) during which the number of attempts specified by the **RestartThreshold** must occur before the group is failed over. The value should be set to 32400 (or 9 hours). Therefore, answer b is incorrect.

The **RestartAction** option defines what action to take if the resource does fail, and the **PendingTimeout** option specifies how long a resource can remain in a pending state before it is considered offline or failed. Therefore, answer a is incorrect.

The **LooksAlivePollInterval** option specifies how often Cluster Service should perform a quick check on the resource. The **IsAlivePollInterval** option specifies how often Cluster Service should perform a more thorough check of the resource's status. Therefore, answer c is incorrect.

Question 45

The correct answer is d. The best way to configure the networks is to set the private network for Internal Cluster Communication only and the public network for All Communications. This isolates node-to-node communication while ensuring that the public network can be used as a backup in case the private network fails. Therefore, answers a, b, and c are incorrect.

Glossary

active

A component that requires power to give it the ability to function properly. For example, a SCSI card often requires power to maintain its termination state.

address bus

A PC pathway that transmits component addresses to read or write to.

archive attribute

A file property that is turned on when the file is changed or modified and is turned off when the file is backed up during a full or incremental backup.

Backup log

A report of the backup process that shows successes and errors.

basic storage

A storage device (such as a hard disk) that can be divided into partitions, extended partitions, and logical drives. A storage device that is initialized as "basic" can contain up to four primary partitions or three primary partitions and one extended partition.

boot disk

A disk used to boot a PC to a specific operating system.

bottleneck

A situation in which a device or resource cannot keep up with client use.

bus width

The number of pathways that transmit data between devices in a PC.

Checkpoint Manager

Saves logs on the Quorum resource.

client access

The ability of a workstation (client) on a network to access a server.

client affinity

In Network Load Balancing, client affinity is a process in which a client is directed to a specific server every time the client makes a request.

client-to-cluster communication

For client-to-cluster communication to take place, one of the network cards in each of the cluster nodes must be connected to the public network. This allows the clients on the public network to access the cluster and its resources.

Clusrest.exe
This command restores the Quorum Log file and cluster database to a node's Registry.

cluster
Created when multiple servers act together as one server.

Cluster Administrator (Cluadmin.exe)
Cluster Administrator is the main utility used for managing and configuring a cluster.

Cluster Group command
The **Cluster Group** command is used to manage and configure groups within a cluster. The syntax is **Cluster [cluster name] Group [group name] /option.**

cluster group
A collection of resources that act as a unit when they fail to be moved to another node within the cluster.

Cluster IP Address resource
The static IP address and subnet mask assigned to a resource during the installation of Cluster Service on the first node. Administrators can connect to and administer the cluster by using the Cluster IP Address resource.

Cluster Log
A diagnostic log file that records the cluster activity.

cluster name
The NetBIOS name assigned to the cluster during the installation of Cluster Service on the first node. An Administrator can use the cluster name to manage and configure the cluster.

Cluster Network command
The **Cluster Network** command is used to manage and configure the networks used by the cluster. The syntax is **Cluster [cluster name] Network [network name] /option.**

Cluster Node command
The **Cluster Node** command is used to manage and configure cluster nodes from the command prompt. The syntax is **Cluster [cluster name] Node [node name] /option.**

Cluster Resource command
The **Cluster Resource** command is used to manage and configure cluster resources. The syntax is **Cluster [cluster name] Resources [resource name] /option.**

cluster resources
Individual components of a group that provide the access and functionality of clients.

Cluster.exe
A command-line utility used to administer a cluster. Using Cluster.exe, an administrator can manage a cluster across a slow link and automate administrative tasks through scripting.

Comclust.exe
Comclust.exe (Component Cluster Wizard) places the MS-DTC in cluster mode.

Communications Manager
The Communications Manager manages communications between the nodes in a cluster.

Component Load Balancing

The ability of Application Center 2000 to execute individual application services on different servers within a cluster.

Computer Management utility

The utility used to manage various components in a PC. An administrator can use the Computer Management utility to format drives and assign drive letters.

Configuration Database Manager

The Configuration Database Manager manages the changes to the cluster configuration database.

controller card

A device within a PC that controls the data input and output to and from the hard disk and floppy drive.

convergence

The process in which network load-balanced servers determine that another node has gone offline or has come back online.

copy backup

A process that backs up all files without changing the archive attribute.

database

A collection of data, tables, and other objects.

default instance

SQL Server supports multiple instances. The default instance can be accessed by specifying the computer name rather than requiring the server name and instance name.

default SCSI ID

The SCSI ID assigned to a device at the factory.

dependency

A resource that depends on another resource to function. For example, the Network Name resource depends on the IP Address resource.

DHCP resource

An entity that allows the services that issue TCP/IP addresses to clients to be fault tolerant.

differential backup

The partial backup of files that have changed since the last full backup.

disk subsystem

The set of devices that allows a PC to send data to and retrieve data from its hard disks.

distributed partition views

SQL 2000 uses distributed partition views to distribute a database across multiple PCs to allow for fault tolerance.

Distributed Transaction Coordinator resource

An entity that provides the services that manage transactions for clients. It is required by SQL.

Domain Name Service

The service used on networks to track the domain name of each host.

Dumpcfg.exe

This utility restores an old signature file to a new disk.

dynamic storage

Dynamic storage is a new storage system that is only supported by the Windows 2000 platforms. A storage device that is converted to "dynamic" can contain volumes, spanned volumes, striped volumes, mirrored volumes, and striped volumes with parity. It extends the capabilities of basic storage by adding the capability to perform disk-management tasks without the computer needing to be restarted, thus improving the recovery of damaged storage.

equal load distribution

The capability to distribute all requests from clients equally among all servers.

Event Processor

The Event Processor manages all the Cluster Service components.

Event Viewer

A Windows 2000 utility that can be used to view any messages generated by Cluster Service or other services.

Exchange Virtual Server (EVS)

The equivalent of a cluster resource group. It appears to clients as though it is a physical Windows 2000 server, and they can connect to the EVS using the network name assigned to it. The EVS contains all the resources needed to run Exchange in a cluster environment.

Excluadmin.dll

The custom resource DLL provided with Exchange 2000 that is used by the Cluster Administrator to manage and configure Exchange resources.

Exres.dll

The resource DLL provided with Exchange 2000 that is used by Cluster Service to monitor the status of Exchange resources. Exres.dll performs functions on the Exchange resources, such as checking their status through IsAlive calls, reporting any resource failures, and bringing resources online.

failback

The setting that allows a failed group to return to its original node of operation when that node comes back online.

failover

The process by which a group that fails to function on a node and is transferred to another node to operate.

failover cluster

A cluster that allows groups to move from a failed node to an active node.

failover policy

The settings that determine how and when a failover will occur.

fault tolerance

The ability of a system to recover from minor hardware failures.

fiber optic

Glass fibers that use light for the transmission of data.

Fibre Channel

The technology that allows for the transmission of data signals over fiber-optic or copper cables. The signals can include network, SCSI, and video signals.

fixquorum
A Cluster Service startup parameter that can be used to bypass the Quorum resource.

floppy controller
The device in a PC that controls the data signals into and out of the floppy drive.

full backup
A process in which all files on a PC are backed up to an external media type, such as a tape.

fully qualified domain name (FQDN)
The combination of a NetBIOS name and the name of the domain on which the client is connected.

Gigabit Interface Converter (GBIC)
The interface in a Fibre Channel device that can be replaced, depending on the configuration of the Fibre Channel connectivity.

Global Update Manager
The Global Update Manager manages cluster updates made by other components.

group
A collection of resources that acts as a single unit.

handling priority
A setting that allows a priority to placed on a node in Network Load Balancing to allow that node to process requests covered by a port rule.

heartbeat
A message sent between nodes in a cluster to monitor each other's online status. Heartbeats are sent between nodes every 1.2 seconds using UDP port 3343.

hot swap
The ability to replace hardware devices within a PC without having to turn off the power to the PC.

hub
A central connection point for all the network cables in a unit that accepts signals from one connection and transmits these signals to a specific connection or all connections.

Internet Information Services (IIS) Service
Allows WWW and FTP Services to be used in a cluster to make the WWW or FTP site fault tolerant.

incremental backup
A partial backup performed on files that have changed since the last back up.

load weight
The percentage of NLB traffic managed by a node.

Log Manager
The Log Manager manages the Recovery Log on the Quorum resource.

Message Queuing resource
Allows for application message handling for the purposes of fault tolerance.

motherboard
The main electronics board within a PC that transmits signals between devices in the PC.

multicast mode
Allows NLB nodes to work with multicast packets so that all nodes can receive the same client packets.

named instance
An administrator can create named instances to allow multiple instances of SQL to exist on a cluster. Clients connect to a named instance by specifying the computer name and the instance name.

Net View command
This command is used to test connectivity to a computer using its NetBIOS name.

NetBIOS (Network Basic Input/Output System)
A protocol for local area networks that operates at Layers 4 and 5 of the OSI model.

Network Load Balancing (NLB)
The ability to balance client requests for TCP/IP services among 2 to 32 PCs. The balance will be placed on TCP/IP applications or services only, mainly Web sites.

Network Monitor
A network-capture utility used to monitor traffic on a network. Network Monitor can be used to monitor cluster heartbeats and RPC communication.

NNTP Service
The service that allows clients to use newsgroups.

node
A single server within a cluster.

Node Manager
The Node Manager is one of the components of Cluster Service that runs on each cluster node. The Node Manager is responsible for monitoring the status of other cluster members through heartbeat messages.

node-to-node communication
The communication that occurs between cluster nodes, including server heartbeats, calls to monitor resource status, cluster commands, and application commands.

noquorumlogging
This Cluster Service startup parameter allows the service to start without Quorum logging.

passive
The ability of a component to require no power to operate. For example, a SCSI card can stay terminated even without the PC it is installed in turned on.

PC bus
A pathway in a PC that allows for the transmission of information between PC components.

PCI (Peripheral Component Interconnect)
A bus type specification that allows expansion cards to transmit 32 or 64 bits of data at a single time.

Performance Monitor
A tool used to monitor the realtime performance of system components and services.

physical resistor
A physical electrical component that can be placed in or removed from a SCSI adapter to cause termination

when the component is in place and remove termination when the component is removed.

ping
A utility used to verify TCP/IP connectivity.

port rules
Rules that specify how a node acts within a cluster.

preferred node
The node that a resource should be running on. The administrator will define the preferred node for a group, because the physical resources required for the group may be available only when running on a certain node. For example, a certain amount of memory may be required by Group A, and only Node 1 has that much RAM. Node 2 may have sufficient RAM, but not when running other groups, making Node 1 the preferred owner of the group.

preferred owner
The node that a group should be operating on if both nodes are online. If the group fails over to another cluster node, it will fail back to the preferred owner once it comes online if failback is enabled.

print spooler
A file that stores data to be printed on a server.

private network
The network on which the nodes within a cluster communicate with one another.

public network
The network on which the network clients and the nodes within a cluster communicate with one another.

Quorum resource
A hard disk shared by the nodes of a cluster that stores the database of cluster information.

RAID (Redundant Array of Independent Disks)
RAID combines two or more drives for fault tolerance and improved performance. The different levels of RAID include Level 0 (disk striping), Level 1 (disk mirroring), and Level 5 (disk striping with parity).

RAID 1 (disk mirroring)
RAID 1 provides disk-mirroring capabilities and requires two hard drives. Data is written to two drives concurrently. If one of the drives fails, the data can still be accessed from the other drive in the mirror set.

RAID 5 (disk striping with parity)
RAID 5 requires a minimum of three hard drives. Multiple partitions are combined into a logical drive and data is written evenly across all drives in the RAID configuration. Parity information is used for fault tolerance.

resetquorumlog
This startup parameter allows you to reset a corrupt Quorum Log.

Resource Manager
The Resource Manager is responsible for initiating actions such as bringing resources online or offline and initiating failover. It receives informa-

tion for the Node Manager and Resource Monitors to determine what actions to take.

Resource Monitor

The Resource Monitor tracks the status of cluster resources through polling. It does not initiate any action but rather passes the information to the Resource Manager, which, in turn, determines what action to take.

resource owner

The node on which a resource is running.

restore

The process of copying files from the backup media back to the hard disk.

ring network

A network in which all PCs are connected in a loop (circle) of network cables.

rolling upgrade

A rolling upgrade allows the operating system on existing cluster nodes to be upgraded while minimizing the downtime users will experience. The cluster nodes must be running Windows NT Server 4.0 Enterprise Edition with SP4 (or later), Microsoft Cluster Server, and Internet Information Server 4.0. Cluster nodes are upgraded one at a time, so there is always one node available to respond to client requests.

Round-Robin DNS

When multiple PCs with different IP addresses will be accessed equally by clients, they can be given the same DNS name, and the DNS server will issue different server addresses to the requesting clients so that each client receives the next server address in the list.

RPC (remote procedure call)

RPC is a communication mechanism by which applications can make calls on a remote computer. RPC is also the mechanism by which cluster nodes communicate.

scripting

Scripting allows a list of commands to be executed without any user intervention. The commands available with the Cluster.exe command-line utility can be placed into a batch file to automate many of the cluster administration tasks.

SCSI adapter

A device that sends and receives all data to and from the SCSI devices connected to it.

SCSI bus

A connection between SCSI devices that allows the devices to transmit data.

SCSI chain

A collection of SCSI devices connected together.

SCSI termination

To cause the ends of a SCSI bus to have resistance, by using a resistor, in order to absorb data signals so that these signals do not bounce back and forth across the bus.

SMTP Service

The service that allows email to be sent across a network.

statistical mapping algorithm
A mathematical equation that determines which node in NLB will receive a client request.

subnet mask
A set of bits that indicates which part of a TCP/IP address determines the host ID and which part determines the network ID.

system disk
The disk within a PC that contains the operating system files.

Task Manager
A utility used to view which processes are running on a system.

TCP/IP address
A unique address assigned to all network hosts in a TCP/IP network. Each host must have a unique address in order to communicate. The address consists of four numbers ranging from 0 to 255 separated by periods. For example, an IP address for a host could be 10.10.10.1.

Terminal Service
A service that allows clients to send and receive requests to a server, which does all the processing. No processing is done at the client, except for keyboard, mouse, and video processing.

Time Service
A service that synchronizes the system time so that all PCs have the same time.

true cluster
The capability of a cluster to allow all nodes to operate at once with the same shared resources.

UDP (User Datagram Protocol)
UDP is a connectionless protocol used mainly for broadcasting messages on a network.

unicast mode
The mode in which the IP address of the NLB cluster is used to communicate with clients. Unicast mode does not allow node-to-node communication unless secondary network cards are used.

virtual disk
The disk on which the virtual memory is written.

virtual memory
The memory area that is actually swapped to the hard disk to allow for portions of RAM to be cleared for use by applications.

Virtual Private Network (VPN)
A private and secure connection over a public network. For example, clients can access an intranet from the Internet.

virtual server
A node containing a group configured with a network name and IP address, so that resources within the same group can be accessed as a specific server. The node appears to clients as another physical server and not as part of the node on which it is operating.

Windows Internet Naming Service (WINS)
WINS allows a server to maintain a list of all PC NetBIOS names on the network to provide NetBIOS names to IP Address resolution.

Index